Count Basie

SWINGIN' THE BLUES, 1936–1950
KEN VAIL

The Scarecrow Press, Inc.
Lanham, Maryland, and Oxford
2003

SCARECROW PRESS, INC.

Published in the United States of America
by Scarecrow Press, Inc.
A wholly owned subsidiary of
The Rowman & Littlefield Publishing Group, Inc.
4501 Forbes Boulevard, Suite 200, Lanham, Maryland 20706
www.scarecrowpress.com

PO Box 317
Oxford
OX2 9RU, UK

British Library Cataloguing in Publication Information Available

Library of Congress Cataloging-in-Publication Data Available

0-8108-4882-1 (pbk : alk. paper)

♾™ The paper used in this publication meets the minimum
requirements of American National Standard for Information
Sciences—Permanence of Paper for Printed Library Materials,
ANSI/NISO Z39.48-1992.
Manufactured in the United States of America.

Acknowledgments

My grateful thanks to:
My wife, Marian, and my children, Sam and Emily;
Rolf Dahlgren for his generosity in sharing his photographs;
Down Beat and *Metronome* magazines;
Ron Fritts for sharing material and information from his
Washington D.C. and Baltimore M.D. collection;
Franz Hoffmann for his amazing series of books, *Jazz Advertised*;
Bob Inman for his invaluable Swing Era Scrapbooks;
David Nathan of the National Jazz Foundation Archive at
Loughton;
Brian Peerless for sharing his collection of *Metronomes* and *Down
Beats* and much more besides;
Tony Shoppee for sharing his *Down Beat* collection;
Grant Elliott, Bob Frost, Dave Green, Jim Greig, Scott Hamilton,
Dan Morgenstern, Hank O'Neal, Ken Peplowski, Bruce Phillips,
Norman Saks, Randy Sandke and David Smith for help and
encouragement at crucial moments.

I have also been grateful for the writings of W. Bruynincx, Frank
Büchmann-Møller, Stanley Dance, Leonard Feather, Ralph
Gleason, Nat Hentoff, Jorgen Grunnet Jepsen, Bud Kliment, Mike
Levin, Tom Lord, Alun Morgan, Albert Murray, Brian Rust, Chris
Sheridan, Barry Ulanov.

Photographs from the collections of Dan Bied, Rolf Dahlgren, Brian
Foskett, Bob Inman, Duncan Schiedt, Peter Vacher, and the author.

Preface

The Jazz Itineraries set out to provide a fascinating insight into the life and times of some of my favourite jazz musicians, in this case... Count Basie. Using contemporary photographs, newspaper reports, advertisements and reviews, I have attempted to chronicle his life through the birth of his first big band in Kansas City to its demise in early 1950. I have tried to include all known club, concert, television, film and jam session appearances as well as his recordings, although this is not intended to be a discography.

I hope that you will find this book an informative accompaniment when listening to Basie's records or reading any of his biographies.

Ken Vail, Cambridge, March 2003

1904–1925

Sunday 21 August 1904
William Basie is born in Red Bank, New Jersey, the second son of Lilly Ann and Harvey Lee Basie. Harvey Lee Basie is a coachman and caretaker for Judge White who owns a large mansion in the area.

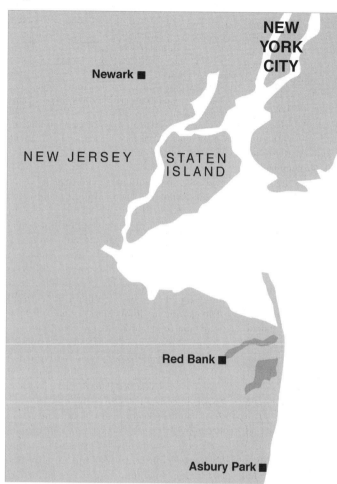

Above: Harry Richardson and his Kings of Syncopation (1924). L to r: Jimmy Hill, Basie, Elmer Williams, Harry Richardson.

Below: Katie Krippen and her Kiddies (1924-5). L to r: Basie, Steve Wright (drums), Freddy Douglas (trumpet), Katie, Elmer Williams (sax), Lou Henry (trombone).

As a boy, Bill Basie has piano lessons, but his first love is drums. He thinks he is pretty good until he hears the drumming of local boy Sonny Greer. Discouraged, he decides to concentrate on piano.

1923
Bill Basie graduates from junior high school. A poor student, he decides not to go on to high school and attempts, unsuccessfully, to make it as a musician in the nearby summer resort of Asbury Park.

Summer 1924
Bill Basie and his friend Elmer Williams return to Asbury Park for the season. They get a job with drummer Harry Richardson in a roadhouse called The Hongkong Inn.

Autumn 1924
Bill Basie (20) and Elmer Williams move to Harlem in New York City. They get a job with Katie Krippen and her Kiddies, part of the *Hippity Hop* vaudeville revue. They tour the United States for a year before the show disbands.

1925
Bill Basie (21) plays at Leroy's in Harlem where sitters-in include James P. Johnson, Willie 'The Lion' Smith and other top Harlem pianists. He also runs into Fats Waller who is accompanying movies on the organ at the Lincoln Theatre. They become friendly and Waller shows Basie a few tricks.

1926

Bill Basie (22) joins Gonzelle White and her Band and sets off on another vaudeville tour.

1927

In Tulsa, Oklahoma, Basie hears the Blue Devils. When Gonzelle White and the Band reach Kansas City the show breaks up and Basie is stranded in Kansas City.

Summer 1927

Basie is hospitalized for a month with spinal meningitis. When he is released he gets a job as organist at the Eblon Theatre, accompanying the silent movies.

July 1928

Basie writes to Walter Page, leader of the Blue Devils, and soon he is invited to join the band in Oklahoma. They tour through Texas and Kansas.

Sunday 25 November 1928

Bill Basie and the Blue Devils play a Battle of Bands with George Lee at the Paseo Hall in Kansas City.

1929

Basie leaves the Blue Devils and returns to Kansas City where he resumes at the Eblon Theatre. He renews his friendship with ex-Blue Devil Eddie Durham who is now playing trombone and guitar with the Bennie Moten Orchestra. Moten asks Basie to join the band as second pianist/arranger.

Wednesday 23 October 1929

Bill Basie (25) makes his recording debut with the Bennie Moten Orchestra for Victor in Chicago.

ED LEWIS, BOOKER WASHINGTON (trumpets); THAMON HAYES (trombone); EDDIE DURHAM (trombone/guitar); HARLAN LEONARD (clarinet/alto sax); JACK WASHINGTON (clarinet/alto sax/baritone sax); WOODY WALDER (clarinet/tenor sax); COUNT BASIE (piano); LEROY BERRY (banjo); VERNON PAGE (tuba); WILLIE McWASHINGTON (drums); BENNIE MOTEN (director)

Rumba Negro (Spanish Stomp) / The Jones Law Blues / Band Box Shuffle / Small Black / Every Day Blues

Thursday 24 October 1929

Bill Basie and the Bennie Moten Orchestra again record for Victor in Chicago.

ED LEWIS, BOOKER WASHINGTON (trumpets); THAMON HAYES (trombone); EDDIE DURHAM (trombone/guitar); HARLAN LEONARD (clarinet/alto sax); JACK WASHINGTON (clarinet/alto sax/baritone sax); WOODY WALDER (clarinet/tenor sax); COUNT BASIE (piano); BUSTER MOTEN (piano accordion); LEROY BERRY (banjo); VERNON PAGE (tuba); WILLIE McWASHINGTON (drums/vocal); BENNIE MOTEN (director)

Boot It / Mary Lee / Rit-Dit-Ray (vWMW) */ New Vine Street Blues* (2 takes) */ Sweetheart Of Yesterday*

Summer 1930

Bill Basie and the Bennie Moten Orchestra play the season as house band at Fairyland Park (*below*) in Kansas City.

Monday 27 October 1930
Bill Basie and the Bennie Moten Orchestra record for Victor in Kansas City.
HOT LIPS PAGE, ED LEWIS, BOOKER WASHINGTON (trumpets), THAMON HAYES (trombone), EDDIE DURHAM (trombone/guitar), HARLAN LEONARD (clarinet/alto sax), JACK WASHINGTON (clarinet/alto sax/baritone sax), WOODY WALDER (clarinet/tenor sax), COUNT BASIE (piano), BUSTER MOTEN (piano accordion), LEROY BERRY (banjo), VERNON PAGE (tuba), WILLIE MCWASHINGTON (drums), JIMMY RUSHING (vocal), BENNIE MOTEN (director),
Won't You Be My Baby? (vJR, 2 takes)

Tuesday 28 October 1930
Bill Basie and the Bennie Moten Orchestra again record for Victor in Kansas City.
I Wish I Could Be Blue / Oh! Eddie / That Too, Do (vJR, 2 takes) */ Mack's Rhythm / You Made Me Happy / Here Comes Marjorie / The Count*

Wednesday 29 October 1930
Bill Basie and the Bennie Moten Orchestra again record for Victor in Kansas City.
Liza Lee (vJR)

Thursday 30 October 1930
Bill Basie and the Bennie Moten Orchestra again record for Victor in Kansas City.
Get Goin' (vJR) */ Professor Hot Stuff / When I'm Alone* (vJR) */ New Moten Stomp / As Long As I Love You (Jeannette)* (vJR)

Friday 31 October 1930
Bill Basie and the Bennie Moten Orchestra again record for Victor in Kansas City.
Somebody Stole My Gal (vCB) */ Now That I Need You* (vJR) */ Bouncin' Round / Break A Day Shuffle*

During the winter Basie and the Bennie Moten band play a series of one-nighters across Missouri, Illinois, Indiana and Ohio, heading for New York City.

Monday 9 March 1931
Bill Basie and the Bennie Moten Orchestra play a dance at the Pythian Temple in Pittsburgh.

Saturday 11 April 1931
Bill Basie and the Bennie Moten Orchestra open a one-week engagement at the Lafayette Theatre in New York City in 'Rhythm Bound' with Minto Cato and Wells, Mordecai & Taylor.

Wednesday 15 April 1931
Bill Basie and the Bennie Moten Orchestra record for Victor in New York City.
HOT LIPS PAGE, ED LEWIS, BOOKER WASHINGTON (trumpets), THAMON HAYES (trombone), EDDIE DURHAM (trombone/guitar), HARLAN LEONARD (clarinet/alto sax), JACK WASHINGTON (clarinet/alto sax/baritone sax), WOODY WALDER (clarinet/tenor sax), COUNT BASIE (piano), BUSTER MOTEN (piano accordion), LEROY BERRY (banjo), VERNON PAGE (tuba), WILLIE MCWASHINGTON (drums), JIMMY RUSHING (vocal), BENNIE MOTEN (director),
Ya Got Love (vJR) */ I Wanna Be Around My Baby All The Time* (vJR)

Friday 17 April 1931
Bill Basie and the Bennie Moten Orchestra close at the Lafayette Theatre in New York City.

Around this time the band also play a dance at the Savoy Ballroom in Harlem opposite Chick Webb's Orchestra. Basie also finds time to visit his family in Red Bank where he is shocked to discover that his father has left home.

Saturday 18 April 1931
Bill Basie and the Bennie Moten Orchestra open a one-week engagement at the Royal Theatre in Baltimore.

Friday 24 April 1931
Bill Basie and the Bennie Moten Orchestra close at the Royal Theatre in Baltimore.

Above: A dim picture of the Bennie Moten Orchestra and their band bus visiting the newspaper offices of the Baltimore Afro-American during an engagement at the Royal Theatre.

Monday 4 May 1931
Bill Basie and the Bennie Moten Orchestra play a Battle Royal of Music with Erskine Tate's Orchestra at the Pythian Temple in Pittsburgh.

Summer 1931
Bill Basie and the Bennie Moten Orchestra play the season as house band at Fairyland Park in Kansas City.

Basie marries Vivian Wynn, but the marriage doesn't last.

Friday 30 September 1931
Bill Basie and the Bennie Moten Orchestra play the Golden Slipper Night Club in Dayton, Ohio.

Thursday 1 October 1931
Bill Basie and the Bennie Moten Orchestra play a dance at the Pythian Temple in Pittsburgh.

The Bennie Moten Orchestra then join a 'Battle of Music' tour featuring the bands of Blanche Calloway, Chick Webb, Zack Whyte and Johnson's Happy Pals. The tour takes in Philadelphia, Baltimore, Richmond Va, Washington DC, Harrisburgh, Pittsburgh, Orange NJ, Wheeling WVa and Cincinnati. Basie's wife Vivian joins him on the tour.

Thursday 15 October 1931
Bill Basie and the Bennie Moten Orchestra play a Battle of Music at the Masonic Auditorium in Washington D.C.

Tuesday 20 October 1931
Bill Basie and the Bennie Moten Orchestra play a Battle of Music at the Pythian Temple in Pittsburgh.

After the band hit New York, Vivian leaves Basie and heads back to Kansas City. It is the end of the marriage.

Saturday 31 October 1931
Bill Basie and the Bennie Moten Orchestra open a one-week engagement at the Lafayette Theatre in New York City. Also on the bill are Garbage Rogers and Alice Harris. The movie presentation is 'Bought' starring Constance Bennett.

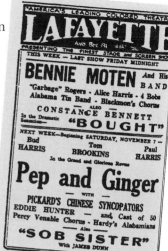

Friday 6 November 1931
Bill Basie and the Bennie Moten Orchestra close at the Lafayette Theatre in New York City.

Saturday 7 November 1931
Bill Basie and the Bennie Moten Orchestra open a one-week engagement at the Pearl Theatre in Philadelphia.

Friday 13 November 1931
Bill Basie and the Bennie Moten Orchestra close at the Pearl Theatre in Philadelphia.

Saturday 14 November 1931
Bill Basie and the Bennie Moten Orchestra open a one-week engagement at the Howard Theatre in Washington, D.C. Also on the bill are The Four Pepper Shakers and Sweet Papa Garbage.

Friday 20 November 1931
Bill Basie and the Bennie Moten Orchestra close at the Howard Theatre in Washington, D.C.

Saturday 12 December 1931

Bill Basie and the Bennie Moten Orchestra open a one-week engagement at the Lafayette Theatre in Harlem and Basie meets Catherine Morgan, a beautiful 16-year-old dancer with the Whitman Sisters, for the first time.

Friday 18 December 1931

Bill Basie and the Bennie Moten Orchestra close at the Lafayette Theatre in New York City.

February 1932

Walter Page, Ben Webster and Eddie Barefield join the Bennie Moten Orchestra. The band rearse for a month before a heavy touring schedule that lasts through the summer. It is in Toledo, during the 1932 summer tour, that Basie has his first encounter with Art Tatum.

Monday 2 May 1932

Bill Basie and the Bennie Moten Orchestra play a Battle of bands with Thamon Hayes at the Annual Musicians Ball at the Labor Temple in Kansas City.

Sunday 26 June 1932

Bill Basie and the Bennie Moten Orchestra play a dance at Harmarville Park in Pittsburgh.

Monday 27 June 1932

Bill Basie and the Bennie Moten Orchestra play a dance at the Pythian Temple in Pittsburgh.

Friday 9 December 1932

Bill Basie and the Bennie Moten Orchestra open a one-week engagement at the Pearl Theatre in Philadelphia.

Tuesday 13 December 1932
Bill Basie and the Bennie Moten Orchestra record for
Victor in Camden, New Jersey.
HOT LIPS PAGE, JOE KEYES, DEE STEWART (trumpets), DAN
MINOR (trombone), EDDIE DURHAM (trombone/guitar),
EDDIE BAREFIELD (clarinet/alto sax), JACK WASHINGTON (alto
sax/baritone sax), BEN WEBSTER (tenor sax), COUNT BASIE
(piano), LEROY BERRY (banjo), WALTER PAGE (bass), WILLIE
MCWASHINGTON (drums), JIMMY RUSHING, STERLING RUSSELL
TRIO (vocal), BENNIE MOTEN (director),
Toby / Moten Swing / Imagination (vSR3) / *New Orleans* (vJR) /
The Only Girl I Ever Loved (vSR3) / *Lafayette / Prince Of Wails*
HOT LIPS PAGE (trumpet), EDDIE BAREFIELD (clarinet/alto
sax), COUNT BASIE (piano), EDDIE DURHAM (guitar), WALTER
PAGE (bass), WILLIE MCWASHINGTON (drums), JOSEPHINE
GARRISON (vocal), BENNIE MOTEN (director),
The Blue Room / Milenberg Joys / Two Times (vJG)

Thursday 15 December 1932
Bill Basie and the Bennie Moten Orchestra close at the
Pearl Theatre in Philadelphia.

The band tour south and then east to Cincinnati for a
Christmas theatre date. There are rumblings of dissent in
the band, Ben Webster leaves and others follow suit. After
a New Year's Eve dance they return to Kansas City.

1933
Things are very slow for the band as the depression bites. In
April a new club called the Cherry Blossom opens at the
remodelled Eblon Theatre at 1822 Vine Street in Kansas
City. The George E. Lee Band are the first band to play in
there but in July the Bennie Moten Band takes over. During
the Cherry Blossom engagement, escalating disputes come
to a head. Several band members decide to break away
from Moten and they elect Basie as their leader. Count
Basie and his Cherry Blossom Orchestra remain at the club
for over nine months, into March 1934.

February 1934
Lester Young joins the Count Basie band at the Cherry
Blossom Club.

Thursday 1 March 1934
Count Basie and his orchestra leave the Cherry Blossom
and open a two-month engagement at Sam Baker's Terrace
Gardens in Little Rock, Arkansas. The line-up of the band is:
Joe Keyes, Hot Lips Page, Dee Stewart (trumpets); Dan
Minor (trombone); Lester Young, Buster Smith, Jack
Washington (saxes); Count Basie (piano); Claude McTear
(guitar); Walter Page (bass); Jo Jones (drums); Jimmy
Rushing (vocals)

c.25 March 1934
Lester Young leaves Basie to join the Fletcher Henderson
Orchestra. Buddy Tate is Lester's replacement but when
the Terrace Gardens engagement ends the band breaks up.

Basie eventually returns to Kansas City and joins the
reorganized Bennie Moten Orchestra. He plays with
Bennie throughout the rest of the year and into the
following spring.

1935
Saturday 9 February 1935
Count Basie and the Bennie Moten Orchestra open a one-
week engagement at the Orpheum Theatre in Lincoln,
Nebraska.

Tuesday 2 April 1935
Count Basie and the Bennie Moten Orchestra open an
important one-week engagement at the Rainbow Gardens in
Denver, Colorado. Bennie Moten, who has stayed behind in
Kansas City for a tonsillectomy, dies on the operating table.
The band finishes the week and returns to Kansas City for a
two-week club date on Troost Avenue. After a week Basie
quits the band. He trawls the local club scene, sitting in
where possible, and is fortunate to be offered the job as
leader of the house band at the Reno Club. He gathers
together several of his former colleagues and soon has a
swinging nine-piece band called Count Basie and his Barons
of Rhythm. The personnel is: Joe Keyes, Carl 'Tatti' Smith
(trumpets); Buster Smith, Jack Washington, Slim Freeman
(saxes); Basie (piano); Walter Page (bass); and Jesse Price
(drums). Jimmy Rushing and Hot Lips Page are booked as
singles. Lips acts as emcee and often joins the trumpet section
to make the classic 3 (trumpets), 3 (saxes) and 3 (rhythm).

1936

The band starts broadcasting from the Reno Club on
W9XBY, a local radio station. Lester Young hears the
broadcasts in Minneapolis and is soon on his way to
Kansas City to replace Slim Freeman.

February 1936
Lester Young joins the Basie band at the Reno Club.

John Hammond is in Chicago with Benny Goodman's
Band when he hears a Basie broadcast on his car radio. He
is knocked out and enthuses in *Down Beat*.

> Benny Goodman, it may interest Basie to know, thinks that he has the
> most powerful drive of any band in the country, judging from his
> nightly performances over W9XBY (Kansas City, 1550 kilocycles)…
> I almost forgot to say that Lester Young's tenor playing in Basie's
> orchestra is so good that it seems impossible that it was the same guy
> who took Hawkins's place in Fletcher's band two years ago and failed
> to distinguish himself.

Spring 1936

John Hammond persuades Willard Alexander of MCA to sign Count Basie and his Barons of Rhythm to an exclusive contract but is horrified when he returns to Kansas City in the summer to find Basie has signed a record deal with Dave Kapp of Decca. Basie has agreed to record 24 sides a year for $750 outright and no royalties! At Alexander's instigation Basie enlarges the band: George Hunt and Dan Minor, trombones, Buck Clayton for Hot Lips Page and Caughey Roberts for Buster Smith. In August, Basie and the band leave the Reno Club and play a few dance hall gigs in Tulsa, Muskogee, Okmulgee, Oklahoma City, Wichita and Omaha.

Monday 7 September 1936

Count Basie and his orchestra play a Musicians Labor Day Ball at the Labor Temple at 14th and Woodlawn in Kansas City. Also on the bill are the bands of Andy Kirk, Harlan Leonard, Bus Moten, Pete Johnson, Clarence Love and Jerome Carrington.

Saturday 31 October 1936

Count Basie and his enlarged 14-piece orchestra play a farewell dance at the Paseo Hall in Kansas City.

Monday 2 November 1936

Count Basie and his Orchestra are again at the Paseo Hall as a warm up for the Duke Ellington Orchestra. Immediately after their set, Basie and the band leave Kansas City en route for New York City, via Chicago.

Tuesday 3 November 1936

The band begin rehearsals in Chicago for their Grand Terrace Café opening. Claude Williams (guitar/violin) joins the band.

Friday 6 November 1936

Count Basie and his Orchestra open at the Grand Terrace Café in Chicago with a Gala Party. The band broadcast over WJZ at 11.00pm.
Streamline Strut / I'm Always In Love With You / I Surrender Dear (vJR)

Monday 9 November 1936

Members of the Count Basie Orchestra record as Jones-Smith Incorporated for Vocalion in Chicago.
CARL 'TATTI' SMITH (trumpet), LESTER YOUNG (tenor sax), COUNT BASIE (piano), WALTER PAGE (bass), JO JONES (drums), JIMMY RUSHING (vocal)
Shoe Shine Boy (2 takes) / *Evenin'* (vJR) / *Boogie Woogie* (vJR) / *Lady Be Good*

Wednesday 11 November 1936

Count Basie and his Orchestra boadcast over WJZ at midnight from the Grand Terrace Café in Chicago.
Moten Swing (theme) / *South Side Stomp / Tea For Two / Glory Of Love* (vJR) / *Shout And Do It / But Definitely / Hot Coffee / Yeah Man*

Saturday 14 November 1936

Count Basie and his Orchestra boadcast over WEAF at 12.10 from the Grand Terrace Café in Chicago.
Yeah Man / Christopher Columbus / Confessin' (vJR) / *Dear Old Southland / Rhythm In My Nursery Rhymes* (vJR)

Monday 16 November 1936

Count Basie and his Orchestra boadcast at 11.30 from the Grand Terrace Café in Chicago.
Moten Swing (theme) / *Jangled Nerves / Ebony Rhapsody / Boogie Woogie / Shout And Scream / House Hop / The Glory Of Love* (vJR) / *Harlem Shout / Moten Swing* (theme)

Saturday 21 November 1936

Count Basie and his Orchestra play a Pre-Thanksgiving Party at the Regal Theatre in Chicago.

Wednesday 25 November 1936

Count Basie and his Orchestra boadcast over WJZ at 12.30 from the Grand Terrace Café in Chicago.
Jangled Nerves / I'll Always Be In Love / Tea On The Terrace (vJR) / *Drop Me Off At Harlem / Rhythm In My Nursery Rhymes* (vJR) / *Limehouse Blues*

Thursday 26 November 1936

Count Basie and his Orchestra boadcast over WJZ at 11.35 from the Grand Terrace Café in Chicago.
Streamline Strut / Drop Me Off At Harlem / Tea On The Terrace (vJR) / *Happy Feet / Shoe Shine Boy / But Definitely / Easy To Love / Ebony Rhapsody*

Friday 27 November 1936

Count Basie and his Orchestra boadcast over WJZ at 11.35 from the Grand Terrace Café in Chicago.
You're Too Good To Be True / Rose Room / It's De-Lovely / Tea On The Terrace (vJR) / *Thanksgiving / Jangled Nerves*

Thursday 3 December 1936

Count Basie and his Orchestra close at the Grand Terrace.

Friday 4 December 1936

Count Basie and his Orchestra leave Chicago to play a series of one-nighters on the way to New York City.

Monday 7 December 1936

Count Basie and his Orchestra play a one-nighter at the Vendome Hotel in Buffalo, New York.

Thursday 24 December 1936

Count Basie and his Orchestra open at the Roseland Ballroom in New York City.

Thursday 31 December 1936

Count Basie and his Orchestra boadcast at 12.10 from the Roseland Ballroom in New York City.
Huff Puff / Organ Grinder's Swing / The Glory Of Love (vJR) / *Limehouse Blues / Jangled Nerves / Thanksgiving / Moten Swing* (theme)

1937

Saturday 9 January 1937

Teenage fan Bob Inman visits NYC with a friend. In the morning they see Fats Waller and his big band on stage at Loew's State Theatre in Times Square. At 6.45pm they see the Saturday Night Swing Broadcast featuring Bunny Berigan and Hazel Scott but, before that, they spend the afternoon at Roseland: *At 2 o'clock we paid 55 cents and went in the Ballroom. Woody Herman's Band and Count Basie's Band played alternately for one hour each from 2 to 6 o'clock.* Basie's Band played: *Too Bad* (vJR) / *Blue Lou* / *If We Never Meet Again* (vJR) / *Wild Party* / *My First Thrill* / *My Blue Heaven* (vJR) / *Tea For Two* / *Riffin' At The Ritz* / *I Surrender Dear* / *Big Chief De Sota* / *Skeleton In The Closet* / *Pennies From Heaven* (vJR) / *But Definitely* (vJR) / *I Ain't Got Nobody* (vJR) / *Dinah* (vJR) / *Nagasaki* (vJR) / *Moten Swing* (theme)

Wednesday 13 January 1937

Count Basie and his Orchestra broadcast (8.15pm) from Roseland Ballroom in New York City.
Yeah Man! / *Walkin' Through The Park* / *Evenin'* (vJR) / *Streamlined Strut* / *Moten Swing* (theme)

Thursday 21 January 1937

Count Basie and his Orchestra record for Decca in New York. BUCK CLAYTON, JOE KEYES, CARL SMITH (trumpets); DAN MINOR, GEORGE HUNT (trombones); CAUGHEY ROBERTS (alto sax); LESTER YOUNG, HERSCHEL EVANS (tenor sax); JACK WASHINGTON (baritone sax); COUNT BASIE (piano); CLAUDE WILLIAMS (guitar); WALTER PAGE (bass); JO JONES (drums); JIMMY RUSHING (vocal)
Honeysuckle Rose / *Pennies From Heaven* (vJR) / *Swinging At The Daisy Chain* / *Roseland Shuffle*

Saturday 23 January 1937

Count Basie and his Orchestra broadcast (5.00pm) on their closing night at the Roseland Ballroom in New York City.
Yeah Man! / *Shoe Shine Boy* / *Mary Had A Little Lamb* / *Margie* (vJR) / *Swinging At The Daisy Chain* / *The Glory Of Love* (vJR) / *Limehouse Blues*

Monday 25 January 1937

Members of the Count Basie Orchestra record with Billie Holiday and Teddy Wilson for Brunswick at 1776 Broadway in New York City. The session producer is John Hammond. BUCK CLAYTON (trumpet), LESTER YOUNG (tenor sax), BENNY GOODMAN (clarinet), TEDDY WILSON (piano), FREDDIE GREEN (guitar), WALTER PAGE (bass), JO JONES (drums), BILLIE HOLIDAY (vocal)
He Ain't Got Rhythm (vBH) / *This Year's Kisses* (vBH) / *Why Was I Born?* (vBH) / *I Must Have That Man* (vBH)

Monday 8 February 1937

Count Basie and his Orchestra open a three-week engagement at the Chatterbox in the William Penn Hotel in Pittsburgh. Drummer Jo Jones is missing for some of this engagement following a nervous breakdown.

Wednesday 10 February 1937

Count Basie and his Orchestra broadcast (12.35) from the Chatterbox in Pittsburgh.
You Do The Darnedest Things, Baby (vJR) / *Swinging At The Daisy Chain* / *Riffin'* / *I Cried For You* (vJR) / *Lady Be Good* / *Yeah Man!* / *Moten Swing* (theme)

Friday 12 February 1937

Count Basie and his Orchestra broadcast (1.00) from the Chatterbox in Pittsburgh.
Margie / *Swing, Brother, Swing* / *You Do The Darnedest Things, Baby* (vJR) / *Streamline Strut* / *Magnolias In The Moonlight* / *My Blue Heaven* (vJR) / *Organ Grinder's Swing* / *I Got Rhythm* / *Moten Swing* (theme)

Wednesday 24 February 1937

Count Basie and his Orchestra broadcast (12.30) from the Chatterbox in Pittsburgh.
Rhythm In My Soul / *Dear Old Southland* / *For Sentimental Reasons* (vJR) / *Lady Be Good* / *Somebody Loves Me* (vJR) / *You Do The Darnedest Things, Baby* (vJR) / *Dancing Derby* / *Yeah Man!*

Saturday 27 February 1937

Count Basie and his Orchestra close at the Chatterbox in the William Penn Hotel in Pittsburgh.

Saturday 13 March 1937

Count Basie and his Orchestra play a one-nighter at Energetic Park in Scranton, Pennsylvania.

Sunday 14 March 1937

Count Basie and his rhythm section attend an afternoon jam session at the new Master Recording Studios in New York City. The session is produced by Helen Oakley for Irving Mills to launch the Master and Variety record labels. Duke Ellington, Artie Shaw, Frankie Newton, Mezz Mezzrow, Ella Fitzgerald, Chick Webb, George Wettling and Eddie Condon are among others taking part.

Lots of swell music was made during the party. Basie's rhythm section started things off, joined by various reeds and brass, achieving at times a colossal drive. Benny Goodman and Chick Webb joined forces while Ella Fitzgerald sang three fast songs; Artie Shaw and George Wettling impressed everybody, and Duke along with Rex Stewart, Harry Carney and a few others of his virtuosi, literally panicked the folk late in the day.

In the evening Billie Holiday makes her debut with the Count Basie Orchestra on a one-nighter at Enna Jettick Park in Binghamton, New York.

Friday 19 March 1937

Count Basie and his Orchestra open a one-week engagement at the Apollo Theatre in New York City.

Above: Billie Holiday and Basie on stage at the Apollo Theatre.

Thursday 25 March 1937

Count Basie and his Orchestra close at the Apollo Theatre in New York City.

Friday 26 March 1937

Count Basie and his Orchestra record for Decca in New York. BUCK CLAYTON, ED LEWIS, BOBBY MOORE (trumpets), DAN MINOR, GEORGE HUNT (trombones), CAUGHEY ROBERTS (alto sax), LESTER YOUNG, HERSCHEL EVANS (tenor sax), JACK WASHINGTON (baritone sax), COUNT BASIE (piano), FREDDIE GREEN (guitar), WALTER PAGE (bass), JO JONES (drums), JIMMY RUSHING (vocal)
Exactly Like You (vJR) / *Boo-Hoo* (vJR) / *The Glory Of Love* / *Boogie-Woogie* (vJR)

Count Basie and his Orchestra embark on a short tour which includes the Cincinnati Cotton Club, the Adams Theatre in Newark and Hartford, Connecticut.

Thursday 1 April 1937

Count Basie and his Orchestra open a two-week engagement at the Savoy Ballroom in New York City.

Wednesday 14 April 1937

Count Basie and his Orchestra close at the Savoy Ballroom in New York City.

Friday 16 April 1937

Count Basie and his Orchestra open a one-week engagement at the Nixon Grand Theatre in Philadelphia. During this engagement, Earle Warren replaces Caughey Roberts.

Saturday 17 April 1937

Count Basie and his Orchestra broadcast (12.30) from the Nixon Grand Theatre in Philadelphia. *Moten Swing* (theme) / *Shout And Feel It* / *Old Fashioned Love* / *Mary Had A Little Lamb* (vJR) / *King Porter Stomp* / *This Year's Kisses* (vBH) / *Dear Old Southland* / *Somebody Loves Me* (vJR) / *Swingin' At The Daisy Chain* / *Yeah Man!*

Thursday 22 April 1937

Count Basie and his Orchestra close at the Nixon Grand Theatre in Philadelphia.

Friday 23 April 1937

Count Basie and his Orchestra open a one-week engagement at the Howard Theatre in Washington, D.C.

Thursday 29 April 1937

Count Basie and his Orchestra close at the Howard Theatre in Washington, D.C.

Tuesday 11 May 1937

Members of the Count Basie Orchestra record with Billie Holiday and Teddy Wilson for Columbia in New York City. The session is produced by John Hammond. BUCK CLAYTON (trumpet), LESTER YOUNG (tenor sax), BENNY GOODMAN (clarinet), JOHNNY HODGES (alto sax), TEDDY WILSON (piano), ALLAN REUSS (guitar), ARTIE BERNSTEIN (bass), COZY COLE (drums), BILLIE HOLIDAY (vocal)
Sun Showers (vBH) / *Yours And Mine* (vBH) / *I'll Get By* (vBH) / *Mean To Me* (vBH)

Tuesday 1 June 1937

Members of the Count Basie Orchestra record with Billie Holiday and Teddy Wilson for Columbia in New York City. The session is produced by John Hammond. BUCK CLAYTON (trumpet), LESTER YOUNG (tenor sax), BUSTER BAILEY (clarinet), TEDDY WILSON (piano), FREDDIE GREEN (guitar), WALTER PAGE (bass), JO JONES (drums), BILLIE HOLIDAY (vocal)
Foolin' Myself (vBH) / *Easy Living* (vBH) / *I'll Never Be The Same* (vBH) / *I Found A New Baby*

Friday 4 June 1937

Count Basie and his Orchestra open a one-week engagement at the Apollo Theatre in New York City.

Thursday 10 June 1937
Count Basie and his Orchestra close at the Apollo Theatre in New York City.

Tuesday 15 June 1937
Members of the Count Basie Orchestra record with Billie Holiday and her Orchestra for Columbia in New York City. The session is produced by Bernie Hanighen.
BUCK CLAYTON (trumpet), LESTER YOUNG (tenor sax), EDMOND HALL (clarinet), JAMES SHERMAN (piano), FREDDIE GREEN (guitar), WALTER PAGE (bass), JO JONES (drums), BILLIE HOLIDAY (vocal)
Me, Myself And I (vBH) / *A Sailboat In The Moonlight* (vBH) / *Born To Love* (vBH) / *Without Your Love* (vBH)

Tuesday 22 June 1937
Count Basie and his Orchestra open a long engagement at the Savoy Ballroom in New York City, opposite Billy Hicks' Sizzling Six. At 12.30 Basie and the band broadcast over WMCA: *Moten Swing* (theme) / *King Porter Stomp* / *Where Are You?* (vBH) / *Blue Ball*

Wednesday 23 June 1937
16-yr-old Bob Inman visits the Savoy:

> We arrived at the Savoy Ballroom at 9:30 p.m. and paid the fifty cent admission fee. …Count Basie was one of the best bands; it's so relaxed with a driving rhythm section behind all the great soloists and the sensational singer, Billie Holiday. Basie's band played:
> *Sometimes I'm Happy* / *I Surrender Dear* (vJR) / *House Hop* / *Boo Hoo* / *My First Thrill* / *Riffin' At The Ritz* / *I've Got My Eye On You* / *Pennies From Heaven* (vJR) / *Jam Session* / *Always* / *Louise* / *Me, Myself And I* (vBH) / *Blue Ball* / *Dreamboat* / *Mayflower*
> Too bad Billie Holiday didn't sing more numbers. After having a very enjoyable evening at the Savoy, we had to catch the 1:15 train from 138th Street to our homes in Bronxville, N.Y.

Saturday 26 June 1937
Count Basie and Jimmy Rushing are guests on CBS's Saturday Night Swing Session (7.30pm) broadcast, playing with the CBS studio band:
Prince Of Wails / *Boogie Woogie* (vJR)

Monday 28 June 1937
Count Basie and his Orchestra broadcast (1.00) from the Savoy Ballroom in New York City: *Yeah Man!* / *You Do The Darnedest Things, Baby* (vJR) / *Dear Old Southland* / *I Can't Get Started* (vBH) / *St. Louis Blues* (vJR) / *Roseland Shuffle* / *Me, Myself And I* (vBH) / *Baby Girl* / *Thanksgiving*

Wednesday 30 June 1937
Count Basie and his Orchestra broadcast from the Savoy Ballroom in New York City.
Moten Swing (theme) / *Shout And Feel It* / *The You And Me That Used To Be* (vJR) / *The Count Steps In* / *They Can't Take That Away From Me* (vBH) / *I'll Always Be In Love With You* / *When My Dreamboat Comes Home* (vJR) / *Swing, Brother, Swing* (vBH) / *Bugle Blues* / *I Got Rhythm* / *Moten Swing* (theme)

Friday 2 July 1937
Count Basie and his Orchestra broadcast (1.00) from the Savoy Ballroom in New York City: *Moten Swing* (theme) / *South Side Stomp* / *Where Are You?* (vJR) / *Happy Feet* / *Too Marvellous For Words* (vBH) / *One O'Clock Jump* / *Boo Hoo* (vJR) / *Whatcha Gonna Do When There Ain't No Swing?* (vBH) / *Moten Swing* (theme)

Monday 5 July 1937
Count Basie and his Orchestra broadcast (1.00) from the Savoy Ballroom in New York City: *I Found A New Baby* / *Never In A Million Years* (vBH)

Wednesday 7 July 1937
Count Basie and his Orchestra record for Decca in New York City.
BUCK CLAYTON, ED LEWIS, BOBBY MOORE (trumpets), DAN MINOR, GEORGE HUNT (trombones), EARLE WARREN (alto sax), LESTER YOUNG, HERSCHEL EVANS (tenor sax), JACK WASHINGTON (baritone sax), COUNT BASIE (piano), FREDDIE GREEN (guitar), WALTER PAGE (bass), JO JONES (drums), JIMMY RUSHING (vocal)
Smarty / *One O'Clock Jump* / *Listen My Children, And You Shall Hear* (vJR) / *John's Idea*
In the evening, the band broadcasts (1.30) over WOR from the Savoy Ballroom: *Yeah Man!* / *Me, Myself And I* (vBH) / *Rhythm In My Nursery Rhymes* (vJR) / *Roseland Shuffle* / *Swinging At The Daisy Chain* / *September In The Rain* / *I Must Have That Man* (vBH) / *Dinah* (vJR) / *Thanksgiving*

The engagement at the Savoy ends some time in July and the band play a few gigs in New England, including a 'Battle of the Bands' with Jimmie Lunceford in Hartford, Connecticut.

Thursday 5 August 1937
Count Basie and his Orchestra play a one-nighter at Fieldston on the Atlantic, Massachusetts.

Friday 6 August 1937
Count Basie and his Orchestra play a one-nighter at Old Orchard Beach, Maine.

Sunday 8 August 1937
Count Basie and his Orchestra open an extended residency at the Hotel Ritz-Carlton in Boston.

Monday 9 August 1937
Count Basie and his Orchestra record for Decca in New York.
BUCK CLAYTON, ED LEWIS, BOBBY MOORE (trumpets), DAN MINOR, BENNY MORTON, EDDIE DURHAM (trombones), EARLE WARREN (alto sax/vocal), LESTER YOUNG, HERSCHEL EVANS (tenor sax), JACK WASHINGTON (baritone sax), COUNT BASIE (piano), FREDDIE GREEN (guitar), WALTER PAGE (bass), JO JONES (drums), JIMMY RUSHING (vocal)
Good Morning Blues (vJR) / *Our Love Was Meant To Be* (vEW) / *Time Out* / *Topsy*

Friday 13 August 1937
Count Basie and his Orchestra broadcast from the Hotel Ritz-Carlton in Boston: *Moten Swing* (theme) / *Yeah Man!* / *Louise* / *I Must Have That Man* (vBH) / *When My Dreamboat Comes Home* (vJR) / *Swinging At The Daisy Chain* / *Me, Myself And I* (vBH) / *Smarty* (vJR) / *Perfidia* / *After You've Gone*

Saturday 14 August 1937
Count Basie and his Orchestra broadcast from the Hotel Ritz-Carlton in Boston: *Moten Swing* (theme) / *I Found A New Baby* / *Too Marvellous For Words* (vBH) / *He Ain't Got Rhythm* (vJR) / *Lady Be Good*

Monday 16 August 1937
Count Basie and his Orchestra broadcast from the Hotel Ritz-Carlton in Boston: *Old Fashioned Love* / *I'll Always Be In Love With You* / *Swing, Brother, Swing* (vBH) / *With Plenty Of Money And You* / *Our Love Was Never Meant To Be* (vEW) / *Energetic Stomp* / *There's A Lull In My Life* (vBH) / *Roseland Shuffle*

Friday 20 August 1937
Count Basie and his Orchestra broadcast from the Hotel Ritz-Carlton in Boston: *Shoot The Likker* / *Easy Living* (vBH) / *The You And Me That Used To Be* (vJR) / *Baby Girl* / *I Cried For You* (vBH) / *Boogie Woogie* (vJR) / *Honeysuckle Rose* / *Swinging At The Daisy Chain*

Saturday 21 August 1937
Count Basie's 33rd birthday.
He and his Orchestra broadcast from the Hotel Ritz-Carlton in Boston: *Bugle Call Rag* / *I Can't Get Started* (vBH) / *Rhythm In My Nursery Rhymes* (vJR) / *Thanksgiving*

Monday 23 August 1937
Count Basie and his Orchestra broadcast from the Hotel Ritz-Carlton in Boston: *Energetic Stomp* / *They Can't Take That Away From Me* (vBH) / *Good Morning Blues* (vJR) / *Moten Twist* / *Tea For Two* / *Whatcha Gonna Do When There Ain't No Swing?* (vBH) / *The Glory of Love* (vJR) / *Lady Be Good* / *One O'Clock Jump*

Friday 27 August 1937
Count Basie and his Orchestra broadcast from the Hotel Ritz-Carlton in Boston: *Abadias* / *Have You Any Castles, Baby?* / *Jivin' The Keys* / *I Don't Know If I'm Coming Or Going* (vBH) / *If You Ever Should Leave* (vJR) / *I Ain't Got Nobody* (vJR) / *A Sailboat In The Moonlight* (vBH) / *Doggin' Around*

Monday 30 August 1937
Count Basie and his Orchestra broadcast from the Hotel Ritz-Carlton in Boston: *Moten Swing* (theme) / *Milenburg Joys* / *Let's Call The Whole Thing Off* (vBH) / *Smarty* (vJR) / *September In The Rain* (vEW) / *You're Precious To Me* / *Them There Eyes* (vBH) / *Boogie Woogie* (vJR) / *Bugle Call Rag*

Friday 3 September 1937
Count Basie and his Orchestra broadcast from the Hotel Ritz-Carlton in Boston: *Lady Be Good* / *Love Is In The Air Tonight* (vEW) / *Heaven Help This Heart Of Mine* (vBH) / *Good Morning Blues* (vJR) / *Study In Brown* (vJR) / *Cabin Of Dreams* (vJR) / *I Got Rhythm* / *Moten Swing* (theme)

Monday 6 September 1937
Count Basie and his Orchestra broadcast from the Hotel Ritz-Carlton in Boston: *Prince Of Wails* / *How Could You?* (vBH) / *Have You Any Castles, Baby?* / *Evenin'* (vJR) / *Abadias* / *Swing, Brother, Swing* (vBH) / *I Ain't Got Nobody* (vJR) / *Doggin' Around* / *Moten Swing* (theme)

Around this time Count Basie and his orchestra close at the Ritz-Carlton Hotel in Boston and return to New York. Apart from recording in New York and a week at the Royal Theatre in Baltimore, the Basie band's whereabouts in late September and October are unknown.

Monday 13 September 1937
Members of the Count Basie Orchestra record with Billie Holiday and her Orchestra for Columbia in New York City. The session is produced by Bernie Hanighen.
BUCK CLAYTON (trumpet), LESTER YOUNG (tenor sax), BUSTER BAILEY (clarinet), CLAUDE THORNHILL (piano), FREDDIE GREEN (guitar), WALTER PAGE (bass), JO JONES (drums), BILLIE HOLIDAY (vocal)
Getting Some Fun Out Of Life (vBH) / *Who Wants Love?* (vBH) / *Trav'lin' All Alone* (vBH) / *He's Funny That Way* (vBH)

Wednesday 13 October 1937
Count Basie and his Orchestra record for Decca in New York City.
BUCK CLAYTON, ED LEWIS, BOBBY HICKS (trumpets), DAN MINOR, BENNY MORTON, EDDIE DURHAM (trombones), EARLE WARREN (alto sax/vocal), LESTER YOUNG, HERSCHEL EVANS (tenor sax), JACK WASHINGTON (baritone sax), COUNT BASIE (piano), FREDDIE GREEN (guitar), WALTER PAGE (bass), JO JONES (drums), JIMMY RUSHING (vocal)
I Keep Remembering (vJR) / *Out The Window* / *Don't You Miss Your Baby?* (vJR) / *Let Me Dream* (vEW)

Count Basie "Clicks" On Baltimore Stage

BALTIMORE, Md., Nov. 4 — Count Basie and his orchestra with James Rushing and Billie Halliday doing the vocals made a hit on their recent appearance at the Royal Theatre here. Press agents gave the band several hundred words of praise.

Thursday 21 October 1937
Count Basie and his Orchestra open a two-week engagement at the Meadowbrook Lounge, Cedar Grove, New Jersey.

Sunday 31 October 1937
Count Basie and his Orchestra play a Sunday Morning Swing Concert (11.00am) at the Criterion Theatre in New York City. *Yours And Mine* (vBH) / *I Ain't Got Nobody* (vJR)

Monday 1 November 1937

Members of the Count Basie Orchestra record with Billie Holiday and Teddy Wilson for Brunswick in New York City. The session is produced by John Hammond.

BUCK CLAYTON (trumpet), PRINCE ROBINSON (clarinet/tenor sax), VIDO MUSSO (clarinet/tenor sax), TEDDY WILSON (piano), ALLAN REUSS (guitar), WALTER PAGE (bass), COZY COLE (drums), BILLIE HOLIDAY (vocal)

Nice Work If You Can Get It (vBH) / *Things Are Looking Up* (vBH) / *My Man* (vBH) / *Can't Help Lovin' Dat Man* (vBH)

Wednesday 3 November 1937

Count Basie and his Orchestra broadcast live from the bandstand on their last night at the Meadowbrook Lounge in Cedar Grove, New Jersey.

BUCK CLAYTON, ED LEWIS, BOBBY MOORE (trumpets), DAN MINOR, BENNY MORTON, EDDIE DURHAM (trombones), EARLE WARREN (alto sax), LESTER YOUNG, HERSCHEL EVANS (tenor sax), JACK WASHINGTON (baritone sax), COUNT BASIE (piano), FREDDIE GREEN (guitar), WALTER PAGE (bass), JO JONES (drums), JIMMY RUSHING, BILLIE HOLIDAY (vocal)

Theme–Moten Swing / *One O'Clock Jump* / *I Can't Get Started* (vBH) / *A Study In Brown* / *Rhythm In My Nursery Rhymes* (vJR) / *John's Idea* / *Good Morning Blues* (vJR) / *Dinah* (vJR)

Lester Young solos at the Meadowbrook Lounge.

Friday 5 November 1937

Count Basie and his Orchestra open a one-week engagement at the Apollo Theatre in New York City. Also appearing on the bill are Butterbeans & Susie, The Three Miller Brothers, Big Time Crip, Hilda Rogers, Paul Bass, Honey Brown, John Mason and John Vigal.

Thursday 11 November 1937

Count Basie and his Orchestra close at the Apollo Theatre in New York City.

Friday 12 November 1937

Count Basie and his Orchestra open a one-week engagement at the Howard Theatre in Washington, D.C.

Thursday 18 November 1937

Count Basie and his Orchestra close at the Howard Theatre in Washington, D.C.

Friday 19 November 1937

Count Basie and his Orchestra play at a dance organised by Elsa Maxwell at Princeton University, Princeton, NJ.

The rest of the year consists of a tour of one-nighters including 1 week at the Fox Theatre in Detroit in early December and the last two weeks of December at the Grand Theatre, Philadelphia.

1938

Saturday 1 January 1938
Count Basie and his Orchestra play a dance at Roseland in Boston.

Sunday 2 January 1938
Count Basie and his Orchestra play a dance at Hamilton Park, Waterbury, Connecticut.

Monday 3 January 1938
Count Basie and his Orchestra record for Decca in New York City.
BUCK CLAYTON, ED LEWIS, KARL GEORGE (trumpets), DAN MINOR, BENNY MORTON, EDDIE DURHAM (trombones), EARLE WARREN (alto sax/vocal), LESTER YOUNG, HERSCHEL EVANS (tenor sax), JACK WASHINGTON (baritone sax), COUNT BASIE (piano), FREDDIE GREEN (guitar), WALTER PAGE (bass), JO JONES (drums), JIMMY RUSHING (vocal)
Georgianna (vJR) / *Blues In The Dark* (vJR)

Friday 7 January 1938
Count Basie and his Orchestra open a two-night engagement at the Astor Theatre on Times Square in New York City.

Saturday 8 January 1938
Count Basie and his Orchestra close at the Astor Theatre on Times Square in New York City.

Friday 14 January 1938
Count Basie and his Orchestra play a one-nighter in Johnson City, New York.

Saturday 15 January 1938
Count Basie and his Orchestra play a one-nighter in Scranton, Pennsylvania.

Sunday 16 January 1938
Members of the Basie band appear at the famous Benny Goodman Carnegie Hall Concert in New York City. Afterwards the Count Basie Orchestra appear at the Savoy Ballroom in Harlem, in a Battle of the Bands with Chick Webb's Orchestra.
Down Beat reports:

The affair drew a record attendance and hundreds were turned away at the box office with the crowd tying up traffic for several blocks in that vicinity. Applause for both bands was tremendous and it was difficult to determine which band was the more popular.

Nevertheless, the ballot taken showed Chick Webb's band well in the lead over Basie's and Ella Fitzgerald well out in front over Billie Holiday and James Rushing…

Feeling ran very high between the supporters of the two bands, and it was a fight to the finish. Both bands played magnificently, with Basie having a particular appeal for the dancers, and Webb consistently stealing the show on the drums. Ella caused a sensation with her rendition of 'Loch Lomond', and Billie Holiday thrilled her fans with 'My Man', When Ella sang she had the whole crowd rocking with her. James Rushing had everybody shouting the blues right along with him. Handkerchiefs were waving, people were shouting, the excitement was intense…

General consensus of opinion agreed that both bands played magnificently making the decision a very close one…

Monday 17 January 1938
Count Basie and his Orchestra play a one-nighter at The Ritz in Pottsville, Pennsylvania.

Thursday 20 January 1938
Count Basie and his Orchestra open a one-week engagement at Loew's State Theatre in Times Square, New York City. The film presentation is 'Nothing Sacred' starring Carole Lombard and Fredric March.

Wednesday 26 January 1938
Count Basie and his Orchestra close at Loew's State Theatre in Times Square, New York City.

Friday 28 January 1938
Count Basie and his Orchestra play a one-nighter at The Casino in Washington, D.C.

Sunday 30 January 1938
Count Basie and his Orchestra play a one-nighter in Harrisburg, Pennsylvania.

Wednesday 2 February 1938
Count Basie and his Orchestra play a Battle of the Bands with Lucky Millinder's Orchestra at The Armory in Baltimore, Maryland. Harry Edison is playing trumpet with Lucky Millinder, impresses Basie, and joins the Basie band shortly afterwards.

Thursday 3 February 1938
Count Basie and his Orchestra play a one-nighter at the High School in Red Bank, New Jersey – Basie's home town.

Friday 4 February 1938
Count Basie and his Orchestra play a one-nighter at Williamstown College in Williamstown, Massachusetts.

Saturday 5 February 1938
Count Basie and his Orchestra play a one-nighter in Portland, Maine.

Thursday 10 February 1938
Count Basie and his Orchestra play a one-nighter at Cornell University in Ithaca, New York.

Friday 11 February 1938
Count Basie and his Orchestra play a one-nighter in Rochester, New York.

Saturday 12 February 1938
Count Basie and his Orchestra play a return one-nighter at Cornell University in Ithaca, New York.

Wednesday 16 February 1938
Count Basie and his Orchestra record for Decca in New York City.
BUCK CLAYTON, ED LEWIS, HARRY EDISON (trumpets), DAN MINOR, BENNY MORTON, EDDIE DURHAM (trombones), EARLE WARREN (alto sax/vocal), LESTER YOUNG, HERSCHEL EVANS (tenor sax), JACK WASHINGTON (baritone sax), COUNT BASIE (piano), FREDDIE GREEN (guitar), WALTER PAGE (bass), JO JONES (drums), JIMMY RUSHING (vocal)
Sent For You Yesterday And Here You Come Today (vJR) / *Every Tub / Now Will You Be Good?* (vJR) / *Swinging The Blues*

Thursday 17 February 1938
Count Basie and his Orchestra play a one-nighter in Wilmington, Delaware.

Friday 18 February 1938
Count Basie and his Orchestra play a one-nighter at the Strand Ballroom in Philadelphia.

Sunday 20 February 1938
Count Basie and his Orchestra play a one-nighter at Club Fordham in the Bronx, New York City.

Tuesday 22 February 1938
Count Basie and his Orchestra play a Battle of Bands at the Roseland Ballroom in New York City. Also involved are the bands of Don Redman, Zinn Arthur and Gene Kardos.

Friday 25 February 1938
Count Basie and his Orchestra open a one-week engagement at the Apollo Theatre in New York City.

Saturday 26 February 1938
Bob Inman and a friend visit the Apollo:

> We got there at 2.45 and saw Basie's Band plus movies and a stage show. Billie Holiday used to have red hair but today it was black. Basie's band played: *Farewell Blues / Swingin' The Blues / Underneath The Stars* (vBH) / *Nice Work If You Can Get It* (vBH) / *I Can't Get Started* (vBH) / *Easy Living* (vBH) / *One Never Knows, Does One?* (vBH) / *One O'Clock Jump / Rosalie* (vJR) / *Boogie Woogie* (vJR) / *Rhythm In My Nursery Rhymes* (vJR)

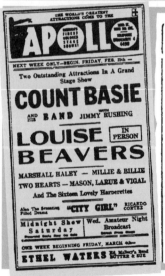

Sunday 27 February 1938
Count Basie and his Orchestra play a Sunday Swing Concert (11.00am) at the Criterion Theatre in New York City. Part of the concert is broadcast over WNEW: *Every Tub / One O'Clock Jump / Rosalie* (vJR) / *Out The Window / Sent For You Yesterday* (vJR) / *Swingin' The Blues / I Ain't Got Nobody* (vJR)

Thursday 3 March 1938
Count Basie and his Orchestra close at the Apollo Theatre. Billie Holiday leaves the Basie band after the final show.

Friday 4 March 1938
Count Basie and his Orchestra play a one-nighter at Wellesley College in Wellesley, Massachusetts.

Saturday 5 March 1938
Count Basie and his Orchestra play a one-nighter in the Bronx, New York City.

Monday 7 March 1938
Count Basie and his Orchestra play a one-nighter in Washington, D.C.

Wednesday 9 March 1938
Count Basie and his Orchestra play a one-nighter in Garden City, New York.

Friday 11 March 1938
Count Basie and his Orchestra play a one-nighter at Yale University in New Haven, Connecticut.

Saturday 12 March 1938
Count Basie and his Orchestra play a one-nighter in Hartford, Connecticut.

Sunday 13 March 1938
Count Basie and his Orchestra open a one-week engagement at the Savoy Ballroom in New York City.

Tuesday 15 March 1938
Count Basie and his Orchestra broadcast from the Savoy Ballroom: *Out The Window / Melody In F / Marie / King Porter Stomp / Good Morning Blues* (vJR) / *I Found A New Baby / Basin Street Blues* (vEW)

Saturday 19 March 1938
Count Basie and his Orchestra close at the Savoy Ballroom in New York City.

Sunday 20 March 1938
Count Basie and his Orchestra play a one-nighter at the Madrid Club in Harrisburg, Pennsylvania.

Tuesday 22 March 1938
Count Basie and his Orchestra play a one-nighter at The Market in Wheeling, West Virginia.

Wednesday 23 March 1938
Count Basie and his Orchestra play a one-nighter at the East Market Gardens in Akron, Ohio.

Thursday 24 March 1938
Count Basie and his Orchestra play a one-nighter in Lexington, Kentucky.

Friday 25 March 1938
Count Basie and his Orchestra play a one-nighter at the Cotton Club in Dayton, Ohio.

Saturday 26 March 1938
Count Basie and his Orchestra play a one-nighter at Vanity Fair in Huntington, West Virginia.

Monday 28 March 1938
Count Basie and his Orchestra play a one-nighter in Mount Hope, West Virginia.

Tuesday 29 March 1938
Count Basie and his Orchestra play a one-nighter at the Genoa High School in Bluefield, West Virginia.

Wednesday 30 March 1938
Count Basie and his Orchestra play a one-nighter in Charleston, West Virginia.

Thursday 31 March 1938
Count Basie and his Orchestra play a one-nighter at The Armory in Louisville, Kentucky.

Friday 1 April 1938
Count Basie and his Orchestra play a one-nighter in Memphis, Tennessee.

Saturday 2 April 1938
Count Basie and his Orchestra get a break from the hectic one-nighters as they open a three-night engagement at the Masonic Temple in Birmingham, Alabama.

Monday 4 April 1938
Count Basie and his Orchestra close at the Masonic Temple in Birmingham, Alabama.

Tuesday 5 April 1938
Count Basie and his Orchestra are back on the bus for the 149-mile drive to play a one-nighter in Chattanooga, Tennessee.

Wednesday 6 April 1938
Count Basie and his Orchestra play a one-nighter at the Sunset Casino in Atlanta, Georgia.

Thursday 7 April 1938
Count Basie and his Orchestra play a one-nighter in Bowling Green, Kentucky.

Friday 8 April 1938
Count Basie and his Orchestra play a one-nighter in St. Louis, Missouri.

Saturday 9 April 1938
Count Basie and his Orchestra play a one-nighter in Kansas City, Missouri.

Sunday 10 April 1938
Count Basie and his Orchestra play a one-nighter in Omaha, Nebraska.

Monday 11 April 1938
Count Basie and his Orchestra play a one-nighter at the New Municipal Auditorium in Kansas City, Missouri.

Tuesday 12 April 1938
Count Basie and his Orchestra play a one-nighter in Topeka, Kansas.

Wednesday 13 April 1938
Count Basie and his Orchestra play a one-nighter in Wichita, Kansas.

Thursday 14 April 1938
Count Basie and his Orchestra play a one-nighter in Tulsa, Oklahoma.

Friday 15 April 1938
Count Basie and his Orchestra play a one-nighter in Muskogee, Oklahoma.

Saturday 16 April 1938
Count Basie and his Orchestra play a one-nighter in Oklahoma City, Oklahoma.

Sunday 17 April 1938
Count Basie and his Orchestra play a one-nighter in Fort Worth, Texas.

Monday 18 April 1938
Count Basie and his Orchestra play a one-nighter in Shreveport, Louisiana.

Tuesday 19 April 1938
Count Basie and his Orchestra play a one-nighter in Waco, Texas.

Wednesday 20 April 1938
Count Basie and his Orchestra play a one-nighter in San Antonio, Texas.

Thursday 21 April 1938
Count Basie and his Orchestra play a one-nighter at the City Auditorium in Houston, Texas.

Friday 22 April 1938
Count Basie and his Orchestra play a one-nighter in Port Arthur, Texas.

Saturday 23 April 1938
Count Basie and his Orchestra play a one-nighter in Houston, Texas.

Monday 25 April 1938
Count Basie and his Orchestra play a one-nighter in Galveston, Texas.

Tuesday 26 April 1938
Count Basie and his Orchestra play a one-nighter in Beaumont, Texas.

Wednesday 27 April 1938
Count Basie and his Orchestra play a one-nighter in Houston, Texas.

Thursday 28 April 1938
Count Basie and his Orchestra play a one-nighter in Dallas, Texas.

Friday 29 April 1938
Count Basie and his Orchestra open a weekend engagement at The Casino in Fort Worth, Texas.

Sunday 1 May 1938
Count Basie and his Orchestra close at The Casino in Fort Worth, Texas.

Monday 2 May 1938
Count Basie and his Orchestra play a one-nighter in Little Rock, Arkansas.

Tuesday 3 May 1938
Count Basie and his Orchestra play a one-nighter in St. Louis, Missouri.

Wednesday 4 May 1938
Count Basie and his Orchestra play a one-nighter in Evansville, Indiana.

Thursday 5 May 1938
Count Basie and his Orchestra play a one-nighter in Louisville, Kentucky.

Friday 6 May 1938
Count Basie and his Orchestra play a one-nighter in Lexington, Kentucky.

Saturday 7 May 1938
Count Basie and his Orchestra play a one-nighter in Charleston, West Virginia.

Monday 9 May 1938
Count Basie and his Orchestra play a one-nighter in Durham, North Carolina.

Friday 13 May 1938
Count Basie and his Orchestra open a one-week engagement at the Apollo Theatre in New York City. Also on the bill are John Hernandez, Avon Long, Moke & Poke, and Mason, LaRue & Vigal.

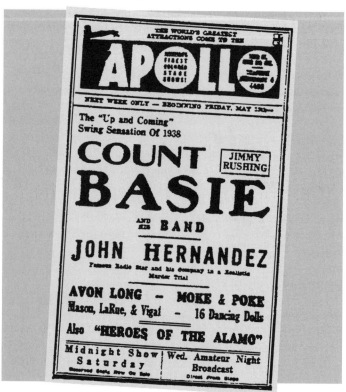

Thursday 19 May 1938
Count Basie and his Orchestra close at the Apollo Theatre in New York City.

Friday 20 May 1938
Count Basie and his Orchestra play a one-nighter in Atlantic City, New Jersey.

Saturday 21 May 1938
Count Basie and his Orchestra play a one-nighter at the New Strand Ballroom in Philadelphia, Pennsylvania.

Sunday 22 May 1938
Count Basie and his Orchestra open a one-week engagement at the Savoy Ballroom in New York City.

Saturday 28 May 1938
Count Basie and his Orchestra close at the Savoy Ballroom in New York City.

Sunday 29 May 1938
Count Basie and his Orchestra play an outdoor benefit for Musicians Union Local 802 at the Randall's Island Stadium in New York City. The 'Carnival of Swing' (11am–4.45pm) organised by Martin Block features more than 20 bands and attracts a crowd of 25,000.
In the evening, they play a concert at Asbury Park, New Jersey.

Monday 30 May 1938
Count Basie and his Orchestra play a one-nighter in Trenton, New Jersey.

Wednesday 1 June 1938
Count Basie and his Orchestra play a one-nighter in Washington, D.C.

Thursday 2 June 1938
Count Basie and his Orchestra play a one-nighter at Edgewater Beach, Turner's Station, Maryland.

Friday 3 June 1938
Count Basie and his Orchestra play a one-nighter in Brooklyn, New York City.

Saturday 4 June 1938
Count Basie and his Orchestra play at the New York Swing Festival on Randall's Island, New York City.

Monday 6 June 1938
Count Basie and his Orchestra record for Decca in New York City.
BUCK CLAYTON, ED LEWIS, HARRY EDISON (trumpets), DAN MINOR, BENNY MORTON, EDDIE DURHAM (trombones), EARLE WARREN (alto sax/vocal), LESTER YOUNG, HERSCHEL EVANS (tenor sax), JACK WASHINGTON (baritone sax), COUNT BASIE (piano), FREDDIE GREEN (guitar), WALTER PAGE (bass), JO JONES (drums), JIMMY RUSHING (vocal)
Mama Don't Want No Peas An' Rice An' Coconut Oil (vJR) / *Blue And Sentimental / Doggin' Around*

Thursday 9 June 1938
Count Basie and his Orchestra play a one-nighter in Allentown, Pennsylvania.

Saturday 11 June 1938
Count Basie and his Orchestra play a one-nighter in Lakewood, Pennsylvania.

Sunday 12 June 1938
Count Basie and his Orchestra play a Swing Festival at Madison Square Garden in New York City.

Monday 13 June 1938
Count Basie and his Orchestra play a one-nighter in Rochester, New York.

Tuesday 14 June 1938
Count Basie and his Orchestra play a one-nighter in Syracuse, New York.

Wednesday 15 June 1938
Count Basie and his Orchestra play a one-nighter in Worcester, Massachusetts.

Thursday 16 June 1938
Count Basie and his Orchestra play a one-nighter in Brunswick, Maine.

Friday 17 June 1938
Count Basie and his Orchestra play a one-nighter in Cambridge, Massachusetts.

Saturday 18 June 1938
Count Basie and his Orchestra play a one-nighter in Narragansett, Rhode Island.

Sunday 19 June 1938
Count Basie and his Orchestra play a one-nighter at the Shady Rest in Plainfield, New Jersey.

Wednesday 22 June 1938
Basie is John Hammond's guest at the Joe Louis-Max Schmeling fight at Yankee Stadium in New York City.

Thursday 23 June 1938
Count Basie and his Orchestra play a one-nighter in Millsboro, Delaware.

Friday 1 July 1938
Count Basie and his Orchestra play a one-nighter in Pittsburgh, Pennsylvania.

Saturday 2 July 1938
Count Basie and his Orchestra play a one-nighter in Jamestown, New York.

Sunday 3 July 1938
Count Basie and his Orchestra play a one-nighter at the Graystone Ballroom in Detroit, Michigan.

Monday 4 July 1938
Count Basie and his Orchestra play a one-nighter in Jamestown, New York.

Saturday 9 July 1938
Count Basie and his Orchestra broadcast on CBS 'America Dances'. Dicky Wells and Helen Humes join the band.

Monday 11 July 1938
Count Basie and his Orchestra open an extended engagement at the Famous Door on 52nd Street in New York City. The band are squeezed onto the bandstand in the tiny club (*below*) during the summer heat wave.

Monday 22 August 1938
Count Basie and his Orchestra record for Decca in New York City.

BUCK CLAYTON, ED LEWIS, HARRY EDISON (trumpets), DAN MINOR, BENNY MORTON, DICKIE WELLS (trombones), EARLE WARREN (alto sax/vocal), LESTER YOUNG, HERSCHEL EVANS (tenor sax), JACK WASHINGTON (baritone sax), COUNT BASIE (piano), FREDDIE GREEN (guitar), WALTER PAGE (bass), JO JONES (drums), JIMMY RUSHING (vocal)

Stop Beatin' Around The Mulberry Bush (vJR, 2 takes) / *London Bridge Is Falling Down* (vJR) / *Texas Shuffle* / *Jumpin' At The Woodside*

Thursday 1 September 1938
Count Basie and his Orchestra take part in a Benefit Bandfest at Randall's Island Stadium in New York City.

Thursday 15 September 1938
Members of the Count Basie Orchestra record with Billie Holiday and her Orchestra for Vocalion/Columbia in New York City.

BUCK CLAYTON (trumpet), LESTER YOUNG (clarinet/tenor sax), DICKIE WELLS (trombone), MARGARET 'QUEENIE' JOHNSON (piano), FREDDIE GREEN (guitar), WALTER PAGE (bass), JO JONES (drums), BILLIE HOLIDAY (vocal)

The Very Thought Of You (vBH) / *I Can't Get Started* (vBH) / *I've Got A Date With A Dream* (vBH) / *You Can't Be Mine* (vBH)

Tuesday 27 September 1938
Members of the Count Basie Orchestra record as the Kansas City Six for Commodore in New York City.

BUCK CLAYTON (trumpet), LESTER YOUNG (clarinet/tenor sax), EDDIE DURHAM (trombone/electric guitar), FREDDIE GREEN (guitar/vocal), WALTER PAGE (bass), JO JONES (drums), BILLIE HOLIDAY (vocal)

Way Down Yonder In New Orleans / *Countless Blues* / *Them There Eyes* (vFG) / *I Want A Little Girl* / *Pagin' The Devil*

Monday 31 October 1938
Members of the Count Basie Orchestra record with Billie Holiday and Teddy Wilson for Brunswick in New York City. John Hammond produces the session.

HARRY JAMES (trumpet), LESTER YOUNG, HERSCHEL EVANS (tenor sax), EDGAR SAMPSON, BENNY CARTER (alto sax), BENNY MORTON (trombone), TEDDY WILSON (piano), AL CASEY (guitar), WALTER PAGE (bass), JO JONES (drums), BILLIE HOLIDAY (vocal)

Everybody's Laughin' (vBH) / *Here It Is Tomorrow Again* (vBH)

Wednesday 9 November 1938
Members of the Count Basie Orchestra record with Billie Holiday and Teddy Wilson for Brunswick in New York City. John Hammond produces the session.

HARRY JAMES (trumpet), LESTER YOUNG, HERSCHEL EVANS (tenor sax), EDGAR SAMPSON, BENNY CARTER (alto sax), BENNY MORTON (trombone), TEDDY WILSON (piano), AL CASEY (guitar), WALTER PAGE (bass), JO JONES (drums), BILLIE HOLIDAY (vocal)

Say It With A Kiss (vBH) / *April In My Heart* (vBH) / *I'll Never Fail You* (vBH) / *They Say* (vBH)

Basie records some piano solos with his rhythm section for Decca in New York City.

COUNT BASIE (piano), FREDDIE GREEN (guitar), WALTER PAGE (bass), JO JONES (drums)

How Long Blues / *The Dirty Dozens* / *Hey Lawdy Mama* / *The Fives* / *Boogie-Woogie*

Saturday 12 November 1938
Count Basie and his Orchestra close at the Famous Door on 52nd Street in New York City.

Sunday 13 November 1938
Count Basie and his Orchestra play a dance at the Savoy Ballroom in New York City.

Wednesday 16 November 1938
Count Basie and his Orchestra record for Decca in New York City.

BUCK CLAYTON, ED LEWIS, HARRY EDISON (trumpets), DAN MINOR, BENNY MORTON, DICKIE WELLS (trombones), EARLE WARREN (alto sax/vocal), LESTER YOUNG, HERSCHEL EVANS (tenor sax), JACK WASHINGTON (baritone sax), COUNT BASIE (piano), FREDDIE GREEN (guitar), WALTER PAGE (bass), JO JONES (drums), JIMMY RUSHING, HELEN HUMES (vocal)

Dark Rapture (vHH) / *Shorty George* / *The Blues I Like To Hear* (vJR) / *Do You Wanna Jump, Children?* (vJR) / *Panassie Stomp*

Wednesday 23 November 1938
Count Basie and his Orchestra open a one-week engagement at the Paramount Theatre in Brooklyn, New York City.

Tuesday 29 November 1938
Count Basie and his Orchestra close at the Paramount Theatre in Brooklyn, New York City.

Wednesday 30 November 1938
Count Basie and his Orchestra open a one-week engagement at the Paramount Theatre in Times Square, New York City. Also on the bill is Sister Rosetta Tharpe. The movie presentation is 'Say it in French' starring Ray Milland.

Tuesday 6 December 1938
Count Basie and his Orchestra close at the Paramount Theatre in Times Square, New York City.

Wednesday 7 December 1938
Count Basie and his Orchestra play a one-nighter at the Earle Theatre in Philadelphia.

Thursday 8 December 1938
Count Basie and his Orchestra play a one-nighter in Trenton, New Jersey.

Friday 9 December 1938
Count Basie and his Orchestra open a one-week engagement at the Hippodrome Theatre in Baltimore.

Thursday 15 December 1938
Count Basie and his Orchestra close at the Hippodrome Theatre in Baltimore.

Friday 16 December 1938
Count Basie and his Orchestra play a one-nighter in Cleveland, Ohio.

Saturday 17 December 1938
Count Basie and his Orchestra play a one-nighter in Huntington, West Virginia.

Sunday 18 December 1938
Count Basie and his Orchestra play a one-nighter in Cleveland, Ohio.

Monday 19 December 1938
Count Basie and his Orchestra play a one-nighter in Dayton, Ohio.

Tuesday 20 December 1938
Count Basie and his Orchestra play a one-nighter in Cincinnati, Ohio.

Wednesday 21 December 1938
Count Basie and his Orchestra play a one-nighter in Cleveland, Ohio.

Thursday 22 December 1938
Count Basie and his Orchestra play a one-nighter in Geneva, New York.

Friday 23 December 1938
Count Basie and his Orchestra appear in the 'From Spirituals to Swing' Concert at Carnegie Hall in New York City.

Saturday 24 December 1938
Count Basie and his Orchestra open a one-week engagement at the Strand Theatre in New York City.

Friday 29 December 1938
Count Basie and his Orchestra close at the Strand Theatre in New York City.

Saturday 30 December 1938
Count Basie and his Orchestra play a one-nighter in Reading, Pennsylvania.

Sunday 31 December 1938
Count Basie and his Orchestra play a one-nighter at the Armory in Geneva, New York.
THEN Breakfast Dance at the New Rockland Palace in New York City opposite Edgar Hayes' Band.

1939

Tuesday 2 January 1939
Count Basie and his Orchestra play a one-nighter in White Plains, New York.

Thursday 5 January 1939
Count Basie and his Orchestra record for Decca in New York City.
BUCK CLAYTON, ED LEWIS, SHAD COLLINS, HARRY EDISON (trumpets), DAN MINOR, BENNY MORTON, DICKIE WELLS (trombones), EARLE WARREN (alto sax/vocal), LESTER YOUNG, HERSCHEL EVANS (tenor sax), JACK WASHINGTON (baritone sax), COUNT BASIE (piano), FREDDIE GREEN (guitar), WALTER PAGE (bass), JO JONES (drums), HELEN HUMES (vocal)
My Heart Belongs To Daddy (vHH) / *Sing For Your Supper* (vHH)

Friday 6 January 1939
Count Basie and his Orchestra open a one-week engagement at the Nixon Grand Theatre in Philadelphia.

Thursday 12 January 1939
Count Basie and his Orchestra close at the Nixon Grand Theatre in Philadelphia.

Friday 13 January 1939
Count Basie and his Orchestra open a one-week engagement at the Howard Theatre in Washington, D.C.

Thursday 19 January 1939
Count Basie and his Orchestra close at the Howard Theatre in Washington, D.C.

Saturday 21 January 1939
Count Basie and his Orchestra play a one-nighter at the Crystal Ballroom in Hartford, Connecticut.

Sunday 22 January 1939
Count Basie and his Orchestra play a one-nighter at the Savoy Ballroom in New York City.

Monday 23 January 1939
Count Basie and his Orchestra play a one-nighter at the Auditorium in Norfolk, Virginia.

Tuesday 24 January 1939
Count Basie and his Orchestra play a one-nighter at the Mosque Ballroom in Richmond, Virginia.

Wednesday 25 January 1939
Count Basie and his Orchestra play a one-nighter in Baltimore, Maryland.

Thursday 26 January 1939
Count Basie and his rhythm section record for Decca in New York City.
COUNT BASIE (piano), FREDDIE GREEN (guitar), WALTER PAGE (bass), JO JONES (drums)
Oh! Red / *Fare Thee Honey, Fare Thee Well* (2 takes) / *Dupree Blues* / *When The Sun Goes Down* (2 takes) / *Red Wagon*

Above: the Count Basie Orchestra on stage at the Apollo. Trumpets: Harry Edison, Shad Collins, Ed Lewis, Buck Clayton (soloing); trombones: Dan Minor, Dickie Wells, Benny Morton; Basie (piano); Jo Jones (drums); Freddie Green (guitar); Walter Page (bass); saxes: Herschel Evans, Earle Warren, Jack Washington, Lester Young.

Friday 27 January 1939

Count Basie and his Orchestra open a one-week engagement at the Apollo Theatre in New York City.

Thursday 2 February 1939

Count Basie and his Orchestra close at the Apollo Theatre in New York City.
Earlier in the day Count Basie and a small group from his Orchestra record for Decca in New York City.
SHAD COLLINS (trumpets), LESTER YOUNG (tenor sax), COUNT BASIE (piano), FREDDIE GREEN (guitar), WALTER PAGE (bass), JO JONES (drums), JIMMY RUSHING (vocal)
You Can Depend On Me (vJR)

Friday 3 February 1939

Count Basie and his Orchestra record for Decca in New York City. Herschel Evans doesn't feel well enough to make the session and Chu Berry deputises.
BUCK CLAYTON, ED LEWIS, SHAD COLLINS, HARRY EDISON (trumpets), DAN MINOR, BENNY MORTON, DICKIE WELLS (trombones), EARLE WARREN (alto sax/vocal), LESTER YOUNG, CHU BERRY (tenor sax), JACK WASHINGTON (baritone sax), COUNT BASIE (piano), FREDDIE GREEN (guitar), WALTER PAGE (bass), JO JONES (drums), HELEN HUMES (vocal)
Cherokee, Part 1 / Cherokee, Part 2 / Blame It On My Last Affair (vHH, 2 takes)

Saturday 4 February 1939

Count Basie and his Orchestra again record for Decca in New York City.
BUCK CLAYTON, ED LEWIS, SHAD COLLINS, HARRY EDISON (trumpets), DAN MINOR, BENNY MORTON, DICKIE WELLS (trombones), EARLE WARREN (alto sax/vocal), LESTER YOUNG, CHU BERRY (tenor sax), JACK WASHINGTON (baritone sax), COUNT BASIE (piano), FREDDIE GREEN (guitar), WALTER PAGE (bass), JO JONES (drums), JIMMY RUSHING, HELEN HUMES (vocal)
Jive At Five / Thursday (vHH) / *Evil Blues* (vJR) / *Oh! Lady Be Good*

Sunday 5 February 1939

Count Basie and his Orchestra play a one-nighter at the Manhattan Club in New York City.

Monday 6 February 1939

Count Basie and his Orchestra play a one-nighter in Hartford, Connecticut. Herschel Evans collapses on the bandstand and is taken to hospital in New York.

Tuesday 7 February 1939

Count Basie and his Orchestra play a one-nighter in Pittsburgh, Pennsylvania.

Wednesday 8 February 1939

Count Basie and his Orchestra play a one-nighter in Youngstown, Ohio.

Thursday 9 February 1939

Count Basie and his Orchestra play a one-nighter in Toledo, Ohio. Herschel Evans dies in Wadsworth Hospital, W185th Street, New York.

HERSCHEL EVANS
9 March 1909 – 9 February 1939

Friday 10 February 1939
Count Basie and his Orchestra play a one-nighter in Ann Arbor, Michigan. Skippy Williams comes in on tenor as a temporary replacement for Herschel Evans.

Saturday 11 February 1939
Count Basie and his Orchestra play a one-nighter in Flint, Michigan.

Sunday 12 February 1939
Count Basie and his Orchestra play a one-nighter at the Savoy Ballroom in Chicago.

Monday 13 February 1939
Count Basie and a small group from his Orchestra record for Columbia in Chicago.
BUCK CLAYTON, SHAD COLLINS (trumpets); DAN MINOR (trombone); LESTER YOUNG (tenor sax); COUNT BASIE (organ); FREDDIE GREEN (guitar); WALTER PAGE (bass); JO JONES (drums); JIMMY RUSHING (vocal)
I Ain't Got Nobody / Goin' To Chicago (vJR) / *Live And Love Tonight / Love Me Or Leave Me*
In the evening, Count Basie and his Orchestra play a one-nighter in Milwaukee, Wisconsin.

Basie on Vocalion

Chicago—Count Basie's band jumped from Decca to the Vocalion record label in February, knocking off their first sides for the new label in mid-February here. The Count also recorded two solos played on a Hammond electric organ. Basie was forced to use a substitute tenor man in place of Herschel Evans, who died suddenly in New York while the band was in Toledo. Lester Young handled all tenor solo work as a result. On his one-nighter at the Savoy here, Basie attracted 6,000 heads to set an all-time record at the spot.

Tuesday 14 February 1939
Count Basie and his Orchestra play a one-nighter in Indianapolis, Indiana.

Wednesday 15 February 1939
Count Basie and his Orchestra play a one-nighter at East Market Gardens in Akron, Ohio.

Thursday 16 February 1939
Count Basie and his Orchestra play a one-nighter in Toronto, Canada.

Friday 17 February 1939
Count Basie and his Orchestra play a one-nighter in Queen's Union, Ontario, Canada.

Saturday 18 February 1939
Count Basie and his Orchestra play a one-nighter at the Paradise Theatre in Detroit, Michigan.

Tuesday 21 February 1939
Count Basie and his Orchestra play a one-nighter in Oxford, Ohio.

Thursday 23 February 1939
Count Basie and his Orchestra open a four-night engagement at the Orpheum Theatre in Memphis, Tennessee.

Sunday 26 February 1939
Count Basie and his Orchestra close at the Orpheum Theatre in Memphis, Tennessee.

Monday 27 February 1939
Count Basie and his Orchestra open a two-night engagement in Nashville, Tennessee.

Tuesday 28 February 1939
Count Basie and his Orchestra play a second night in Nashville, Tennessee.

Thursday 2 March 1939
Count Basie and his Orchestra play a one-nighter in Kansas City, Missouri.

Buddy Tate arrives in Kansas City following a telegram from Basie. For the next two nights he shares the second tenor spot with Skippy Williams.

Friday 3 March 1939
Count Basie and his Orchestra play a campus dance in Lawrence, Kansas.

Saturday 4 March 1939
Count Basie and his Orchestra play a one-nighter in Topeka, Kansas.

Sunday 5 March 1939
Count Basie and his Orchestra play a one-nighter in St. Louis, Missouri.

Monday 6 March 1939
Count Basie and his Orchestra play a one-nighter in Queensboro, Kentucky.

Tuesday 7 March 1939
Count Basie and his Orchestra open a two-night engagement in Chicago.

Wednesday 8 March 1939
Count Basie and his Orchestra play a second night in Chicago.

Thursday 9 March 1939
Count Basie and his Orchestra play a one-nighter at the Paradise Theatre in Detroit, Michigan.

Friday 10 March 1939
Count Basie and his Orchestra open a two-night engagement in Cleveland, Ohio.

Saturday 11 March 1939
Count Basie and his Orchestra play a second night in Cleveland, Ohio.

Monday 13 March 1939
Count Basie and his Orchestra open a three-week engagement at the Southland Café in Boston, Massachusetts.

Sunday 19 March 1939
Count Basie and his Orchestra record for Vocalion in New York City.
BUCK CLAYTON, ED LEWIS, SHAD COLLINS, HARRY EDISON (trumpets); DAN MINOR, BENNY MORTON, DICKIE WELLS (trombones); EARLE WARREN (alto sax/vocal); LESTER YOUNG, BUDDY TATE (tenor sax); JACK WASHINGTON (baritone sax); COUNT BASIE (piano); FREDDIE GREEN (guitar); WALTER PAGE (bass); JO JONES (drums); JIMMY RUSHING, HELEN HUMES (vocal)
What Goes Up Must Come Down (vJR) / *Rock-A-Bye Basie* / *Baby, Don't Tell On Me* (vJR) / *If I Could Be With You (One Hour Tonight)* (vHH) / *Taxi War Dance*

Monday 20 March 1939
Count Basie and his Orchestra record for Vocalion in New York City.
BUCK CLAYTON, ED LEWIS, SHAD COLLINS, HARRY EDISON (trumpets); DAN MINOR, BENNY MORTON, DICKIE WELLS (trombones); EARLE WARREN (alto sax/vocal); LESTER YOUNG, BUDDY TATE (tenor sax); JACK WASHINGTON (baritone sax); COUNT BASIE (piano); FREDDIE GREEN (guitar); WALTER PAGE (bass); JO JONES (drums); HELEN HUMES (vocal)
Don't Worry 'Bout Me (vHH) / *Jump For Me*

Friday 31 March 1939
Count Basie and his Orchestra close at the Southland Café in Boston.

Monday 3 April 1939
Count Basie and his Orchestra play a one-nighter in Portland, Maine.

Tuesday 4 April 1939
Count Basie and his Orchestra play a one-nighter at the Roseland Ballroom in Boston, Massachusetts.

Wednesday 5 April 1939
Count Basie and his Orchestra record for Vocalion in New York City.
BUCK CLAYTON, ED LEWIS, SHAD COLLINS, HARRY EDISON (trumpets); DAN MINOR, BENNY MORTON, DICKIE WELLS (trombones); EARLE WARREN (alto sax/vocal); LESTER YOUNG, BUDDY TATE (tenor sax); JACK WASHINGTON (baritone sax); COUNT BASIE (piano); FREDDIE GREEN (guitar); WALTER PAGE (bass); JO JONES (drums); HELEN HUMES (vocal)
And The Angels Sing (vHH) / *If I Didn't Care* (vHH) / *Twelfth Street Rag* / *Miss Thing, Part 1* / *Miss Thing, Part 2*

Friday 7 April 1939
Count Basie and his Orchestra open a one-week engagement at the Apollo Theatre in New York City.

Thursday 13 April 1939
Count Basie and his Orchestra close at the Apollo Theatre in New York City.

Friday 14 April 1939
Count Basie and his Orchestra open a one-week engagement at the Royal Theatre in Baltimore, Maryland.

Thursday 20 April 1939
Count Basie and his Orchestra close at the Royal Theatre in Baltimore, Maryland.

Friday 21 April 1939
Count Basie and his Orchestra open a one-week engagement at the Howard Theatre in Washington, D.C.

Thursday 27 April 1939
Count Basie and his Orchestra close at the Howard Theatre in Washington, D.C.

Friday 28 April 1939
Count Basie and his Orchestra play a one-nighter in Durham, North Carolina.

Sunday 30 April 1939
Count Basie and his Orchestra play a one-nighter in Danville, Virginia.

Monday 1 May 1939
Count Basie and his Orchestra play a one-nighter at the Civic Auditorium in Raleigh, North Carolina.

In the May issue of *Down Beat*, Barrelhouse Dan reviews Basie's Vocalion releases:

Count Basie
BLUES I LIKE TO HEAR and BLAME IT ON MY LAST AFFAIR, (Decca); ROCKABYE BASIE; BABY, DON'T TELL ON ME; DON'T WORRY ABOUT ME; WHAT GOES UP; THURSDAY and SHORTY GEORGE, (Vocalion).

Get these, if only to marvel at the Count's rhythm section.

Lester Young appears to be working overtime since Herschel Evans' death, but the Young tenor is still thrilling. Harry Edison and Buck Clayton contribute sterling trumpet choruses. Basie's piano, backed as it is by Walter Page's lifting bass, is delightful. *Blues, Rockabye* and *Shorty George* are especially excellent. And I glory in the way Rushing sings the blues. Earl Warren's alto dominates the sax ensemble a trifle strongly, but it's a minor complaint.

Tuesday 2 May 1939
Count Basie and his Orchestra play a one-nighter in Petersburg, Virginia.

Wednesday 3 May 1939
Count Basie and his Orchestra play a one-nighter in Roanoke, Virginia.

Thursday 4 May 1939
Count Basie and his Orchestra play a one-nighter in Asheville, North Carolina.

Friday 5 May 1939
Count Basie and his Orchestra play a one-nighter at the Columbia Auditorium in Columbia, South Carolina.

Monday 8 May 1939
Count Basie and his Orchestra play a one-nighter in Savannah, Georgia.

Tuesday 9 May 1939
Count Basie and his Orchestra play a one-nighter in Macon, Georgia.

Wednesday 10 May 1939
Count Basie and his Orchestra play a one-nighter in Charlotte, North Carolina.

Friday 12 May 1939
Count Basie and his Orchestra play a one-nighter in Columbus, Georgia.

Monday 15 May 1939
Count Basie and his Orchestra play a one-nighter in Augusta, Georgia.

Tuesday 16 May 1939
Count Basie and his Orchestra play a one-nighter in Atlanta, Georgia.

Wednesday 17 May 1939
Count Basie and his Orchestra play a one-nighter in Chattanooga, Tennessee.

Friday 19 May 1939
Count Basie and his Orchestra record for Columbia in Chicago.
BUCK CLAYTON, ED LEWIS, SHAD COLLINS, HARRY EDISON (trumpets); DAN MINOR, BENNY MORTON, DICKIE WELLS (trombones); EARLE WARREN (alto sax); LESTER YOUNG, BUDDY TATE (tenor sax); JACK WASHINGTON (baritone sax); COUNT BASIE (piano/organ); FREDDIE GREEN (guitar); WALTER PAGE (bass); JO JONES (drums); JIMMY RUSHING, HELEN HUMES (vocal)
Lonesome Miss Pretty / Nobody Knows (vJR, orgCB) / *Pound Cake*
SHAD COLLINS (trumpets), LESTER YOUNG (tenor sax), COUNT BASIE (piano), FREDDIE GREEN (guitar), WALTER PAGE (bass), JO JONES (drums), HELEN HUMES (vocal)
Bolero At The Savoy (vHH)

Saturday 20 May 1939
Count Basie and his Orchestra open a six-week engagement at the Panther Room of the Hotel Sherman in Chicago. They broadcast nightly, except Monday, on NBC at 1.30am. In addition, they broadcast nightly, except Monday, at midnight over National Red, National Blue or WMAQ. Muggsy Spanier's Ragtimers alternate the dance sets with Basie and also play the Wednesday and Saturday afternoon sessions. With Muggsy are Rod Cless (clarinet), George Brunis (trombone), Eddie Pripps (tenor sax), George Zack (piano), Pat Pattison (bass) and Russ Winslow (drums).

June 1939
In the new issue of *Down Beat* Barrelhouse Dan reviews the latest batch of Basie issues:

> **Count Basie**
> TAXI WAR DANCE, IF I COULD BE WITH YOU, HOW LONG BLUES, BOOGIE-WOOGIE, CHEROKEE (two sides) on Vocalion, Decca.
>   A great group of records.
>   Basie is more convincing with every one he makes. Studio balance on the Vocalion sides which I've heard so far has been, most unfortunately, discouraging. But the Decca sides show the band better, especially the saxes. Lester Young helped write *Taxi* and you'll hear one of Young's typically unorthodox tenor choruses right after Basie's piano intro; a robust style that grows on one. Joe Jones' tasty, but simple, drumming also is excellent, so good, in fact, that I confess I have grown to prefer his work to that of the more publicized percussionists. Basie's piano is up to par; Helen Humes gets the best vocal in her career with the Count on *If I Could*; the same tune slips off to almost a carbon copy of Chick Webb's stuff on the last chorus.

Saturday 24 June 1939
Count Basie and his Orchestra record for Vocalion in Chicago.
Buck Clayton, Ed Lewis, Shad Collins, Harry Edison (trumpets), Dan Minor, Benny Morton, Dickie Wells (trombones), Earle Warren (alto sax/vocal), Lester Young, Buddy Tate (tenor sax), Jack Washington (baritone sax), Count Basie (piano/organ), Freddie Green (guitar), Walter Page (bass), Jo Jones (drums), Jimmy Rushing, Helen Humes (vocal)
You Can Count On Me (vHH) / *You And Your Love* (vHH) / *How Long Blues* (vJR) / *Sub-Deb Blues* (vHH)

Friday 30 June 1939
Count Basie and his Orchestra close at the Panther Room of the Hotel Sherman in Chicago.

Count Basie, following an old Bob Crosby custom, passed out numbered cards to nightly guests of the Sherman Hotel's Panther Room recently. Then later in the evening a drawing was held, the dozen holders of "lucky numbers" being given Basie Vocalion records. But the Count went Crosby one better. In the event some guests didn't care to walk out on the floor under the bright lights, to possible embarrassment, the Count mailed the records to the address on the winning stubs. Stunt worked up lots of interest in Basie's waxings around Chicago town.

Saturday 1 July 1939
Count Basie and his Orchestra play a one-nighter at the Lake Shore Club in Chicago.

In the July issue of *Down Beat* Barrelhouse Dan reviews the latest Basie releases:

> **Count Basie**
> *The Dirty Dozen* and *When the Sun Goes Down*, piano solos on Decca; *Miss Thing*, with entire band, on Vocalion.
>   Excellent Basie samples.
>   The solos are abetted by Joe Jones' drums, Freddie Green's guitar and Walter Page's bass. Both tunes are old standbys; both show off the Count as few of his band records do. Vocalion's publicity releases state that *Miss Thing* was waxed, unknown to the band, while it was improvising in the studios between recordings. I doubt that, but the tune (taking both sides) *does* sound relaxed, and the solos by Lester Young, tenor; Buck Clayton, trumpet, and Buddy Tate (who comes in for the second tenor solo on the "A" side), have plenty to interest jazz fans. The riff the band uses becomes monotonous, but not the rhythm section, which stands out here as usual, a habit which convinces one it's the best on records today.

Sunday 2 July 1939
Count Basie and his Orchestra play a one-nighter in Gary, Indiana.

Monday 3 July 1939
Count Basie and his Orchestra play a one-nighter in South Bend, Indiana.

Around this time, Harry Edison marries Birtie Sanford, a showgirl from St. Louis, in Crown Point, Indiana

Tuesday 4 July 1939
Count Basie and his Orchestra play a one-nighter in Youngstown, Ohio.

Wednesday 5 July 1939
Count Basie and his Orchestra play a one-nighter in Columbus, Ohio.

Saturday 8 July 1939
Count Basie and his Orchestra play a one-nighter in Brooklyn, New York.

Monday 10 July 1939
Count Basie and his Orchestra play a one-nighter in Atlantic City, New Jersey.

Tuesday 11 July 1939

Count Basie and his Orchestra open a nine-week stay at the Famous Door on 52nd Street in New York City.

Monday 31 July 1939

Coleman Hawkins, straight off the boat from Europe, turns up at the Famous Door to hear Lester Young and the Basie band. A few days later, Hawk and Lester Young are involved in a cutting contest at Puss Johnson's Tavern in Harlem.

Hawk and Les Young In Carving Contest

New York—When Les Young of Count Basie's band took out his tenor the other night at Puss Johnson's Tavern, on St. Nicholas avenue in Harlem, Coleman Hawkins was ready. The two aces tangled for an hour in a carving contest, and according to members of Fats Waller's band, it stopped when Les said he'd had enough. Hawkins is making plans to have a band of his own.

'Les Young Wasn't Carved' -- Holiday

Chicago—Refuting statements made by members of Fats Waller's band and other colored musicians who were there, Billie Holiday last week branded reports that Coleman Hawkins "carved" Les Young in a tenor duel at Puss Johnson's tavern in Harlem as "unfair" to Les. "Young really cut the Hawk," said Billie, "and most everyone there who saw them tangle agreed on that."

August 1939

In the new issue of *Down Beat* Barrelhouse Dan reviews the latest Basie releases:

Count Basie

Jump For Me, Twelfth Street Rag, on Vocalion.

What intriguing satire on *Rag*! The Count works with Jo Jones admirably, and one can imagine the kicks the two got when they knocked out the first chorus together. Basie's piano is Wallerish, however, and not as effective on *Rag* as *Jump*. Lester Young's tenor cuts through occasionally to add brilliance to the Count's rhythm section. The band has made better records, but this one is a gem because of its subtlety.

Friday 4 August 1939

Count Basie and his Orchestra record for Vocalion in New York City.

BUCK CLAYTON, ED LEWIS, SHAD COLLINS, HARRY EDISON (trumpets); DAN MINOR, BENNY MORTON, DICKIE WELLS (trombones); EARLE WARREN (alto sax); LESTER YOUNG, BUDDY TATE (tenor sax); JACK WASHINGTON (baritone sax); COUNT BASIE (piano); FREDDIE GREEN (guitar); WALTER PAGE (bass); JO JONES (drums); JIMMY RUSHING, HELEN HUMES (vocal)

Moonlight Serenade (vHH) / *Song Of The Islands* / *I Can't Believe That You're In Love With Me* (vJR) / *Clap Hands, Here Comes Charlie*

September 1939

In the new issue of *Down Beat* Barrelhouse Dan reviews the latest Basie releases:

Count Basie

You Can Count On Me, Lady Be Good, on Decca.

Another chance to hear the late Herschel Evans' tenor. It's there, brilliantly, on the first portion of *Lady* and reestablishes him as a master of the instrument. One of the last Basie performances left in Decca's unreleased files, this disc is badly balanced. The rhythm section, especially, is difficult to hear. But with excellent solos by Evans, Les Young (who also plays solo after Herschel on *Lady*), Shad Collins and the Count, and because both arrangements are superb examples of hot jazz on paper, discophiles should not overlook the results.

Jimmy Rushing's vocal on *Count* is poor. His forte is straight blues, and as recent Vocalion sides by him indicate, he should stick to that form and let others sing the pops.

Sunday 3 September 1939

Count Basie and his Orchestra close at the Famous Door on 52nd Street in New York City.

Monday 4 September 1939

Count Basie and his Orchestra play a one-nighter in Youngstown, Ohio.

Tuesday 5 September 1939

Count Basie and his Kansas City Seven record for Vocalion in New York City.

BUCK CLAYTON (trumpet); DICKIE WELLS (trombone); LESTER YOUNG (tenor sax); COUNT BASIE (piano); FREDDIE GREEN (guitar); WALTER PAGE (bass); JO JONES (drums)

Dickie's Dream (2 takes) / *Lester Leaps In* (2 takes)

Thursday 7 September 1939
Count Basie and his Orchestra open a two-week engagement at the Roseland Ballroom in New York City.

Tuesday 19 September 1939
Count Basie and his Orchestra play an afternoon concert at the Manhattan Center in New York City.

Wednesday 20 September 1939
Count Basie and his Orchestra close at the Roseland Ballroom in New York City.

Thursday 21 September 1939
Count Basie and his Orchestra play a one-nighter in Stamford, Connecticut.

Friday 22 September 1939
Count Basie and his Orchestra play a one-nighter in Newark, New Jersey.

Saturday 23 September 1939
Count Basie and his Orchestra play a one-nighter at the Savoy Ballroom in New York City.

Sunday 24 September 1939
Count Basie and his Orchestra play a one-nighter in Buffalo, New York.

Monday 25 September 1939
Count Basie and his Orchestra play a one-nighter in Cleveland, Ohio.

Tuesday 26 September 1939
Count Basie and his Orchestra play a one-nighter in Indianapolis, Indiana.

Wednesday 27 September 1939
Count Basie and his Orchestra play a one-nighter in St. Louis, Missouri.

Thursday 28 September 1939
Count Basie and his Orchestra play a one-nighter at the Municipal Auditorium in Kansas City, Missouri.

Friday 29 September 1939
Count Basie and his Orchestra play a one-nighter in Omaha, Nebraska.

Saturday 30 September 1939
Count Basie and his Orchestra play a one-nighter in Denver, Colorado.

Morton Leaves Basie

Los Angeles—Benny Morton, ace hot trombonist with Count Basie, left the band last week. His place was taken by Jimmy Young, Jimmie Lunceford's singer-trombonist. Morton pulled out, it was said, because Basie felt he couldn't feature the Morton trombone as it deserved to be featured. Basie's band opens the Palomar Oct. 4.

Monday 2 October 1939
Count Basie and his Orchestra play a one-nighter at Sweets Ballroom in Oakland, California.

They are due to open at the Palomar Ballroom in Los Angeles on 4th October, but it is destroyed in a fire on the 2nd. They are signed instead for the Paramount Ballroom.

Thursday 5 October 1939
Count Basie and his Orchestra play a one-week engagement at the Paramount Ballroom in Los Angeles, California.

Wednesday 11 October 1939
Count Basie and his Orchestra close at the Paramount Ballroom in Los Angeles, California.

Thursday 12 October 1939
Count Basie and his Orchestra play a one-nighter at the Vogue Ballroom in Los Angeles, California.

Saturday 14 October 1939
Count Basie and his Orchestra play a one-nighter in San Diego, California.

Monday 16 October 1939
Count Basie and his Orchestra open a two-week engagement at the World's Fair, Treasure Island, in San Francisco, California.

Above: Lester Young solos at the World's Fair, Treasure Island, in San Francisco, California.

Friday 27 October 1939
Count Basie and his Orchestra appear on a CBS radio show promoting Columbia records.

Sunday 29 October 1939
Count Basie and his Orchestra close at the World's Fair in San Francisco, California.

Tuesday 31 October 1939
Count Basie and his Orchestra play a one-nighter in Sacramento, California.

Wednesday 1 November 1939
Count Basie and his Orchestra play a one-nighter in Stockton, California.

Thursday 2 November 1939
Count Basie and his Orchestra play a one-nighter in Los Angeles, California.

Friday 3 November 1939
Count Basie and his Orchestra play a one-nighter in Glendale, California.

Saturday 4 November 1939
Count Basie and his Orchestra play a one-nighter in San Bernardino, California.

Monday 6 November 1939
Count Basie and his Orchestra record for Columbia in Los Angeles.
BUCK CLAYTON, ED LEWIS, SHAD COLLINS, HARRY EDISON (trumpets); DAN MINOR, BENNY MORTON, DICKIE WELLS (trombones); EARLE WARREN (alto sax); LESTER YOUNG, BUDDY TATE (tenor sax); JACK WASHINGTON (baritone sax); COUNT BASIE (piano); FREDDIE GREEN (guitar); WALTER PAGE (bass); JO JONES (drums); JIMMY RUSHING (vocal)
The Apple Jump / I Left My Baby (vJR) / *Riff Interlude / Volcano*

Tuesday 7 November 1939
Count Basie and his Orchestra record for Columbia in Los Angeles.
BUCK CLAYTON, ED LEWIS, SHAD COLLINS, HARRY EDISON (trumpets); DAN MINOR, BENNY MORTON, DICKIE WELLS (trombones); EARLE WARREN (alto sax); LESTER YOUNG, BUDDY TATE (tenor sax); JACK WASHINGTON (baritone sax); COUNT BASIE (piano); FREDDIE GREEN (guitar); WALTER PAGE (bass); JO JONES (drums); HELEN HUMES (vocal)
Between The Devil And The Deep Blue Sea (vHH) / *Ham'n'Eggs / Hollywood Jump / Someday, Sweetheart* (vHH)

Thursday 9 November 1939
Count Basie and his Orchestra play a one-nighter in El Paso, Texas.

Saturday 11 November 1939
Count Basie and his Orchestra open a two-night engagement in Fort Worth, Texas.

Sunday 12 November 1939
Count Basie and his Orchestra close in Fort Worth, Texas.

Monday 13 November 1939
Count Basie and his Orchestra play a one-nighter in San Antonio, Texas.

Tuesday 14 November 1939
Count Basie and his Orchestra play a one-nighter in Galveston, Texas.

Wednesday 15 November 1939
Count Basie and his Orchestra play a one-nighter in Houston, Texas.

Down Beat's Barrelhouse Dan reviews Basie's new batch of records:

Four Basie Sides Highlight Lists
BY BARRELHOUSE DAN
Taking a powder on his band, and rounding up a handful of his boys for a special session, Count Basie comes through with two new records which get the nod as the most unique of the entire batch to be released in the last two weeks.

Solos With Rhythm
With Freddie Green on guitar, Walter Page on bass, and Jo Jones at the traps, the Count unleashes his talent to cut two solo sides on Decca 2780 which reveal hitherto unappreciated talent. Titles are "Oh, Red" and "Fare Thee, Honey," and although they were waxed last winter, are sterling samples of what four men can accomplish when they set out to produce a different kind of jazz. "Fare Thee" is nothing more than the ancient "How Long Blues" with a new title. Equally as pure are "Lester Leaps In" and "Dickie's Dream," on Vocalion 5118, by Basie and the same group with Les Young, Dickie Wells and Buck Clayton added to form the Kansas City Seven. Here, on "Leaps," Les plays the most unusual and stirring tenor he's shown on records—and the way he and Basie play back to each other throughout the 10 inches is a kick not often experienced. "Dream" also shows fine Young samples, plus a quiet, restrained chorus by Clayton and one by Dickie to boot. Both sides are definite "musts" for collectors as well as musicians.

Thursday 16 November 1939

Count Basie and his Orchestra play a one-nighter in Henderson, Texas.

Friday 17 November 1939

Count Basie and his Orchestra play a one-nighter in Port Arthur, Texas.

Saturday 18 November 1939

Count Basie and his Orchestra play a one-nighter in Baton Rouge, Louisiana.

Sunday 19 November 1939

Count Basie and his Orchestra play a one-nighter in New Orleans, Louisiana.

Monday 20 November 1939

Count Basie and his Orchestra play a one-nighter in Monroe, Louisiana.

Tuesday 21 November 1939

Count Basie and his Orchestra play a one-nighter in Little Rock, Arkansas.

Wednesday 22 November 1939

Count Basie and his Orchestra play a one-nighter in Birmingham, Alabama.

Thursday 23 November 1939

Count Basie and his Orchestra play a one-nighter in Atlanta, Georgia.

Friday 24 November 1939

Count Basie and his Orchestra open a two-nighter in Jacksonville, Florida.

Saturday 25 November 1939

Count Basie and his Orchestra close in Jacksonville, Florida.

Monday 27 November 1939

Count Basie and his Orchestra play a one-nighter in Macon, Georgia.

Tuesday 28 November 1939

Count Basie and his Orchestra play a one-nighter in Knoxville, Tennessee.

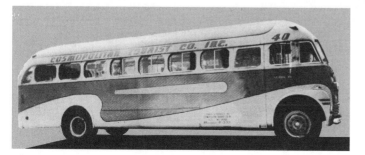

Wednesday 29 November 1939

Count Basie and his Orchestra play a one-nighter in Louisville, Kentucky.

Thursday 30 November 1939

Count Basie and his Orchestra play a one-nighter in Bowling Green, Kentucky.

Friday 1 December 1939

Count Basie and his Orchestra play a one-nighter in Evansville, Indiana.

Saturday 2 December 1939

Count Basie and his Orchestra play a one-nighter at the Casa Loma Ballroom in St. Louis, Missouri.

Sunday 3 December 1939

Count Basie and his Orchestra play a dance at the Savoy Ballroom in Chicago.

Monday 4 December 1939

Count Basie and his Orchestra play a one-nighter in Detroit, Michigan.

Tuesday 5 December 1939

Count Basie and his Orchestra play a one-nighter in Columbus, Ohio.

Wednesday 6 December 1939

Count Basie and his Orchestra play a one-nighter in Huntington, West Virginia.

Thursday 7 December 1939

Count Basie and his Orchestra play a one-nighter in Pittsburgh, Pennsylvania.

Friday 8 December 1939

Count Basie and his Orchestra play a one-nighter at the New Albert Auditorium in Baltimore, Maryland.

SUN-DEC-3
IN PERSON
Presented by MCA
The Sepia Swing Sensation

COUNT BASIE
and his ORCHESTRA
with
James Rushing

SAVOY
South Parkway at 47th St.
ADM. 60c BEFORE 8:30

"THE COUNT OF SWING"
COUNT BASIE
AND HIS ORCHESTRA
with JAMES RUSHING and HELEN HUMES
FRIDAY, DEC. 8th — 9 P.M. - 2 A.M.
NEW ALBERT AUDITORIUM
1224 PENNSYLVANIA AVE.   BALTIMORE, MD.
55c Before Date   —   65c On Date
TICKETS ON SALE AT NEW ALBERT, 1224 PENNSYLVANIA AVE.

Saturday 9 December 1939

Count Basie and his Orchestra arrive back in New York City after a gruelling four-month tour.

Sunday 10 December 1939
Count Basie and his Orchestra play a one-nighter in Bridgeport, Connecticut.

Wednesday 13 December 1939
Members of the Count Basie Orchestra record with Billie Holiday and her Orchestra for Vocalion/Columbia in New York City.
BUCK CLAYTON, HARRY EDISON (trumpets); LESTER YOUNG (tenor sax); EARLE WARREN (alto sax); JACK WASHINGTON (baritone sax); JOE SULLIVAN (piano); FREDDIE GREEN (guitar); WALTER PAGE (bass); JO JONES (drums); BILLIE HOLIDAY (vocal)
Night And Day (vBH) / *The Man I Love* (vBH) / *You're Just A No-Account* (vBH) / *You're A Lucky Guy* (vBH)

Thursday 14 December 1939
Count Basie and his Orchestra play a one-nighter in Trenton, New Jersey.

Friday 15 December 1939
Count Basie and his Orchestra play a one-nighter in Wilmington, Delaware.

Down Beat's Barrelhouse Dan reviews Basie's latest release:

Count Basie
"Nobody Knows" and "Song of the Islands," on Vocalion 5169.
Basie plays a heavy organ on *Knows* which spoils an excellent blues side and a vocal by Jimmy Rushing. The arrangement would have been marvelous had the Count been at the Steinway. Reverse is a well-played standard with Basie back where he belongs and aided by superb Jo Jones drums, Les Young tenor and highly-perfected ensemble. Excellent jazz, although Basie's band has turned out better.

Friday 22 December 1939
Count Basie and his Orchestra play a one-nighter at Kreuger's Auditorium in Newark, New Jersey.

Sunday 24 December 1939
Count Basie and his Orchestra appear in the 'Spirituals To Swing' concert (8.45pm) at Carnegie Hall in New York City. The concert, organised by John Hammond, also features The Boogie-Woogie Boys, Sister Rosetta Tharpe, Benny Goodman, Ida Cox and James P. Johnson.

Monday 25 December 1939
Count Basie and his Orchestra play a one-nighter at the Sunnybrook Ballroom in Pottstown, Pennsylvania.

Wednesday 27 December 1939
Count Basie and his Orchestra play a one-nighter in Charleston, West Virginia.

Thursday 28 December 1939
Count Basie and his Orchestra play a one-nighter in Strassburg, Virginia.

Friday 29 December 1939
Count Basie and his Orchestra play a one-nighter in Richmond, Virginia.

Sunday 31 December 1939
Count Basie and his Orchestra play a one-nighter in Worcester, Massachusetts.

1940

Monday 1 January 1940
Count Basie and his Orchestra play a one-nighter in Philadelphia, Pennsylvania.

Friday 5 January 1940
Count Basie and his Orchestra play a dance at the Golden Gate Ballroom in New York City.

Saturday 6 January 1940
Count Basie and his Orchestra play a one-nighter in Brooklyn, New York.

Friday 12 January 1940
Count Basie and his Orchestra open a one-week engagement at the Apollo Theatre in New York City.

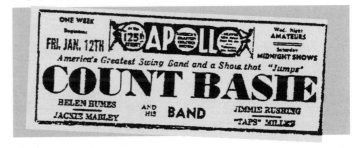

Thursday 18 January 1940
Count Basie and his Orchestra close at the Apollo Theatre in New York City.

Friday 19 January 1940
Count Basie and his Orchestra open a one-week engagement at the Howard Theatre in Washington, D.C.

Thursday 25 January 1940
Count Basie and his Orchestra close at the Howard Theatre in Washington, D.C.

Friday 26 January 1940
Count Basie and his Orchestra open at the Golden Gate Ballroom in New York City.

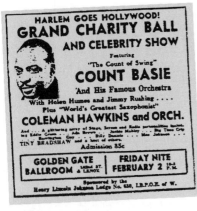

Friday 2 February 1940
Count Basie and his Orchestra play a Grand Charity Ball at the Golden Gate Ballroom in New York City. Coleman Hawkins and his Orchestra share the bill.

Friday 9 February 1940
Count Basie and his Orchestra close at the Golden Gate Ballroom in New York City.

Saturday 10 February 1940
Count Basie and his Orchestra play a dance at the Manhattan Center in New York City.

Sunday 11 February 1940
Count Basie and his Orchestra play a one-nighter in Baltimore, Maryland.

Monday 12 February 1940
Count Basie and his Orchestra play a one-nighter in Orange, New Jersey.

Tuesday 13 February 1940
Count Basie and his Orchestra play a dance at the Roseland State Ballroom in Boston.

Friday 16 February 1940
Count Basie and his Orchestra play a one-nighter in Hamilton, New York.

Saturday 17 February 1940
Count Basie and his Orchestra play a one-nighter in Rochester, New York.

Sunday 18 February 1940
Count Basie and his Orchestra play a one-nighter at Hamilton Park in Waterbury, Connecticut.

Monday 19 February 1940
Count Basie and his Orchestra open a four-week engagement at the Southland Café in Boston, Massachusetts. Vic Dickenson joins the band, replacing Benny Morton.

Tuesday 20 February 1940
Count Basie and his Orchestra broadcast from the Southland Café in Boston, Massachusetts.
BUCK CLAYTON, ED LEWIS, AL KILLIAN, HARRY EDISON (trumpets), DAN MINOR, VIC DICKENSON, DICKIE WELLS (trombones), EARLE WARREN (alto sax), LESTER YOUNG, BUDDY TATE (tenor sax), JACK WASHINGTON (baritone sax), COUNT BASIE (piano), FREDDIE GREEN (guitar), WALTER PAGE (bass), JO JONES (drums), JIMMY RUSHING, HELEN HUMES (vocal)
Ebony Rhapsody / Riff Interlude / Darn That Dream (vHH) / *Take It, Prez / Baby, Don't You Tell On Me* (vJR) / *If I Could Be With You One Hour Tonight* (vHH) / *I Got Rhythm / One O'Clock Jump*

Monday 18 March 1940
Count Basie and his Orchestra close at the Southland Café in Boston, Massachusetts.

Tuesday 19 March 1940
Count Basie and his Orchestra record for Columbia in New York City.
BUCK CLAYTON, ED LEWIS, AL KILLIAN, HARRY EDISON (trumpets), DAN MINOR, VIC DICKENSON, DICKIE WELLS (trombones), EARLE WARREN (alto sax), LESTER YOUNG, BUDDY TATE (tenor sax), JACK WASHINGTON (baritone sax), COUNT BASIE (piano), FREDDIE GREEN (guitar), WALTER PAGE (bass), JO JONES (drums)
I Never Knew / Tickle Toe / Let's Make Hey! While The Moon Shines / Louisiana (2 takes)

Wednesday 20 March 1940
Count Basie and his Orchestra record for Columbia in New York City.
BUCK CLAYTON, ED LEWIS, AL KILLIAN, HARRY EDISON (trumpets), DAN MINOR, VIC DICKENSON, DICKIE WELLS (trombones), EARLE WARREN (alto sax), LESTER YOUNG, BUDDY TATE (tenor sax), JACK WASHINGTON (baritone sax), COUNT BASIE (piano), FREDDIE GREEN (guitar), WALTER PAGE (bass), JO JONES (drums), JIMMY RUSHING (vocal)
Easy Does It / Let Me See / Blues (I Still Think Of Her) (vJR) / *Somebody Stole My Gal* (vJR)

Saturday 23 March 1940
Count Basie and his Orchestra play a one-nighter in Springfield, Massachusetts.

Sunday 24 March 1940
Count Basie and his Orchestra play a one-nighter in Harrisburg, Pennsylvania.

Monday 25 March 1940
Count Basie and his Orchestra play a one-nighter in Philadelphia, Pennsylvania.

Tuesday 26 March 1940
Count Basie and his Orchestra play a one-nighter in Milford, Delaware.

Wednesday 27 March 1940
Count Basie and his Orchestra play a one-nighter in Newark, New Jersey.

Thursday 28 March 1940
Count Basie and his Orchestra play a one-nighter in Wrentham, Massachusetts.

Friday 29 March 1940
Count Basie and his Orchestra play a one-nighter in Portland, Maine.

Saturday 30 March 1940
Count Basie and his Orchestra play a one-nighter in Lawrence, Massachusetts.

Sunday 31 March 1940
Count Basie and his Orchestra play a one-nighter in Waterbury, Connecticut.

Monday 1 April 1940
Count Basie and his Orchestra play a one-nighter in Albany, New York.

Tuesday 2 April 1940
Count Basie and his Orchestra play a one-nighter at the Roseland State Ballroom in Boston, Massachusetts.

Thursday 4 April 1940
Count Basie and his Orchestra open a one-week engagement at Loew's State Theatre in New York City. The movie presentation is 'The Shop Around The Corner' starring James Stewart and Margaret Sullavan.

Wednesday 10 April 1940
Count Basie and his Orchestra close at Loew's State Theatre in New York City.

Thursday 11 April 1940
Count Basie and his Orchestra open a one-week engagement at the Flatbush Theatre in Brooklyn.

Wednesday 17 April 1940
Count Basie and his Orchestra close at the Flatbush Theatre in Brooklyn.

Thursday 18 April 1940
Count Basie and his Orchestra open a one-week engagement at the Windsor Theatre in the Bronx.

Wednesday 24 April 1940
Count Basie and his Orchestra close at the Windsor Theatre in the Bronx.

Thursday 25 April 1940
Count Basie and his Orchestra open a four-day engagement at the Carlton Theatre in Jamaica, Queens, New York.

Sunday 28 April 1940
Count Basie and his Orchestra close at the Carlton Theatre in Jamaica, Queens, New York.

Then it's back on the bus for another tour of one-nighters starting in Virginia.

Tuesday 30 April 1940
Count Basie and his Orchestra play a one-nighter in Abingdon, Virginia.

Wednesday 1 May 1940
Count Basie and his Orchestra play a one-nighter in Bluefield, West Virginia.

Thursday 2 May 1940
Count Basie and his Orchestra play a one-nighter in Beekley, West Virginia.

Friday 3 May 1940
Count Basie and his Orchestra play a one-nighter in Charleston, West Virginia.

Saturday 4 May 1940
Count Basie and his Orchestra open a two-night engagement in Cincinnati, Ohio.

Sunday 5 May 1940
Count Basie and his Orchestra close in Cincinnati, Ohio.

Monday 6 May 1940
Count Basie and his Orchestra play a one-nighter in Lexington, Kentucky.

Tuesday 7 May 1940
Count Basie and his Orchestra play a one-nighter in Wheeling, West Virginia.

Wednesday 8 May 1940
Count Basie and his Orchestra play a one-nighter in Morgantown, West Virginia.

Thursday 9 May 1940
Count Basie and his Orchestra play a one-nighter in Logan, West Virginia.

Friday 10 May 1940
Count Basie and his Orchestra play a one-nighter in Dayton, Ohio.

Saturday 11 May 1940
Count Basie and his Orchestra play a one-nighter in Cleveland, Ohio.

Sunday 12 May 1940
Count Basie and his Orchestra play a one-nighter in Buffalo, New York.

Monday 13 May 1940
Count Basie and his Orchestra play a one-nighter in Pittsburgh, Pennsylvania.

Tuesday 14 May 1940
Count Basie and his Orchestra play a one-nighter in Akron, Ohio.

Wednesday 15 May 1940
Count Basie and his Orchestra play a one-nighter in Bradford, Pennsylvania.

Thursday 16 May 1940
Count Basie and his Orchestra play a one-nighter in Baltimore, Maryland.

Friday 17 May 1940
Count Basie and his Orchestra play a one-nighter in Philadelphia, Pennsylvania.

Saturday 18 May 1940
Count Basie and his Orchestra play a one-nighter in Paterson, New Jersey.

Monday 20 May 1940
Count Basie and his Orchestra play a one-nighter in Lancaster, Pennsylvania.

Tuesday 21 May 1940
Count Basie and his Orchestra play a one-nighter in Atlantic City, New Jersey.

Friday 24 May 1940
Count Basie and his Orchestra open a one-week engagement at the Apollo Theatre in New York City. Also on the bill are 'Hotcha' Drew, Willie Jackson, Alex Lovejoy and Tommy & Al.
In the morning, before the first show, Basie presides over a million dollar jam session on the stage of the Apollo where he is joined by Benny Carter, Coleman Hawkins and Charlie Barnet.

Thursday 30 May 1940
Count Basie and his Orchestra close at the Apollo Theatre in New York City.

Friday 31 May 1940
Count Basie and his Orchestra record for Columbia in New York City.
BUCK CLAYTON, ED LEWIS, AL KILLIAN, HARRY EDISON (trumpets), DAN MINOR, VIC DICKENSON, DICKIE WELLS (trombones), EARLE WARREN (alto sax/vocal), TAB SMITH (alto sax), LESTER YOUNG, BUDDY TATE (tenor sax), JACK WASHINGTON (baritone sax), COUNT BASIE (piano), FREDDIE GREEN (guitar), WALTER PAGE (bass), JO JONES (drums), JIMMY RUSHING (vocal)
Blow Top (2 takes) / *Gone With What Wind* (2 takes) / *Super Chief* / *You Can't Run Around* (vJR)

Tab Smith May Join Basie Band

New York—Tab Smith, noted reed man, sat in on alto with Basie's band for the recording of his own number, *Blow-Top*, before the Basie band left for its 2-week vacation. Tab was originally hailed as an alto find with Lucky Millinder's bunch but was recently heard on tenor with Frankie Newton and Teddy Wilson. Count is considering adding him to the band permanently as fifth sax.

Other sides waxed on the date were *Gone With What Wind*, an Elton Hill arrangement of the Goodman Sextet original, which featured Dan Minor in his first recorded solo with the band; also *Stardust* and a Jimmy Rushing blues, featuring Tab, the four trumpets and rhythm. Basie and Goodman will get together soon, geography permitting, for another Sextet session. MCA has been dickering to keep the Count in town during the summer at a famous hotel spot. The deal to switch the band to William Morris under Willard Alexander's aegis seems to have fallen through, and chances are that Basie will remain with MCA.

Saturday 1 June 1940
The Count Basie Orchestra start a two-week vacation.

Friday 7 June 1940
Members of the Count Basie Orchestra record with Billie Holiday and her Orchestra for Columbia in New York City.
ROY ELDRIDGE (trumpet), LESTER YOUNG, KERMIT SCOTT (tenor sax), BILL BOWEN, JOE ELDRIDGE (alto sax), TEDDY WILSON (piano), FREDDIE GREEN (guitar), WALTER PAGE (bass), J. C. HEARD (drums), BILLIE HOLIDAY (vocal)
I'm Pulling Through (vBH) / *Tell Me More* (vBH) / *Laughing At Life* (vBH) / *Time On My Hands* (vBH)

Friday 14 June 1940
Count Basie attends Coleman Hawkins' opening at the Apollo Theatre. He takes part in a jam session with Hawkins and other visiting bandleaders: Pete Brown (alto sax), Joe Marsala (clarinet), Bunny Berigan, Roy Eldridge (trumpets), Tommy Dorsey, Jack Jenney (trombones), John Kirby (bass) and Gene Krupa (drums).

Saturday 15 June 1940
Count Basie and his Orchestra play a one-nighter in Newark, New Jersey.

Monday 17 June 1940
Count Basie and his Orchestra play a one-nighter in Rocky Mount, North Carolina.

Tuesday 18 June 1940
Count Basie and his Orchestra play a one-nighter in Charleston, North Carolina.

Wednesday 19 June 1940
Count Basie and his Orchestra play a one-nighter in Charlotte, North Carolina.

Thursday 20 June 1940
Count Basie and his Orchestra play a one-nighter in Roanoke, Virginia.

Friday 21 June 1940
Count Basie and his Orchestra play a one-nighter in Winston-Salem, North Carolina.

Saturday 22 June 1940
Count Basie and his Orchestra play a one-nighter in Washington, D.C.

Sunday 23 June 1940
Count Basie and his Orchestra play an open air Swing Jamboree (3.00pm–8.00pm) at Carr's Beach in Annapolis, Maryland.

Monday 24 June 1940
Count Basie and his Orchestra play a one-nighter in Buckaroo Beach, Virginia.

Tuesday 25 June 1940
Count Basie and his Orchestra play a one-nighter in Petersburg, Virginia.

Wednesday 26 June 1940
Count Basie and his Orchestra play a one-nighter in Asheville, North Carolina.

Thursday 27 June 1940
Count Basie and his Orchestra play a one-nighter in Johnson City, Tennessee.

Friday 28 June 1940
Count Basie and his Orchestra play at the Moonlite Gardens and also at the Cotton Club in Cincinnati, Ohio.

Saturday 29 June 1940
Count Basie and his Orchestra play a one-nighter in Jamestown, New York.

Sunday 30 June 1940
Count Basie and his Orchestra play a one-nighter in Vermillion, Ohio.

Monday 1 July 1940
Count Basie and his Orchestra play a one-nighter in Yankee Lake, Ohio.

Wednesday 3 July 1940
Count Basie and his Orchestra play a one-nighter in Evansville, Indiana.

Friday 5 July 1940
Count Basie and his Orchestra open a one-week engagement at the Regal Theatre in Chicago.

Earl Hines Retires as Leader

Chicago—Freed of his contract with Ed Fox, mogul of the dark Grand Terrace, Earl Hines has temporarily "retired" as a leader. Walter Fuller, singing trumpeter with Hines, has taken over Earl's band and will work under a contract with Fox. Hines, shown (top) here with Count Basie, plans to

Thursday 11 July 1940

Count Basie and his Orchestra close at the Regal Theatre in Chicago. After the show, Basie is photographed with Benny Goodman who is due for surgery on his back the next day at the Mayo Clinic in Rochester, Minnesota.

Friday 12 July 1940

Count Basie and his Orchestra open a one-week engagement at Coney Island in Cincinnati, Ohio.

Monday 15 July 1940

Down Beat reviews Basie's latest Columbia release:

Count Basie
"Let's Make Hey While the Moon Shines" & "Somebody Stole My Gal," Columbia 35509.

Screwy title is another Basie riff compo with the Count and Lester Young doing the heavy individually. Last two choruses mimic Basie's *One O'Clock Jump* ending…. The coupling is mostly Jimmy Rushing vocal, but Jack Washington, playing exciting baritone sax, bursts through for a grand chorus reminiscent of his bary work with Paul Banks 10 years ago. Harry Edison's trumpet (what's happened to Buck Clayton's masterful muted horn) winds it up. On the whole, excellent Basie samples, and certainly, not commercial.

Friday 19 July 1940

Count Basie and his Orchestra close at Coney Island in Cincinnati, Ohio.

Saturday 20 July 1940

Count Basie and his Orchestra play a one-nighter in Dayton, Ohio.

Monday 22 July 1940

Count Basie and his Orchestra play a one-nighter at the Greystone Ballroom in Detroit, Michigan.

Tuesday 23 July 1940

Count Basie and his Orchestra play a one-nighter in South Bend, Indiana.

Wednesday 24 July 1940

Count Basie and his Orchestra play a one-nighter in Richmond, Indiana.

Thursday 25 July 1940

Count Basie and his Orchestra play a one-nighter in Paducah, Kentucky.

Friday 26 July 1940

Count Basie and his Orchestra play a one-nighter in Memphis, Tennessee.

Saturday 27 July 1940

Count Basie and his Orchestra play a one-nighter in St. Louis, Missouri.

Sunday 28 July 1940

Count Basie and his Orchestra play a one-nighter in Tulsa, Oklahoma.

Monday 29 July 1940

Count Basie and his Orchestra play a one-nighter at the Municipal Auditorium in Kansas City, Missouri.

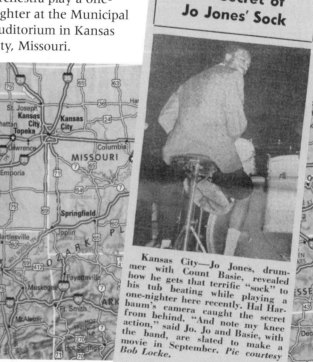

The Secret of Jo Jones' Sock

Kansas City—Jo Jones, drummer with Count Basie, revealed how he gets that terrific "sock" to his tub beating while playing a one-nighter here recently. Hal Harbaum's camera caught the secret from behind. "And note my knee action," said Jo. Jo and Basie, with the band, are slated to make a movie in September. Pic courtesy Bob Locke.

Tuesday 30 July 1940

Count Basie and his Orchestra play a one-nighter in Tulsa, Oklahoma.

Wednesday 31 July 1940

Count Basie and his Orchestra play a one-nighter in Little Rock, Arkansas.

Thursday 8 August 1940

Count Basie and his Orchestra record for Columbia in Chicago.

Buck Clayton, Ed Lewis, Al Killian, Harry Edison (trumpets), Dan Minor, Vic Dickenson, Dickie Wells (trombones), Earle Warren (alto sax/vocal), Tab Smith (alto sax), Lester Young, Buddy Tate (tenor sax), Jack Washington (baritone sax), Count Basie (piano/organ), Freddie Green (guitar), Walter Page (bass), Jo Jones (drums), Jimmy Rushing, Helen Humes (vocal)

Evenin' (vJR) / *The World Is Mad, Pt 1* / *The World Is Mad, Pt 2* / *Moten Swing* / *It's Torture* (vHH) / *I Want A Little Girl* (vJR)

Friday 9 August 1940

Count Basie and his Orchestra open a one-week engagement at the State Lake Theatre in Chicago, Illinois.

Saturday 10 August 1940

Count Basie and his Orchestra play at the Mayor of Bronzeville Ball at the Savoy Ballroom in Chicago.

Thursday 15 August 1940

Count Basie and his Orchestra close at the State Lake Theatre in Chicago, Illinois.

Thursday 15 August 1940

Down Beat reviews Basie's latest Columbia release:

> **Count Basie**
> **"Gone With 'What' Wind" & "Blow Top," Okeh 5629.**
> The leader's red wagon piano-stylings, Dickie Wells' trombone and the rhythm section which many musicians nowadays take too much for granted all jell perfectly on the first side. Ensembles are precise, clean and filled with guts. The coupling was written and arranged by Tab Smith, alto man, but Les Young's tenor gets more of a play than Smith's sax, which, of course, is as it should be. Right up to par on both counts.

Friday 16 August 1940

Count Basie and his Orchestra play a one-nighter in Gary, Indiana.

Saturday 17 August 1940

Count Basie and his Orchestra play a one-nighter in Kansas City, Missouri.

Sunday 18 August 1940

Count Basie and his Orchestra play a one-nighter in Topeka, Kansas.

Monday 19 August 1940

Count Basie and his Orchestra play a one-nighter in Denver, Colorado.

Thursday 22 August 1940

Count Basie and his Orchestra open an 18-day engagement at the Paramount Theatre in Los Angeles, California.

Monday 2 September 1940

Count Basie and his Orchestra play on a Labor Day street parade prior to their evening engagement at the Paramount Theatre in Los Angeles, California. Jimmy Lunceford and his Orchestra are also in the parade.

Sunday 8 September 1940

Count Basie and his Orchestra close at the Paramount Theatre in Los Angeles, California.

Monday 9 September 1940

Count Basie and his Orchestra play a one-nighter in Oakland, California.

Tuesday 10 September 1940

Count Basie and his Orchestra play a one-nighter in Hollywood, California.

Friday 13 September 1940

Count Basie and his Orchestra play a one-nighter in Oklahoma City, Oklahoma.

Saturday 14 September 1940

Count Basie and his Orchestra play a one-nighter in Wichita Falls, Texas.

Sunday 15 September 1940
Count Basie and his Orchestra play a one-nighter in Dallas, Texas.

Down Beat reviews Basie's latest release:

Count Basie
"You Can't Run Around" & "Super Chief," Okeh 5690.
Best blues Count Basie has recorded since he jumped the Decca label pops up this week under the title *You Can't Run Around* which allows plenty of space for Jimmy Rushing's vocal, the leader's soft piano, and a full Tab Smith chorus on alto. Reverse, a Jimmy Mundy special tagged *Super Chief*, is just a series of riffs with Buddy Tate's tenor prominent. The Count has done better, but his disadvantage is that he already has set a tremendous par and unless his wax output is terrifically outstanding it automatically becomes subject to adverse criticism.

Monday 16 September 1940
Count Basie and his Orchestra play a one-nighter in Houston, Texas.

Tuesday 17 September 1940
Count Basie and his Orchestra play a one-nighter in Henderson, Texas.

Wednesday 18 September 1940
Count Basie and his Orchestra play a one-nighter in Galveston, Texas.

Thursday 19 September 1940
Count Basie and his Orchestra play a one-nighter in Shreveport, Louisiana.

Friday 20 September 1940
Count Basie and his Orchestra play a one-nighter in Port Arthur, Texas.

Sunday 22 September 1940
Count Basie and his Orchestra play a one-nighter in New Orleans, Louisiana.

Monday 23 September 1940
Count Basie and his Orchestra play a one-nighter in Monroe, Louisiana.

Tuesday 24 September 1940
Count Basie and his Orchestra play a one-nighter in Greenville, Mississippi.

Wednesday 25 September 1940
Count Basie and his Orchestra play a one-nighter in Birmingham, Alabama.

Thursday 26 September 1940
Count Basie and his Orchestra play a one-nighter in Atlanta, Georgia.

Sunday 29 September 1940
Count Basie and his Orchestra play a one-nighter in Auburn, Alabama.

Monday 30 September 1940
Count Basie and his Orchestra play a one-nighter in Savannah, Georgia.

Tuesday 1 October 1940
Count Basie and his Orchestra play a one-nighter in Columbus, Georgia.

Wednesday 2 October 1940
Count Basie and his Orchestra play a one-nighter in Greenville, South Carolina.

Thursday 3 October 1940
Count Basie and his Orchestra play a one-nighter in Florence, South Carolina.

Friday 4 October 1940
Count Basie and his Orchestra play a one-nighter in Washington, D.C.

Saturday 5 October 1940
Count Basie and his Orchestra play a one-nighter in Rochester, New York.

Sunday 6 October 1940
Count Basie and his Orchestra play a one-nighter in Canton, Ohio.

Monday 7 October 1940
Count Basie and his Orchestra play a one-nighter in Detroit, Michigan.

Tuesday 8 October 1940
Count Basie and his Orchestra play a one-nighter in Cleveland, Ohio.

Wednesday 9 October 1940
Count Basie and his Orchestra play a one-nighter in Cincinnati, Ohio.

Thursday 10 October 1940
Count Basie and his Orchestra play a one-nighter in Bluefield, West Virginia.

Friday 11 October 1940
Count Basie and his Orchestra play a one-nighter in Beekley, West Virginia.

Saturday 12 October 1940
Count Basie and his Orchestra play a one-nighter in Charleston, West Virginia.

Monday 14 October 1940
Count Basie and his Orchestra play a one-nighter in Raleigh, North Carolina.

NEW YORK ►►►►►►

Tuesday 15 October 1940

Count Basie and his Orchestra play a one-nighter in Richmond, Virginia.

Friday 18 October 1940

Count Basie and his Orchestra open a one-week engagement at the Apollo Theatre in New York City.

Thursday 24 October 1940

Count Basie and his Orchestra close at the Apollo Theatre in New York City.

Bottom: The Count Basie Orchestra on stage at the Apollo Theatre.
Right: Recording with Benny Goodman.

Friday 25 October 1940

Count Basie and his Orchestra play a one-nighter in Baltimore, Maryland.

Sunday 27 October 1940

Count Basie and his Orchestra play a one-nighter at the Lyric Theatre in Bridgeport, Connecticut.

Monday 28 October 1940

Count Basie and members of his Orchestra rehearse with Benny Goodman and Charlie Christian in New York City. The results are recorded.

DAN MINOR, BENNY GOODMAN (clarinet); BUCK CLAYTON (trumpet); LESTER YOUNG (tenor sax); COUNT BASIE (piano); CHARLIE CHRISTIAN, FREDDIE GREEN (guitars); WALTER PAGE (bass); JO JONES (drums)

Ad-Lib Blues / I Never Knew / Charlie's Dream / Wholly Cats / Lester's Dream

Tuesday 29 October 1940
Count Basie and his Orchestra play a one-nighter in Lake Champagne, Connecticut.

Wednesday 30 October 1940
Count Basie and his Orchestra record for Columbia in New York City.
BUCK CLAYTON, ED LEWIS, AL KILLIAN, HARRY EDISON (trumpets); DAN MINOR, VIC DICKENSON, DICKIE WELLS (trombones); EARLE WARREN (alto sax); TAB SMITH (alto sax); LESTER YOUNG, BUDDY TATE (tenor sax); JACK WASHINGTON (baritone sax); COUNT BASIE (piano); FREDDIE GREEN (guitar); WALTER PAGE (bass); JO JONES (drums); JIMMY RUSHING, HELEN HUMES (vocal)
All Or Nothing At All (vHH) / *The Moon Fell In The River* (vHH) / *What's Your Number?* / *Draftin' Blues* (vJR)

Friday 1 November 1940
Down Beat reviews Basie's latest Okeh release:

Count Basie
"I Want a Little Girl" & "It's Torture," Okeh 5773.
 When a better performance of an old pop tune—a good one at that—is done, Basie will have to do it. *Little Girl* is not only Jimmy Rushing's greatest vocal since *Good Morning Blues*, but it's also spiced with dirty Buck Clayton trumpet and a mess of weird sax figures behind JR's vocal. Jo Jones' beat is mighty. Reverse is a pop, despite it's alluring title, but it's well sung by Helen Humes and again Clayton's horn is heard.

'I'll Break Up My Band' Basie Says

 New York—Threatening to break up his band and join Benny Goodman as pianist, Count Basie last week lashed at MCA for that agency's alleged failure to book the Basie band into spots with radio wires. Basie and his road manager, Milton Ebbins, claimed MCA's handling of the band was "crazy" and pointed out how the band recently was booked for the Paramount Theater, Los Angeles, for two weeks. "It was the only date we played out there," said Ebbins, "and it cost us $2,000 to send the band there. That doesn't make sense."
500-Mile Jump Hurts
 Unbelievably long jumps also were a point of contention. "500 miles a night isn't unusual for us," Basie said. "We've jumped from New York to Chicago in one night."
 Ebbins said Basie's band was a big grosser everywhere it played. On its recent southern tour it broke records in almost every city. "And yet we don't make money," he said. "MCA got some $19,000 in commission money last year, Basie got $7,000 himself, and the band got some $5,000. Does that make sense?"
 Basie has been playing with Benny Goodman the last couple of weeks, doing one-nighters. The boys in his band loafed around New York. Also in the picture is Willard Alexander, Basie's manager, who is with Wm. Morris agency but who okays all the band's bookings. He has refused several lately offered by MCA.
Taking Case to Petrillo
 Observers believe Basie's threat to join Goodman was just a threat. A proven money-maker, the Basie band is too great a musical organization, and a box-office attraction, to be abandoned. Most persons believed that Basie, who has been trying to get out of his MCA contract for a year and go to the Wm. Morris office, was simply putting pressure on MCA.
 "We are taking the case to James Petrillo Nov. 16," said Ebbins. "We'll lay all the figures in front of him and the AFM. Basie and his band have been getting a rotten deal all along and it is high time the picture changed. We haven't had a location job with air time for a year. Some weeks we work every night, jumping 500 miles a night. Other weeks we lay off. No one seems to be interested in Basie at MCA. We feel that Mr. Petrillo should know the facts."

Monday 4 November 1940
Count Basie, Walter Page and Jo Jones join with Benny Goodman and Charlie Christian to play at a Democratic Rally in New York. Part of the show is broadcast.
Gone With 'What' Wind

Thursday 7 November 1940
Count Basie records with Benny Goodman's Sextet for Columbia in New York City.
BENNY GOODMAN (clarinet); COOTIE WILLIAMS (trumpet); GEORGE AULD (tenor sax); COUNT BASIE (piano); CHARLIE CHRISTIAN (guitar); ARTIE BERNSTEIN (bass); HARRY JAEGER (drums)
Wholly Cats / *Royal Garden Blues* / *As Long As I Live* / *Benny's Bugle*

Friday 8 November 1940
Count Basie and his Orchestra play a one-nighter in Manchester, New Hampshire.

Saturday 9 November 1940
Count Basie and his Orchestra play a one-nighter in Portland, Massachusetts.

Sunday 10 November 1940
Count Basie and his Orchestra play a Dawn Dance at the Roseland Ballroom in Taunton, Massachusetts.

Monday 11 November 1940
Count Basie and his Orchestra play a dance at Egleston Square Gardens in Boston, Massachusetts.

Tuesday 12 November 1940
Count Basie and his Orchestra play a one-nighter in Gardner, Massachusetts.

Wednesday 13 November 1940
Count Basie and his Orchestra play a one-nighter in Claremont, Massachusetts.

Tuesday 19 November 1940
Count Basie and his Orchestra record for Columbia in New York City.
BUCK CLAYTON, ED LEWIS, AL KILLIAN, HARRY EDISON (trumpets); DAN MINOR, VIC DICKENSON, DICKIE WELLS (trombones); EARLE WARREN (alto sax); TAB SMITH (alto sax); LESTER YOUNG, BUDDY TATE (tenor sax); JACK WASHINGTON (baritone sax); COUNT BASIE (piano); FREDDIE GREEN (guitar); WALTER PAGE (bass); JO JONES (drums); HELEN HUMES (vocal)
Five O'Clock Whistle (3 takes) / *Love Jumped Out* (3 takes) / *My Wanderin' Man* (vHH, 3 takes) / *Broadway* (2 takes)
In the evening, Count Basie and Benny Goodman's Sextet broadcast on Martin Block's 'Make Believe Ballroom':
Benny's Bugle / *Wholly Cats* / *Honeysuckle Rose*

Saturday 23 November 1940
Count Basie and his Orchestra play a one-nighter in New Haven, Connecticut.

EXTRA
BIG HOLIDAY EVE DANCE
COME ONE AND ALL!
DAWN DANCE
Sun., Nov. 10, '40
COUNT BASIE
AND HIS ORCHESTRA
ROSELAND BALLROOM
TAUNTON, MASS.
Sun., Nov. 10, '40

Esquire Club
Presents
COUNT BASIE
AND HIS
ORCHESTRA
at
EGLESTON SQUARE GARDENS
MONDAY EVE., NOVEMBER 11
— ADMISSION —
85c UNTIL 9 P. M.
Afterward Admission will be $1.00

Basie Asks Petrillo Help In Squabble

New York—Punches are still being thrown at MCA by Count Basie and his staff of managers and advisers. Reported as being "extremely dissatisfied" with the way MCA has been booking the Basie band, Basie and his handlers have been huddling with James C. Petrillo with an eye toward having the union break off the band's contract with MCA.

Basie's band has been working off and on recently. It is slated to go into the new uptown Cafe Society east, run by Barney Josephson, sometime this month. Basie has been recording with Benny Goodman and doing an occasional one-nighter with BG's new band, but his threat to abandon his band and join Benny permanently is not being taken seriously by those close to him. In the picture with Basie, in the fight against MCA, are Willard Alexander, of the Wm. Morris agency; Goodman, and Milton Ebbins, Basie road manager, among others. They are seeking to have Basie's binder with MCA broken because of dissatisfaction with the way that agency has been handling the band this year.

Monday 25 November 1940

Count Basie and his Orchestra play a one-nighter in Salisbury, Maryland.

Thursday 28 November 1940

Count Basie and his Orchestra play a one-nighter in Philadelphia, Pennsylvania.

Saturday 30 November 1940

Count Basie and his Orchestra open a two-week engagement at the Savoy Ballroom in New York City.

Sunday 1 December 1940

Down Beat reviews Basie's latest Okeh release:

Count Basie
"The World is Mad" in two parts, Okeh.

Not unlike his *One O'Clock Jump*, Basie composed and "head" arranged this 5-minute jump opus with an eye toward spotting all his best soloists. The first tenor is by Buddy Tate, Les Young comes in at the close of the first side and starts out alone on the second. Solos are interesting all the way, but even better is the way Basie paces his rhythm section, and how neatly that section is recorded. Really solid stuff for Basie's legions of followers even if the material is not strong.

Tuesday 10 December 1940

After finishing at the Savoy Ballroom, Count Basie and his Orchestra play a Xmas Basket Fund Breakfast Dance at the Renaissance Casino in New York City. Also appearing are the bands of Earl Bostic, Hot Lips Page and Vernon Andre.

Thursday 12 December 1940

Count Basie and his Orchestra close at the Savoy Ballroom in New York City.

Friday 13 December 1940

Count Basie and his Orchestra record for Columbia in New York City.
BUCK CLAYTON, ED LEWIS, AL KILLIAN, HARRY EDISON (trumpets); DAN MINOR, VIC DICKENSON, DICKIE WELLS (trombones); EARLE WARREN, TAB SMITH (alto sax); PAUL BASCOMB, BUDDY TATE (tenor sax); JACK WASHINGTON (baritone sax); COUNT BASIE (piano); FREDDIE GREEN (guitar); WALTER PAGE (bass); JO JONES (drums); HELEN HUMES (vocal)
It's The Same Old South (vJR, 3 takes) / *Stampede In G Minor* (3 takes) / *Who Am I?* (vHH) / *Rockin' The Blues* (2 takes)
Lester Young fails to show up for the Friday 13th date and is replaced by Paul Bascomb.

Basie Band Won't Break Up

New York—Count Basie's band will not break up!

After fighting with his booker, MCA, for a re-arrangement of the commission monies MCA has been taking for its dates, an agreement was reached whereby a "sliding scale" will be used in the future.
Commish 'Take' Cut Down

Attempts were made by Basie and his staff of managers and handlers to have James C. Petrillo, chief of the AFM, to enter the dispute and hear Basie's side of it. But Basie's meetings with Petrillo, although arranged, always were postponed until the final agreement was reached without Petrillo ever actually stepping in. New setup, instead of allowing MCA a straight 20 per cent take, brings the average cut to 12 per cent. Basie will give MCA 10 per cent on a gross up to $500, 15 per cent up to $750, and 20 per cent for anything above that.

Sunday 15 December 1940

Down Beat reviews Basie's latest Okeh release:

Count Basie
"Blues" & "Apple Jump", Okeh 5862.

Jimmy Rushing's fine vocal is the highspot of *Blues* with Les Young and the Count managing to be heard, too. The brass ensembles on the last chorus sound flat; at least all four trumpets can't be heard. Tempo is much faster than usual for a Rushing showcase. *Apple* is also bright. It's a nice riff number, in which Basie never allows the riff to get monotonous, and there are fine bits by Young and Harry Edison. Well worth the 35 cents asked.

Thursday 19 December 1940

Count Basie and his Orchestra broadcast on Martin Block's *Make Believe Ballroom* over WNEW in New York City.

Friday 20 December 1940

Count Basie and his Orchestra play a one-nighter in Brunswick, Massachusetts.

Saturday 21 December 1940

Count Basie and his Orchestra play a one-nighter in Boston, Massachusetts.

Wednesday 25 December 1940

Count Basie and his Orchestra play a one-nighter in Harrisburgh, Pennsylvania.

Thursday 26 December 1940

Count Basie records 2 takes of *It Counts A Lot* with Sam Donahue's Orchestra in New York City before joining his Orchestra to play a one-nighter in Baltimore, Maryland.

Lester Young, Count Basie Part Company

New York—Lester Young and Count Basie, friends and co-workers for the last five years in Basie's band, parted two weeks ago. The split came as a terrific surprise to followers of Basie and the band.

Basie said he would rather not comment. Young, one of the most distinctive and inventive of all the tenor sax men, likewise refused to discuss the change and said he wasn't sure what he would do. Basie is looking for an unknown youngster to fill Les' shoes. Also leaving the band is Victor Dickinson, who several months ago took Benny Morton's trombone chair. Like Young, Dickinson knew Basie back in Kansas City, although he didn't join the Count until 1940 after working with Cab Calloway and others. Basie is reported to be cutting his brass section down to five instead of seven he has been using.

Les, who failed to show up for a record date on Friday the 13th, said "go 'way and lemme sleep—a man's got no business makin' music on Friday the 13th." Tab Smith is joining the band and Ed Cuffe is temporarily in on trombone.

Friday 27 December 1940

Count Basie and his Orchestra play a one-nighter in Norfolk, Virginia.

Saturday 28 December 1940

Count Basie and his Orchestra play a one-nighter in Richmond, Virginia.

Monday 30 December 1940

Count Basie and his Orchestra play a one-nighter in Durham, North Carolina.

Tuesday 31 December 1940

Count Basie and his Orchestra play a one-nighter in Roanoke, Virginia.

1941

Wednesday 1 January 1941
Count Basie and his Orchestra play a one-nighter in Washington, D.C.

Count Basie Pays $10,000 For His Band Contract; Joins William Morris

Friday 3 January 1941
Count Basie buys his managerial rights from MCA and signs with the William Morris Agency. The Orchestra open a one-week engagement at the Apollo Theatre in New York City. Don Byas takes over from Paul Bascomb.

Thursday 9 January 1941
Count Basie and his Orchestra close at the Apollo Theatre in New York City.

Friday 10 January 1941
Count Basie and his Orchestra play a one-nighter in Wrentham, Massachusetts.

Saturday 11 January 1941
Count Basie and his Orchestra play a one-nighter in Lowell, Massachusetts.

Sunday 12 January 1941
Count Basie and his Orchestra play a one-nighter in Waterbury, Connecticut.

Tuesday 14 January 1941
Count Basie and his Orchestra play a dance at the Roseland State Ballroom in Boston.

Wednesday 15 January 1941
Down Beat reviews Basie's latest Okeh releases:

Count Basie
"Draftin' Blues" & "What's Your Number?", Okeh 5897; "The Moon Fell in the River" & "All Or Nothing at All", Okeh 5884.
Jimmy Rushing's vocal features the blues. It's not up to his standard—*How Long, Good Mornin'*, etc. Buck Clayton wrote *Number* and it's the best in this group, taken at bright tempo. The two others are sorrowful pops, the type Basie shouldn't try. Let Lombardo handle 'em. But *Draftin'* and *Number* are in that Basie groove. With material he chooses himself the Count is hard to beat.

Thursday 16 January 1941
Count Basie records with the Metronome All-Stars for Victor in New York City.
HARRY JAMES, ZIGGY ELMAN, COOTIE WILLIAMS (trumpets); TOMMY DORSEY, J. C. HIGGINBOTHAM (trombones); BENNY GOODMAN (clarinet); TOOTS MONDELLO, BENNY CARTER (alto sax); COLEMAN HAWKINS, TEX BENEKE (tenor sax); COUNT BASIE (piano); CHARLIE CHRISTIAN (guitar); ARTIE BERNSTEIN (bass); BUDDY RICH (drums)
Bugle Call Rag / *One O'Clock Jump*

Friday 17 January 1941
Count Basie and his Orchestra play a dance at the Roseland Ballroom in Taunton, Massachusetts.

Saturday 18 January 1941
Count Basie and his Orchestra play a one-nighter in Portland, Maine.

Monday 20 January 1941
Count Basie and his Orchestra record for Columbia in New York City.
BUCK CLAYTON, ED LEWIS, AL KILLIAN, HARRY EDISON (trumpets), DAN MINOR, VIC DICKENSON, DICKIE WELLS (trombones), EARLE WARREN (alto sax/vocal), TAB SMITH (alto sax), PAUL BASCOMB, BUDDY TATE (tenor sax), JACK WASHINGTON (baritone sax), COUNT BASIE (piano), FREDDIE GREEN (guitar), WALTER PAGE (bass), JO JONES (drums), HELEN HUMES (vocal)
It's Square But It Rocks (vHH. 4 takes) / *I'll Forget* (vHH)

Tuesday 21 January 1941
Count Basie records one track with the Benny Goodman Orchestra for Columbia in New York City.
I'm Not Complainin' (4 takes)

Wednesday 22 January 1941
Count Basie and his Orchestra record for Columbia in New York City.
You Lied To Me (vHH) / *Wiggle Woogie* / *Beau Brummel*

Thursday 23 January 1941
Count Basie and his Orchestra play a one-nighter at the Palais Royale in Toronto, Canada.

Sunday 26 January 1941
Count Basie and his Orchestra play a one-nighter at the Memorial Auditorium in Buffalo, New York.

Monday 27 January 1941
Count Basie and his rhythm section broadcast on NBC's 'Chamber Music Society of Lower Basin Street' in New York City.
There'll Be Some Changes Made / *Rockin' Chair*

Tuesday 28 January 1941
Count Basie and his Orchestra record for Columbia in New York City. Trombonist Ed Cuffee replaces Vic Dickenson, Don Byas comes in on tenor sax.
BUCK CLAYTON, ED LEWIS, AL KILLIAN, HARRY EDISON (trumpets), DAN MINOR, ED CUFFEE, DICKIE WELLS (trombones), EARLE WARREN (alto sax/vocal), TAB SMITH (alto sax), DON BYAS, BUDDY TATE (tenor sax), JACK WASHINGTON (baritone sax), COUNT BASIE (piano), FREDDIE GREEN (guitar), WALTER PAGE (bass), JO JONES (drums), JIMMY RUSHING (vocal)
Music Makers / *Jump The Blues Away* / *Deep In The Blues* / *The Jitters* / *Tuesday At Ten* / *Undecided Blues* (vJR)

Thursday 30 January 1941
Count Basie and his Orchestra play a one-nighter at the Community Center in Wilson, North Carolina.

Monday 3 February 1941
Count Basie and his Orchestra play a one-nighter at the Two Spot Nite Club in Jacksonville, Florida.

Tuesday 4 February 1941
Count Basie and his Orchestra play a one-nighter at the South Street Casino in Orlando, Florida.

Wednesday 5 February 1941
Count Basie and his Orchestra play a one-nighter at the Apollo Ballroom in Tampa, Florida.

Thursday 6 February 1941
Count Basie and his Orchestra play a one-nighter at the New Elite Dance Hall in Winter Haven, Florida.

Friday 7 February 1941
Count Basie and his Orchestra play a one-nighter at the Sunset Auditorium in West Palm Beach, Florida.

Saturday 8 February 1941
Count Basie and his Orchestra play a one-nighter at the City Auditorium in Orlando, Florida.

Sunday 9 February 1941
Count Basie and his Orchestra play a one-nighter at the Harlem Square Club in Miami, Florida.

Monday 10 February 1941
Count Basie and his Orchestra play a one-nighter at the Windsor Club in Fort Lauderdale, Florida.

Tuesday 11 February 1941
Count Basie and his Orchestra play a one-nighter in Savannah, Georgia.

Thursday 13 February 1941
Count Basie and his Orchestra play a one-nighter in Atlanta, Georgia.

Friday 14 February 1941
Count Basie and his Orchestra play a one-nighter at Furman University in Greenville, South Carolina.

Wednesday 19 February 1941
Count Basie and his Orchestra play a one-nighter at the Market Auditorium in Wheeling, West Virginia.

Thursday 20 February 1941
Count Basie and his Orchestra play a one-nighter in Chester, Pennsylvania.

Friday 21 February 1941
Count Basie and his Orchestra play a dance at the Roseland State Ballroom in Boston.

Saturday 22 February 1941
Count Basie and his Orchestra play a one-nighter at the Orange Armory in Orange, New Jersey.

Sunday 23 February 1941
Count Basie and his Orchestra play a one-nighter in White Plains, New York.

Tuesday 25 February 1941
Count Basie and his Orchestra play a one-nighter in Washington, D.C.

Wednesday 26 February 1941
Count Basie and his Orchestra play a one-nighter in Cleveland, Ohio.

Thursday 27 February 1941
Count Basie and his Orchestra open a three-night engagement at the Century Theatre in Buffalo, New York.

Saturday 1 March 1941
Count Basie and his Orchestra close at the Century Theatre in Buffalo, New York.

Sunday 2 March 1941
Count Basie and his Orchestra play a one-nighter in Fremont, Ohio.

Monday 3 March 1941
Count Basie and his Orchestra play a one-nighter in Detroit, Michigan.

Tuesday 4 March 1941
Count Basie and his Orchestra play a one-nighter in Milwaukee, Wisconsin.

Wednesday 5 March 1941
Count Basie and his Orchestra play a one-nighter in Madison, Wisconsin.

Thursday 6 March 1941
Count Basie and his Orchestra play a one-nighter at the Tromar Ballroom in Des Moines, Iowa.

Friday 7 March 1941
Count Basie and his Orchestra play a one-nighter in Lincoln, Nebraska.

Saturday 8 March 1941
Count Basie and his Orchestra play a one-nighter in St. Joseph, Missouri.

Sunday 9 March 1941
Count Basie and his Orchestra play a one-nighter in Topeka, Kansas.

Monday 10 March 1941
Count Basie and his Orchestra play a one-nighter in Omaha, Nebraska.

Tuesday 11 March 1941
Count Basie and his Orchestra play a one-nighter in Cranbery, Kansas.

Thursday 13 March 1941
Count Basie and his Orchestra play a one-nighter in Tulsa, Oklahoma.

Friday 14 March 1941
Count Basie and his Orchestra open a two-night engagement in Oklahoma City, Oklahoma.

Saturday 15 March 1941
Count Basie and his Orchestra close in Oklahoma City.

Sunday 16 March 1941
Count Basie and his Orchestra play a one-nighter in Dallas, Texas.

Monday 17 March 1941
Count Basie and his Orchestra play a one-nighter in Shreveport, Louisiana.

Tuesday 18 March 1941
Count Basie and his Orchestra play a one-nighter in Alexandria, Louisiana.

Thursday 20 March 1941
Count Basie and his Orchestra play a one-nighter in Houston, Texas.

Friday 21 March 1941
Count Basie and his Orchestra play a one-nighter in Austin, Texas.

Saturday 22 March 1941
Count Basie and his Orchestra play a one-nighter in Bunkie, Louisiana.

Monday 24 March 1941
Count Basie and his Orchestra play a one-nighter in Monroe, Louisiana.

Wednesday 26 March 1941
Count Basie and his Orchestra play a one-nighter in Little Rock, Arkansas.

Thursday 27 March 1941
Count Basie and his Orchestra play a one-nighter in Jonesboro, Arkansas.

Friday 28 March 1941
Count Basie and his Orchestra play a one-nighter in Memphis, Tennessee.

Monday 31 March 1941
Count Basie and his Orchestra open a one-week engagement at the Tune Town Ballroom in St. Louis, Missouri.

Sunday 6 April 1941
Count Basie and his Orchestra close at the Tune Town Ballroom in St. Louis, Missouri.

Monday 7 April 1941
Count Basie and his Orchestra play a one-nighter in Owensboro, Kentucky.

Tuesday 8 April 1941
Count Basie and his Orchestra open a two-day engagement at the Comet Theatre in St. Louis, Missouri.

Wednesday 9 April 1941
Count Basie and his Orchestra close at the Comet Theatre in St. Louis, Missouri.

Thursday 10 April 1941
Count Basie and his Orchestra record for Columbia in Chicago.
BUCK CLAYTON, ED LEWIS, AL KILLIAN, HARRY EDISON (trumpets), DAN MINOR, ED CUFFEE, DICKIE WELLS (trombones), EARLE WARREN (alto sax/vocal), TAB SMITH (alto sax), DON BYAS, BUDDY TATE (tenor sax), JACK WASHINGTON (baritone sax), COUNT BASIE (piano), FREDDIE GREEN (guitar), WALTER PAGE (bass), JO JONES (drums), JIMMY RUSHING (vocal)
I Do Mean You / H And J / Goin' To Chicago Blues (vJR)
COLEMAN HAWKINS (tenor sax) added:
9.20 Special / Feedin' The Bean

Man Behind the Counter in soda-jerk getup is that cat, Lionel Hampton, who showed the fountain boys out at the Ritz Hotel in Chi how things really should be done. His customer here is Count Basie, who stopped in to have a snack on Lionel a couple of weeks ago. Hamp was right at home in the jerk surroundings, as he used to mix 'em in drug stores in his home town, Los Angeles, before he got into the jazz business only a few years ago. *Ray Rising clicked it.*

Friday 11 April 1941
Count Basie and his Orchestra play a one-nighter in Hannibal, Missouri.

Saturday 12 April 1941
Count Basie and his Orchestra play a one-nighter in Burlington, Iowa.

Easter Sunday 13 April 1941
Count Basie and his Orchestra play a dance at the Savoy Ballroom in Chicago.

Monday 14 April 1941
Count Basie and his Orchestra play a one-nighter in Minneapolis, Minnesota.

Tuesday 15 April 1941
Count Basie and his Orchestra play a one-nighter in St. Paul, Minnesota.
Down Beat reviews Basie's latest Okeh release:

Count Basie

Tab Smith's sprightly alto sax makes *Undecided Blues* a winner. Jimmy Rushing sings a better vocal than he has been turning out of late despite a cold which bothers the bulky shouter not in the least. Probably because he composed the blues himself. Coupling is a Skippy Martin tune and arrangement, *Tuesday at Ten*, with more fine Smith alto. Basie himself has never played better. But the recording is not good. Okeh 6071.

Thursday 17 April 1941
Count Basie and his Orchestra play a one-nighter in Anderson, Indiana.

Friday 18 April 1941
Count Basie and his Orchestra open a weekend engagement at the Palace Theatre in Fort Wayne, Indiana.

Sunday 20 April 1941
Count Basie and his Orchestra close at the Palace Theatre in Fort Wayne, Indiana.

Tuesday 22 April 1941
Count Basie and his Orchestra play a one-nighter in Pittsburgh, Pennsylvania.

Wednesday 23 April 1941
Count Basie, Buck Clayton, Don Byas and Jo Jones appear in a jam session at the close of the Café Society Concert at Carnegie Hall in New York City. The concert itself features Pete Johnson, Albert Ammons, Lena Horne, Kenneth Spencer, John Kirby's Band, Art Tatum, Hazel Scott, Red Allen's Band and Eddie South. Dave Dexter reviews the concert for *Down Beat*:

Nitery Concert at Carnegie Dull but Grosses $3,000

New York—Cafe Society's recent concert at Carnegie Hall was an artistic failure. Not until Count Basie and a group of "outsiders" paraded onto the platform at the concert's close was there any semblance of spontaneity and warmth. Not until Basie began beating out *One O'Clock Jump* with Bunny Berigan, Will Bradley, Buck Clayton, Ray McKinley, Henry Levine and others helping was there anything which deserved unqualified praise.

Above: Backstage at Carnegie are (l to r) Don Byas, Buck Clayton, Red Allen, Specs Powell, Basie, J. C. Higginbotham, Pete Johnson, Ken Kersey and Lena Horne.

Friday 25 April 1941
Count Basie and his Orchestra open a one-week engagement at the Apollo Theatre in New York City.

Thursday 1 May 1941
Count Basie and his Orchestra close at the Apollo Theatre in New York City.

Helen Humes out of Basie Band

New York—Helen Humes was slated to leave the Count Basie band at press time, and it looked as though Lena Horne might take her place. Billie Holiday also was being considered. Report had it that Miss Humes was "not commercial enough." Miss Horne, currently singing solo at Cafe Society Downtown, was recently with Charlie Barnet.

Pete Johnson, Al Ammons Join Basie

New York—Pete Johnson and Albert Ammons, boogie-woogie pianists, join forces with Count Basie and his band May 2 for a theater tour to be known as the "Count Basie and Cafe Society Boogie-Woogie Revue." Johnson and Ammons have been working for the two Cafe Society niteries here since December, 1938.

Friday 2 May 1941
Count Basie and the Cafe Society Boogie-Woogie Revue open a three-day engagement at the State Theatre in Hartford, Connecticut.

Sunday 4 May 1941
Count Basie and the Cafe Society Boogie-Woogie Revue close at the State Theatre in Hartford, Connecticut.

Monday 5 May 1941
Count Basie and his orchestra broadcast on NBC's Chamber Music Society of Lower Basin Street in New York.
Gone With 'What' Wind / Basie Special

Friday 9 May 1941
Count Basie and his Orchestra open a weekend engagement at the Strand Theatre in Syracuse, New York.

Put the 'Jump' in One O'Clock Jump . . . Strong men of the Count Basie brass section, these four powerful-lipped gents are Buck Clayton, Ed Lewis, Albert Killian, and Harry Edison. Jump purveyors par excellence, they are responsible for a large part of the drive that comes out of the grooves of the band's Okeh records. They'll be pushing on the Basie date at Boston's Ritz Carlton next month, and at the Surf Beach Club, Virginia Beach, Va., starting July 29. *Pic by Werner Wolff.*

ESQUIRE CLUB
Presents
COUNT BASIE
AND
HIS ORCHESTRA
AT
EGLESTON SQUARE GARDENS
FRI., MAY 30th
8 P.M. TO 2 A.M.
ADMISSION
TILL 9 P.M. . . . $ .85
AFTER 9 P.M. . . . $1.00

Sunday 11 May 1941

Count Basie and his Orchestra close at the Strand Theatre in Syracuse, New York.

Monday 12 May 1941

Count Basie and his Orchestra open a four-day engagement at the Plymouth Theatre in Worcester, Massachusetts.

Thursday 15 May 1941

Basie band manager Milt Ebbins marries vocalist Lynne Sherman in Worcester. Count Basie and his Orchestra close at the Plymouth Theatre in Worcester, Massachusetts.

Friday 16 May 1941

Count Basie and his Orchestra open a three-day engagement at the Adams Theatre in Newark, New Jersey.

Sunday 18 May 1941

Count Basie and his Orchestra close at the Adams Theatre in Newark, New Jersey.

Monday 19 May 1941

Count Basie and his Orchestra play a one-nighter in Boston, Massachusetts.

Wednesday 21 May 1941

Count Basie and his Orchestra record for Columbia in New York City.
BUCK CLAYTON, ED LEWIS, AL KILLIAN, HARRY EDISON (trumpets), DAN MINOR, ED CUFFEE, DICKIE WELLS (trombones), EARLE WARREN (alto sax/vocal), TAB SMITH (alto sax), DON BYAS, BUDDY TATE (tenor sax), JACK WASHINGTON (baritone sax), COUNT BASIE (piano), FREDDIE GREEN (guitar), WALTER PAGE (bass), JO JONES or KENNY CLARKE (drums)
You Betcha My Life (vEW, dKC) / *Down, Down, Down* (dKC) / *Tune Town Shuffle* (dJJ) / *I'm Tired Of Waiting For You* (dJJ)

Friday 30 May 1941

Count Basie and his Orchestra play a dance at Egleston Square Gardens in Boston, Massachusetts.

Monday 2 June 1941

Count Basie is present for Teddy Wilson's opening at Café Society Uptown in New York City.

Sunday 8 June 1941

Count Basie and his Orchestra play an afternoon engagement at Sparrow's Beach in Annapolis, Maryland.

Monday 23 June 1941

Count Basie and his Orchestra take a vacation until July 3 when they open at the Ritz-Carlton Hotel in Boston. Dickie Wells is having a tonsillectomy and Dan Minor leaves. Trombonists Eli Robinson and Robert Scott replace them. Maxine Johnson takes over the Helen Humes spot.

Wednesday 2 July 1941

Count Basie and his Orchestra record for Columbia in New York City.
BUCK CLAYTON, ED LEWIS, AL KILLIAN, HARRY EDISON (trumpets), ROBERT SCOTT, ED CUFFEE, ELI ROBINSON (trombones), EARLE WARREN (alto sax/vocal), TAB SMITH (alto sax), DON BYAS, BUDDY TATE (tenor sax), JACK WASHINGTON (baritone sax), COUNT BASIE (piano), FREDDIE GREEN (guitar), WALTER PAGE (bass), JO JONES (drums), JIMMY RUSHING (vocal)
One, Two, Three O'Leary (vJR) / *Basie Boogie* / *Fancy Meeting You* (vEW) / *Diggin' For Dex*

Count Basie Band gets a Dicty Date

Boston—The Ritz-Carlton Hotel roof, stand of bands such as Lombardo, Ruby Newman and the gamut of society-sweet orks, breaks precedent for three weeks starting July 3, when Count Basie brings in his jumpers. Band also has a week at the swank Surf Club, Virginia Beach, Va. starting July 29. At the Ritz-Carlton the band is slated to get six NBC shots a week.

Thursday 3 July 1941

Count Basie and his Orchestra open a three-week engagement at the Ritz-Carlton Hotel in Boston.

George Frazier Debuts as Composer

Boston—When Count Basie and the band played the Ritz roof here recently, jazz analyst and *Beat* columnist George Frazier was inspired to composition, but musical this time, instead of literary. He batted out a jumpy little thing called *Harvard Indifference Blues*, especially for the Basie boys. The Count is due to record it for Okeh this month. Vocalist James Rushing is at the left here, George in the center, and the Count at right.

Basie Rests his famous right hand as Hazel Scott shows him the latest trick from Hollywood. It's called 'tanglefinger' and can only be accomplished through diligent abstinence from practice. Hazel, who was tested recently for a major part in a forthcoming music movie, appeared with the Count at his recent Ritz Carlton engagement in Boston. Lynn Sherman, wife of Basie's manager, Milt Ebbins, will do the vocals on a couple of pop sides at Basie's next recording date for Columbia.

Basie-Scott Romance A Boston Dream

of a press-agent, who hopped up the beantown newspapers over the mythical love affair during the dual appearance of the Count Basie band and Hazel Scott at the Ritz-Carlton Roof. The Boston papers did more than just pick up this publicity material, they blew it up to feature space importance.

Basie's appearance at the Ritz put his music beyond the purses of many of his local devotees, but they were able to obtain a clear impression of it by gathering in the Boston Common just outside the hotel. Every note the band played was audible on the greensward center of the city.

Wednesday 23 July 1941

Count Basie and his Orchestra close at the Ritz-Carlton Hotel in Boston.

Friday 25 July 1941

Count Basie and his Orchestra play a dance at the Roseland State Ballroom in Boston.

Tuesday 29 July 1941

Count Basie and his Orchestra open a one-week engagement at the Surf Beach Club in Virginia Beach.

Monday 4 August 1941

Count Basie and his Orchestra close at the Surf Beach Club in Virginia Beach.
Around this time, Count Basie and his Orchestra film two 'soundies' in New York.
Airmail Special / Take Me Back Baby (vJR)

Friday 15 August 1941

Count Basie and his Orchestra open a one-week engagement at the Regal Theatre in Chicago.

Young Won't Rejoin Basie

Los Angeles—Lester Young will not return to Count Basie's band.

Hopes of Basie followers that a reconciliation could be made were crushed last week when Lester who is now playing tenor in his brother Lee Young's band at the Capri Club here, told *Down Beat* he "wouldn't even consider" returning to the Basie fold.

Basie and Young split last fall. But recently Basie and his handlers admitted they "might take Lester back in the band if Les would go to work and be good." Informed of Basie's willingness, Young fluffed off the offer and declared that under no circumstances would he go back.

Buddy Tate and Don Byas have been holding the tenor chairs with Basie since Young departed. Basie is now on tour in the Chicago area.

Thursday 21 August 1941

Count Basie and his Orchestra close at the Regal Theatre in Chicago.

Lynn Sherman To Record With Basie

Chicago—When the Count Basie band makes its next records for Columbia, Lynn Sherman, wife of Basie manager Milt Ebbins, will be brought in to do a couple of pop vocals, according to John Hammond, who has been in town during the past few weeks.

Lynn, who retired from chirping after having been with the Sonny Burke-Sam Donahue band, sang a few tunes with the Basie crew in Boston while the band played the Ritz-Carlton. Tunes for her hadn't been decided upon.

The Basiemen broke its own one-day record at the Regal theater here during its recent week. Doubling the original record figure of $1,600 gross, the band pulled $3,100 on a Sunday.

Sunday 14 September 1941

Count Basie and his Orchestra play a dance at the Renaissance Ballroom in New York City.

Monday 15 September 1941

Dave Dexter reviews the latest Basie releases in *Down Beat*:

Count Basie

They've got the Base jumping now, turning out two sides a week and one-nighting it all over before hitting N. Y. for a fall location. Most recent Basie couplings are *H & J*, a Harry Edison compo which gives Earl Warren, Tab Smith and Buddy Tate leeway for their saxings, at up tempo, and *Diggin' For Dex*, an original by Eddie Durham which spots the Basie ivory ingenuity and a mess o' mellow Buck Clayton horn. A whacky title, that, and named for some screwball whose recent pacing the floor with a new baby has left him all too little time for disc-spinning. Okeh 6365, and thanks for the plug. Okeh 6330 pairs *Basie Boogie*, a Milton Ebbins masterpiece, with *Let Me See*, still another Harry (trumpeter) Edison job which comes off the turntable as jazz of the finest sort. How Les Young could have gone on this one.

Skip the Count's *One, Two, Three O'Leary* and *Fancy Meetin' You*, with Rushing and Warren vocals. They are so far below the standard of the previous four sides that they're hardly worth hearing. Warren's singing doesn't match his recent *You Betcha' My Life*. But *H & J, Diggin' For Dex, Basie Boogie* and *Let Me See* are in there— zoots! Really the Basieites at their best.

Tuesday 16 September 1941
Count Basie and his Orchestra open at Café Society
Uptown in New York City.
Barry Ulanov reviews the band for *Metronome*:

COUNT BASIE (A-1)

COUNT BASIE and his Orchestra. Reviewed at Café Society Uptown, New York City.

Saxes: (1) Earl Warren, (2) Buddy Tate, (3) Tab Smith, (4) Don Byas, (5) Jack Washington. Trumpets: (1) Ed Lewis, (2) Buck Clayton, (3) Al Killian, (4) Harry Edison. Trombones: (1) Dickie Wells, (2) Robert Scott, (3) Eli Robinson. Guitar: Freddie Greene. Bass: Walter Page. Drums: Joe Jones. Vocals: Jimmy Rushing and Earl Warren. Leader and piano: Count Basie.

A tremendously exciting band to begin with, the Count Basie organization has progressed to the point where it is entirely consonant with all the musical laws of taste and tone and intonation and the rules of commerce. This band kicks at every conceivable tempo and volume, really reaches jazz heights, and still keeps the customer of little mind for these soul-stretching things happy. That's a remarkable achievement for any group, but it's particularly wonderful for a colored orchestra, which is usually a great hot band or a strictly commercial one, but very rarely both.

The greatness of Basie jazz is easy to spot. There are soloists of extraordinary distinction, almost as many as there are men in the band, Buck and Harry Edison, Dickie Wells and Eli Robinson, Buddy Tate, Don Byas, Tab Smith, the Count; Freddie Greene is beginning to branch out as an electric guitarist; Earl Warren and Jack Washington have their fine moments; so do Ed Lewis and Al Killian and Robert Scott. In only one other band can every man be cited for similar jazz laurels, that of Duke Ellington.

But then there's something else here, too. There's a great ensemble. The Basie band plays with inspired drive. The sections have a free-phrasing style, a relaxation as teams, that makes their work together as thrilling as that of the soloists. For this they are fortunate in getting first-rate manuscript. That hasn't always been the case with them, but right now the new arrangements supplied the band are almost uniformly first-rate. Jimmy Mundy, Margie Gibson and other free-lance scripters are partly responsible. But some stalwart arranging talent in the band like Buck Clayton (*Love Jumped Out* and others) and Earl Warren (*9:20 Special* and others) and the strident directing head of the Count himself are really the main reasons for this supply of tiptop jazz scores.

The commercial appeal of the band rests in two or three factors. There is that wonderful personality, Jimmy Rushing. Jimmy's a blues singer of prevailing excellence and a rotund figure that never fails to capture audience fancy, singing, dancing or mock-leading the band. Then there is Earl Warren, a much-improved singer, whose legato phrasing of pop tunes and handsomeness both sell himself, the band and the songs they do together. Beyond that there is the attractive use of subdued performances to contrast with the all out jazz and then—the little band that plays dinner sets at the Café.

The Kansas City Six, they call this small Count Basie unit. It consists of Buck, Buddy and Dickie for melody and Joe, Walter Page and the Count for Rhythm. They hold down hard, getting a light ensemble tone that makes for a genuinely airy atmosphere. The music thay produce is keynoted by Buck's most restrained muted work, complemented by the similar lacy delicacy of the Basie piano, and remarkably lovely trombone and tenor passages. Having a small unit like this one gives Basie a prime commercial attraction for diners, a wonderful contrast to what comes after, when the powerhouse, big band comes on the stand, and a stand out attraction to those who come for strictly jazz kicks.

The intonation of the big band has improved so much, it's hard to remember that the brass and saxes ever played out of tune. Ed Lewis is still playing a lusty trumpet lead, and the three other guys are shelling out beautifully with him. The prevailing tone of the quartet is Buck's, but an awful lot must be said for the firm hold of musical values Killian, Lewis and Edison keep. The latter, Harry Edison, is a thrilling soloist, who sounds too much alike from solo to solo, but every once in a while hits a number that fits his style like the proverbial glove, and vice versa. But, of course, it's Buck's solos, open with his beautiful tone and simple, pretty phrasing, or his subtle, supple muted stuff, that create the really great trumpet moments for the band.

No section is as much improved as the trombones. Here, Scott and Robinson have maintained the heavy body of the trio and added a respect for keeping in tune. Dickie's choppy phrasing is still a great jazz style, particularly as he alternates it with long, sustained cadences. Eli Robinson's gutty work is more infrequent, but is too a leavener

of topnotch music.

The saxes have an unorthodox lead man in Earl Warren, whose tone is in the alto register by definition, but sounds more like a clarinet in its attractive lightness. Tab Smith has given fine body to the group, with his distinctive, noteful playing, and his really beautiful, Hodges-like phrasing of solo choruses. Don Byas is a Coleman Hawkins stylist, with big tone and audible push to his playing. Buddy Tate occasionally suggests Herschel Evans' pretty tenor, and always expresses a vital sax jazz. Both are excellent on their instruments, and work well with the altos and the fine, fleshy Jack Washington baritone to produce a vigorous section blend.

The rhythm is the most highly touted team in the band. It isn't as consistent in maintaining tempos as such a reputation would suggest, but it can, and most often does, get a really magnificent beat. Joe Jones seems most at fault in the decreasing moments of slowdown, but Joe also is most responsible for the moments of impeccable drumming, hard on one beat, not too hard on the cymbals and closely behind and with everyone else in the band.

Perhaps the clearest identification of the Count Basie orchestra to the average listener is its leader's witty piano fill-ins, on the first and third or second and fourth beats of each bar or multiple divisions thereof. That helps to give the band a clear tag. But even more important are the overall qualities of the ensemble, the soloists and the collective and individual spirit that fires them all, and even in the relentless repetition of the same riffs, the same ideas, produces jazz of unquestionable distinction.

Latest Photo of Basie Band . . . Here is the latest pic of Count Basie's ork now receiving much-deserved attention at Cafe Society Uptown in New York. Band is heard on remotes over CBS and mutual and records for Okeh. Shown here from left to right and excluding rhythm section, are Buck Clayton, Ed Lewis, Al Killian and Harry Edison, trumpets; Eli Robinson, Dick Wells, and Bob Scott, trombones, and Buddie Tate, Tab Smith, Earle Warren, Jack Washington, and Don Byas, saxes. In the rhythm section are Fred Greene, guitar; Walter Page, bass; Jo Jones, drums, and Count Basie, piano.

Above: Jo Jones and the trumpets at Café Society Uptown.

Friday 19 September 1941

Count Basie and his Orchestra broadcast from Café Society Uptown in New York City.
There'll Be Some Changes Made (vJR) / *Tuesday At Ten*

Saturday 20 September 1941

The band again broadcast from Café Society Uptown.
Yes Indeed (vJR) / *Tom Thumb* / *9.20 Special* / *I Guess I'll Have To Dream The Rest* (vEW) / *There'll Be Some Changes Made* (vJR)

Tuesday 23 September 1941

The band again broadcast from Café Society Uptown.
Diggin' For Dex / *Love Jumped Out* / *Tune Town Shuffle* / *My Melancholy Baby* (vJR) / *Every Tub*

Wednesday 24 September 1941

Count Basie and his Orchestra record for Columbia in New York City.
BUCK CLAYTON, ED LEWIS, AL KILLIAN, HARRY EDISON (trumpets), ROBERT SCOTT, DICKY WELLS, ELI ROBINSON (trombones), EARLE WARREN (alto sax/vocal), TAB SMITH (alto sax), DON BYAS, BUDDY TATE (tenor sax), JACK WASHINGTON (baritone sax), COUNT BASIE (piano), FREDDIE GREEN (guitar), WALTER PAGE (bass), JO JONES (drums), LYNN SHERMAN, JIMMY RUSHING (vocal)
My Old Flame (vLS) / *Fiesta In Blue* / *Tom Thumb* / *Take Me Back, Baby* (vJR)

Monday 29 September 1941

The band again broadcast from Café Society Uptown.
You Can't Run Around (vJR) / *Jumpin' At The Woodside* / *One O'Clock Jump* (theme)

Paul Robeson Records Blues With Basie

New York—The stentorian voice of Paul Robeson, whose hefty bass chanting has thrilled royalty in the capital cities of Europe, was captured on two 10-inch record sides last week singing a down-to-earth blues with Count Basie's band behind him.

Basie composed the music and Richard Wright, the author, the lyrics to *The Joe Louis Blues*. Robeson sang it, his first jazz performance on wax. The disc soon will be issued on Columbia's red label.

The session came just a few days after Louis, the heavyweight king, belted the daylights out of challenger Lou Nova at the Polo Grounds.

Basie also made a pop, *Something New*, on the session.

Wednesday 1 October 1941

Count Basie and his Orchestra record with Paul Robeson for Okeh in New York City.
King Joe, Part 1 (vPR) / *King Joe, Part 2* (vPR) / *Moon Nocturne* (vEW) / *Something New* (2 takes)

Thursday 2 October 1941
Count Basie and his Orchestra broadcast from Café Society Uptown in New York City.
I Want A Little Girl (vJR) / *Rockin' The Blues* / *Something New* / *Topsy*

Monday 6 October 1941
The band again broadcast from Café Society Uptown.
Wiggle Woogie / *Flamingo* / *Tom Thumb* / *One-Two-Three-O'Leary* (vJR) / *I Do Mean You* / *Tuesday At Ten* / *Moten Swing* (theme)

Tuesday 7 October 1941
The band again broadcast from Café Society Uptown.
Untitled / *Down, Down, Down* / *Take Me Back Baby* (vJR) / *Blue Lou* / *I Found You In The Rain* (vEW) / *Broadway* / *Sweet Georgia Brown*

Friday 10 October 1941
The band again broadcast from Café Society Uptown.
Down For Double / *This Time The Dream's On Me* (vEW) / *Elmer's Tune* / *Yes, Indeed!* (vJR) / *Moon Nocturne*

Monday 13 October 1941
Count Basie and his Orchestra star in a First Anniversary Celebration at Café Society Uptown, when the combined shows from the Uptown and Downtown clubs perform.

Tuesday 14 October 1941
The band broadcast on WOR's 'Men Behind The Guns' with vocalist Dinah Shore.
Air Mail Special / *Love Me Or Leave Me* (vDS) / *Bugle Call Rag*

Saturday 18 October 1941
Count Basie appears at a Gigantic Midnite Benefit for the Brooklyn Branch of N.A.A.C.P. at Loew's Brevoort Theatre in Brooklyn.

Sunday 19 October 1941
The band broadcast on NBC's 'Freedom's People'.
Basie Boogie

Monday 20 October 1941
The band again broadcast from Café Society Uptown.
Wiggle Woogie / *Rockin' The Blues* / *9.20 Special* / *Moten Swing* (closing theme)

Tuesday 21 October 1941
The band again broadcast from Café Society Uptown.
H & J / *Diggin' For Dex* / *Goin' To Chicago* (vJR)

Saturday 25 October 1941
The band again broadcast from Café Society Uptown.
Baby, Don't Tell On Me (vJR) / *Swingin' The Blues* / *One O'Clock Jump* (theme)

Thursday 30 October 1941
Count Basie's mother dies in New York City.

Count's Mother, His 88 Teacher, Dies In N. Y.

New York—Manhattan's finest physicians failed to save the life of Mrs. Lillian Basie, mother of Count Basie, who died here Oct. 30 after a short illness. Basie, playing at Uptown Cafe Society with his famous band at the time of her death, was at her bedside when the time came.

Mrs. Basie was the Count's teacher when he was just a youngster. She influenced his musical education more than anyone else, even in later years after her son "Bill" became prominent throughout the world. Services were held in Red Bank, N. J., Nov. 1 with many musicians and friends of the Basies attending.

Saturday 1 November 1941
Funeral services are held for Count Basie's mother in Red Bank, New Jersey.

Monday 3 November 1941
Count Basie and his Orchestra record for Columbia in New York City.
BUCK CLAYTON, ED LEWIS, AL KILLIAN, HARRY EDISON (trumpets), ROBERT SCOTT, DICKY WELLS, ELI ROBINSON (trombones), EARLE WARREN (alto sax/vocal), TAB SMITH (alto sax), DON BYAS, BUDDY TATE (tenor sax), JACK WASHINGTON (baritone sax), COUNT BASIE (piano), FREDDIE GREEN (guitar), WALTER PAGE (bass), JO JONES (drums), LYNN SHERMAN (vocal)
I Struck A Match In The Dark (vEW) / *Platterbrains* / *All Of Me* (vLS)
In the evening, Count Basie and his Orchestra close at Café Society Uptown.

Count Basie Makes Three New Sides

New York—A sparkling Hug Winterhalter arrangement of *Struck a Match in the Dark* wa cut by Count Basie's band fo Okeh Nov. 3, along with tw others. Lynne Sherman sang *A Of Me* and an instrumental als was made. Earl Warren voca *Dark*. Basie recorded the day left the Cafe Society Uptow Winterhalter, former Raymor Scott arranger, has been doir much work lately for Basie ar Will Bradley.

Monday 17 November 1941
Count Basie and his Orchestra record for Columbia in New York City.
Feather Merchant / *Down For Double* (2 takes) / *More Than You Know* (vLS) / *Harvard Blues* (vJR) / *Coming-Out Party*

Thursday 20 November 1941
Count Basie and his Orchestra play a dance at Symphony Hall in Boston.

Three-Way Combo

New York—Count Basie, at the piano, is managed by Milton Ebbins, former Massachusetts trumpeter. Ebbins' wife, right, is Basie's vocalist on Okeh records. Her name is Lynne Sherman. Hear her on Basie's *My Old Flame*, one of the band's best pop performances of 1941. Basie now is on the road. So is Ebbins. And Lynne stays home in her New York apartment until the next record date. *Pic by Harold Stein.*

AT SYMPHONY HALL
THURSDAY, NOV. 20
THE ESQUIRE CLUB
Presents
A Seven-Star Attraction
COUNT BASIE
and His Orchestra
Featuring
JAMES RUSHING
and
EARLE WARREN
Also a Big Surprise
Dancing from 8 P.M.
'Til 2 A.M.
ADMISSION $1.00. Tax 10c

Sunday 7 December 1941
Japanese aircraft attack the U.S. Fleet at Pearl Harbour in Hawaii. 3000 Americans are killed and 19 ships sunk.

Tuesday 9 December 1941

Count Basie and his Orchestra play at a Christmas Basket Fund Breakfast Dance (10.00pm–6.00am) at the Renaissance Casino in New York City.

Friday 12 December 1941

Count Basie and his Orchestra open a two-week engagement at the Strand Theatre in New York City. They play six shows a day from noon until midnight. Also appearing is Hattie McDaniel. The movie presentation is 'Blues in the Night' starring Priscilla Lane and Betty Field.

SEASON'S GREETINGS

COUNT BASIE
AND HIS ORCHESTRA
Featuring
Jo Jones • Jimmy Rushing • Earle Warren
★ Voted 1941's Sepia King of Swing in Martin Block-WNEW Poll
★ Listen to "KING JOE"—Recorded with Paul Robeson
★ Columbia—Okeh Records
Exclusive Management
WILLIAM MORRIS AGENCY, INCORPORATED
New York • Chicago • Hollywood • London

After the opening they play at Star News Fifth Annual Midnight Benefit Show at the Apollo Theatre in New York City.

Monday 15 December 1941

Dave Dexter reviews the latest Basie release on Okeh in *Down Beat*:

Count Basie

Similar in more than one way to the mood expressed in Thornhill's *Autumn Nocturne* is Basie's moody *Moon Nocturne*, which contains the greatest Tab Smith alto artistry ever cut by the pudgy Basie sideman plus a pleasant Earl Warren vocal. Backer, *Something New*, is well below the Count's standard although it has its good points, as does every Basie release. No vocal. Tab *Moon Nocturne* not only a jazz classic but also as one of Basie's most important discs from a commercial standpoint. On Okeh 6449.

Thursday 25 December 1941

Count Basie and his Orchestra close at the Strand Theatre in New York City.
After the final show, the band travel up to the Savoy Ballroom in Harlem, to play a breakfast dance.

Basie Finds It A Case Of All Work

NEW YORK—The demand for Count Basie's style of "jump rhythm" is proving a continuous workshop for the genial orchestra leader. A decided hit at the Broadway Strand theatre where he culminated a two week's engagement Christmas day by playing six shows from noon until midnight. At midnight Count and his crew descended on the Savoy ballroom to keep a breakfast dance date, and boarding a bus immediately following for a Boston engagement the same night.

Count Basie has been booked for several dance dates throughout New England before returning to New York for a short rest and proceed to the West Coast, all providing the war doesn't change his plans.

Friday 26 December 1941

Count Basie and his Orchestra play a one-nighter in Boston.

Wednesday 31 December 1941

Count Basie records with the Metronome All-Stars for Columbia in New York City.
HARRY JAMES, COOTIE WILLIAMS, ROY ELDRIDGE (trumpets), J. C. HIGGINBOTHAM, LOU MCGARITY (trombones), BENNY GOODMAN (clarinet), TOOTS MONDELLO, BENNY CARTER (alto sax), VIDO MUSSO, TEX BENEKE (tenor sax), COUNT BASIE (piano), FREDDIE GREEN (guitar), DOC GOLDBERG (bass), GENE KRUPA (drums)
Royal Flush (2 takes) / *Dear Old Southland*

1942

Friday 9 January 1942
Count Basie and his Orchestra open a one-week engagement at the Apollo Theatre in New York City.

Thursday 15 January 1942
Count Basie and his Orchestra close at the Apollo Theatre in New York City.

Friday 16 January 1942
Count Basie records with the Metronome All-Stars for Columbia in New York City. The session takes place in the early hours of Friday morning, Basie going straight from his stint at the Apollo Theatre.
COOTIE WILLIAMS (trumpet), J. C. HIGGINBOTHAM (trombone), BENNY GOODMAN (clarinet), BENNY CARTER (alto sax), CHARLIE BARNET (tenor sax), COUNT BASIE (piano), ALVINO REY (guitar), JOHN KIRBY (bass), GENE KRUPA (drums)
I Got Rhythm (2 takes)

Monday 19 January 1942
Count Basie and his Orchestra play a one-nighter USO-Camp show at Windsor Locks in Connecticut.

Wednesday 21 January 1942
Count Basie and his Orchestra record for Columbia in New York City.
BUCK CLAYTON, ED LEWIS, AL KILLIAN, HARRY EDISON (trumpets), ROBERT SCOTT, DICKY WELLS, ELI ROBINSON (trombones), EARLE WARREN (alto sax/vocal), TAB SMITH (alto sax), DON BYAS, BUDDY TATE (tenor sax), JACK WASHINGTON (baritone sax), COUNT BASIE (piano), FREDDIE GREEN (guitar), WALTER PAGE (bass), JO JONES (drums), HENRY NEMO, JIMMY RUSHING (vocal)
One O'Clock Jump / Blue Shadows And White Gardenias (vEW) / *'Ay Now* (vHN) / *For The Good Of The Country* (vJR)

Friday 23 January 1942
Count Basie and his Orchestra open a one-week engagement at the Earle Theatre in Philadelphia.

Thursday 29 January 1942
Count Basie and his Orchestra close at the Earle Theatre in Philadelphia.

Basie Rocks Philly; Then Holds Ball
Philadelphia—Philly rocked recently when Count Basie brought his crew to the stage of the Earle theater here and proceeded to smash all existing opening day attendance records. The management was quite amazed when Basie's week was up—they really drew the customers. The Count's flack, Jim McCarthy, should be credited with doing a terrific exploitation job.
Basie's sidemen got a big boot from Buddy Williams, tenor at Wagner's ballroom here, and especially did Count's tenorist, Don Byas. Basie himself, had a large session at the Down Beat cafe with Dynamite Joe Hooker, former Lunceford and Calloway scat singer.

Thursday 12 February 1942
Count Basie and his Orchestra play a 'Homecoming and Victory' dance at the Municipal Auditorium in Kansas City.

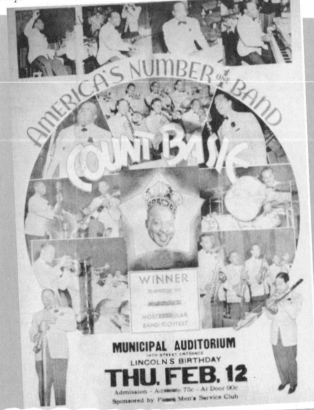

The Count Plays Own Homecoming
Kansas City— Count Basie and his ork finally got home town recognition here February 12. The band which got its start in Kaycee's old Reno club over six years ago played for a "Homecoming and Victory" dance at the Muny Auditorium, sponsored by the Paseo Men's Service Club. A record crowd for sepia dances attended.
An elaborate ceremony was held preceding the dance, during which tribute was paid to Basie by civic leaders, musicians, and a *Down Beat* representative. Robert L. Sweeney and Maceo Birch were in charge of arrangements.

Sunday 15 February 1942

Dave Dexter reviews the latest Basie release on Okeha in *Down Beat*:

Count Basie

My Old Flame and *Tom Thumb*, **Okeh 6527**

An epochal recording, highly significant for several treasons, the most important of which is the fact that Basie reveals for the first time (aside from slow blues) that he and his men can play slow ballads, and excitingly well. *Flame* has a pleasant Lynne Sherman vocal which comes as no surprise to the many who followed this girl's work with the old Sonny Burke band two and three years ago. And eight bars of Buck Clayton, muted, are well worth the 35 centavos asked for the platter. Note the eight bars immediately preceding Buck's entrance—a touch of Lunceford there, but wonderfully executed.

Thumb, an Earle Warren original, once again shows this band's love of a new riff, and how they develop it. Solos are at a minimum, with Basie's piano doing the heavy, but the big and brilliant brass team is conspicuous with its accuracy, attack and intonation. The Leiderkranz echo helps the recording in this case.

Dig Basie on these. The guy and his gang get greater with time!

Friday 27 February 1942

Count Basie and his Orchestra open a one-week engagement at the Oriental Theatre in Chicago.

NEW BASIE CHIRP is Dolly White, the Count's first girl singer in many months. She joined the band the last week in February.

Thursday 5 March 1942

Count Basie and his Orchestra close at the Oriental Theatre in Chicago.

Friday 6 March 1942

Count Basie and his Orchestra open a one-week engagement at the Palace Theatre in Cleveland, Ohio.

Thursday 12 March 1942

Count Basie and his Orchestra close at the Palace Theatre in Cleveland, Ohio.

Friday 13 March 1942

Count Basie and his Orchestra open a one-week engagement at the Paradise Theatre in Detroit.

Sunday 15 March 1942

Dave Dexter reviews the latest Basie release on Okeh in *Down Beat*:

Count Basie

More Than You Know and *Down For Double*, **Okeh 6584**

The Count's been flying high lately, and his every release has packed a barrelhouse wallop. Lynne Sherman chants the ballad—a great old song—in superb style, getting fine assistance from the band all the way out. Buck Clayton's heard briefly also. *Double* is a jumper with trombone, trumpet and tenor all getting off. Basie plays a better solo than any of his men. And the rhythm section is incomparable.

Thursday 19 March 1942

Count Basie and his Orchestra close at the Paradise Theatre in Detroit.

Friday 20 March 1942

Count Basie and his Orchestra open a one-week engagement at the Regal Theatre in Chicago.

Crown Basie King At Chi's Regal

Chicago—Count Basie was crowned King of Swing in a ceremony at the Regal Theater here last week. Basie was chosen in a poll conducted by the *Pittsburgh Courier*. After the coronation, Basie and his band indulged in a jam session in which Cootie Williams, Gene Krupa and other prominent jazz musicians now playing in Chicago joined in.

Thursday 26 March 1942

Count Basie and his Orchestra close at the Regal Theatre in Chicago.

Friday 27 March 1942

Count Basie and his Orchestra open a one-week engagement at the Riverside Theatre in Milwaukee.

Thursday 2 April 1942

Count Basie and his Orchestra close at the Riverside Theatre in Milwaukee.

Friday 3 April 1942

Count Basie and his Orchestra record for Columbia in Chicago.
BUCK CLAYTON, ED LEWIS, AL KILLIAN, HARRY EDISON (trumpets), ROBERT SCOTT, DICKY WELLS, ELI ROBINSON (trombones), EARLE WARREN (alto sax/vocal), JERRY BLAKE (alto sax), DON BYAS, BUDDY TATE (tenor sax), JACK WASHINGTON (baritone sax), COUNT BASIE (piano), FREDDIE GREEN (guitar), WALTER PAGE (bass), JO JONES (drums), JIMMY RUSHING (vocal)
Basie Blues / I'm Gonna Move To The Outskirts Of Town (vJR) / *Time On My Hands* (vEW)

Tuesday 7 April 1942

Count Basie and his Orchestra play a dance at the Convention Hall in Camden, New Jersey.

Friday 17 April 1942

Count Basie and his Orchestra open a one-week engagement at the RKO Theatre in Boston, Massachusetts.

Joe Jones Ill Lovetts Sub

New York—Count Basie's rhythm section suffered its first substitution in five years with Joe Jones out for six weeks due to illness. Jones, famed for his hi-hat stick work, has had a bad case of flu, complicated with a nervous condition that made the med men advise the lay-off.

Subbing is Baby Lovetts, Kansas City drummer formerly with the Harlan Leonard band. Basie's boys are currently roaming the Eastern theaters.

Thursday 23 April 1942

Count Basie and his Orchestra close at the RKO Theatre in Boston.

Friday 24 April 1942

Count Basie and his Orchestra open a one-week engagement at the Civic Theatre in Portland, Maine.

Thursday 30 April 1942

Count Basie and his Orchestra close at the Civic Theatre in Portland, Maine.

Monday 4 May 1942

Count Basie is awarded an Honorary Degree as 'Doctor of Swingology' at Harvard University in Cambridge, Massachusetts. After the ceremony, Count and several of his bandsmen jam with students at a party at Dunster House.

Thursday 7 May 1942

Count Basie and his Orchestra play a dance at the Roseland Ballroom in Taunton, Massachusetts.

Sunday 10 May 1942

Count Basie and his Orchestra play a battle of music with the Lionel Hampton Band at the Savoy Ballroom in New York City.

Friday 15 May 1942

Count Basie and his Orchestra open a one-week engagement at the Howard Theatre in Washington, D.C.

Thursday 21 May 1942

Count Basie and his Orchestra close at the Howard Theatre in Washington, D.C.

Count Basie, Hampton In Band Battle

Such a Bang-up Ball Could Only Happen in The Music Business

New York—One of those bang-up balls that can happen only in the music business busted here May 10th at the Basie-Hampton battle of music at the Savoy. Some 2000 people were turned away, in a jam reminiscent of the Chick Webb-Benny Goodman days, knowing nothing of the confusion that prevailed about the "battle."

When Hampton was booked in for four weeks, his contract specifically provided that he lay off [...]

After the Howard Theatre engagement Basie and the Band continue with a series of one-nighters including Millsboro, Delaware and the Strand ballroom in Philadelphia.

This Lobster Took the Count

New York—Just mention Millburo, Delaware, to Count Basie, and he will give you a fast brush. Seems that while the band was setting up for a date there, recently, Freddie Green, Buster Scott, and Dickie Wells went lobster potting. They returned, putting their catch in a bucket behind the piano,

Half an hour later, "Base" noticed Jimmy Rushing eying his shoes with interest. Of course, one of the real big ones was lying on Count's shoe, twitching his eyes in a most ickie fashion, off-the-beat. Count immediately did a fast kicking act which landed the lobster in tenor saxman Buddy Tate's lap. This broke the sax section up for a good fifteen minutes.

When order was finally restored, Count discovered the exertion had busted his suspenders. When half an hour later the lobster got loose again, Basie had to retreat across the platform, shooing with one hand, and grabbing his pants with the other. At this point, he fell flat on his face across one of the stands. Only Freddie Green's quick interception prevented the lobster, a thorough square, from making a flank attack.

Next night at the Strand in Philly, all the lights went off unexpectedly, leaving the band in total darkness for half an hour with a very uneasy crowd. One of the guys in the band yelled, "There's a lobster loose." Count didn't appreciate the humor.

Count Meets Lieutenant

Fort Bragg, N. C.—Two officers of the field artillery replacement center went backstage for a chat with Count Basie, when the latter's band played in the armory at Charlotte. On the left is former *Down Beater*, Lieut. Edward J. Flynn, and on the right is Lieut. Chuck Beach. *Photo by Bill Belch.*

Monday 1 June 1942
Count Basie and his Orchestra play a one-nighter at the City Auditorium in Atlanta, Georgia.

Tuesday 2 June 1942
Count Basie and his Orchestra play a one-nighter at the City Auditorium in Macon, Georgia.

Wednesday 3 June 1942
Count Basie and his Orchestra play a one-nighter at the Municipal Auditorium in Savannah, Georgia.

Thursday 4 June 1942
Count Basie and his Orchestra play a one-nighter at the Township Auditorium in Columbus, Georgia.

Friday 5 June 1942
Count Basie and his Orchestra play a one-nighter at the City Armory in Augusta, Georgia.

Saturday 6 June 1942
Count Basie and his Orchestra play a one-nighter at the City Auditorium in Montgomery, Alabama.

Sunday 21 June 1942
Count Basie and his Orchestra play a dance at the Savoy Ballroom in Chicago.

SAVOY BALLROOM
So. Parkway at 47th Street
SUN., JUNE 21
Adm. 75c

COUNT BASIE

AND HIS ORCHESTRA
JAMES RUSHING
VOCALIST
GRADUATION DANCE, THURSDAY, JUNE 25
2 POPULAR BANDS
KING KOLAX plus JOHN KIRBY
AND THEIR ORCHESTRAS

The performance is reviewed by George Hoefer for *Down Beat*:

COUNT BASIE
(Reviewed at the Savoy Ballroom, Chicago)

Hot night—hot music. The Basie machine, stripped down to their suspenders, started rather listlessly in keeping with the humidity, but slowly built up momentum to the midnight intermission. After the short rest, they returned to induce that "electric shock" to course through the tightly packed crowd out front. Shouts of "Count B-a-s-i-e and Joe J-o-n-e-s" began to emanate from the dance floor and you knew the band "was in." From then on the usual driving rhythm from that great section inspired sax ensembles and horn choruses on the Basie catalogue of jazz arrangements. The Savoy and Regal are the only places in the city where the bands can devote an entire evening to all jazz numbers. Basie went down the line through *One O'Clock Jump, Jumpin' at the Woodside, Out the Window, Good Morning Blues*, etc.

Conducive to the jazz performance was the lack of polished sheen evidenced during their last Chicago appearance at a downtown movie castle. There they showcased Glen Millerish military formations with Lunceford horn waving in unison and were impeccably garbed. At the Savoy they sat comfortably in relaxed posture and played music.

Missing were several faces familiar to Basie adherents. Buck Clayton was in New York sick and Tab Smith is out. Most lamented gap was the year old one left by "the leaning tower of the tenor" Lester Young.

Personnel on this date: Count, piano; Jo Jones, drums; Walter Page, bass; Freddie Green, guitar; trumpets—Snooky Young (late of the Lunceford band) 3rd, Ed Lewis 1st, Al Killian 2nd, Harry Edison 4th. Reeds—Earl Warren 1st alto, Jack Washington baritone, Johnny Brown 2nd alto, Don Byas 1st tenor, Buddy Tate 2nd tenor. Trombones—Dicky Wells 1st, Buster Scott 2nd, and Eli Robinson 3rd.

Monday 29 June 1942
Count Basie and his Orchestra open a two-week engagement at the Tune Town Ballroom in St.Louis, Missouri.

Tab Smith Out Of Basie Band

St. Louis—Alto saxist Tab Smith is out of the Count Basie reed section with Johnny Brown, a Kansas City toooter, in as a temporary replacement. The Basie band opened here this week for a two-week engagement.

Wednesday 1 July 1942

Mike Levin reviews the latest Basie release in *Down Beat*:

Count Basie
I'm Going to Move Way Out On the Outskirts of Town and *Basie Blues*
(Columbia)

Jimmy Rushing wails about various intruders muscling in on his chick and what he proposes to do about it. Should be a big seller, if Columbia can catch up to the hundreds of thousands of copies Louis Jordan's Decca version sold. *Blues*, outside of a pleasant trumpet trio opening, consists of Count sparingly stroking the ivories. Very nice, but twenty-five cents worth of wax should give you more.

Saturday 11 July 1942

Count Basie and his Orchestra close at the Tune Town Ballroom in St. Louis, Missouri.

Basie Seeks Film

New York—Count Basie, now on the coast, is angling for an MGM picture. It will not be *Cabin in the Sky*, but an all-ofay revue, with Basie skedded in as a special act. *Cabin* was slated to have Cab Calloway, but the deal fell through for reasons of dough, while MGM is now talking to Duke Ellington about the pic, which will star Ethel Waters and Paul Robeson.

Friday 24 July 1942

Count Basie and members of his Orchestra record for Columbia in Los Angeles.
COUNT BASIE (piano), FREDDIE GREEN (guitar), WALTER PAGE (bass), JO JONES (drums)
How Long Blues / Farewell Blues / Café Society Blues / Way Back Blues
BUCK CLAYTON (trumpet), DON BYAS (tenor sax) added:
Royal Garden Blues / Bugle Blues / Sugar Blues / St. Louis Blues

Lester Young Nixes Basie

Los Angeles—Count Basie spent a nice chunk of dough calling here from Dayton, Ohio, via long distance telephone in an effort to get Lester Young, currently at the Trouville club here, to rejoin him.

Lester declined the offer. He and Brother Lee are slated to take their combo into the Cafe Society, New York, this fall.

Though Basie didn't get Lester, he did get a good man here in Couchy Roberts. Just which one of the present Basie tenor men Couchy would replace wasn't known here. Basie is en route to Los Angeles. He'll play the Orpheum theatre here and opens at the Trianon around August 15.

Monday 27 July 1942

Count Basie and his Orchestra record for Columbia in Los Angeles.
BUCK CLAYTON, ED LEWIS, AL KILLIAN, HARRY EDISON (trumpets), ROBERT SCOTT, DICKY WELLS, ELI ROBINSON (trombones), EARLE WARREN (alto sax/vocal), CAUGHEY ROBERTS (alto sax), DON BYAS, BUDDY TATE (tenor sax), JACK WASHINGTON (baritone sax), COUNT BASIE (piano), FREDDIE GREEN (guitar), WALTER PAGE (bass), JO JONES (drums), JIMMY RUSHING (vocal)
Rusty Dusty Blues (vJR) / *Ride On* (vEW) / *Ain't It The Truth? / It's Sand Man / For The Good of The Country* (vEW) / *Blue Jazz*

Wednesday 29 July 1942

Count Basie and his Orchestra open a one-week engagement at the Orpheum Theatre in Los Angeles.

Saturday 1 August 1942

A recording ban imposed by AFM president James Petrillo commences.

ALL RECORDING STOPS TODAY

Basie Under Wire, Records 8 Blue Sides

Los Angeles—The batch of recordings put on ice here by numerous bands, just before the July 31 "deadline" was so large that no one knows yet what was included in it.

Recording execs, who had literally been working night and day during the last two weeks of July, were still too busy ot tired to stop and give out accurate information.

Basie's 15 Sides

Here, as everywhere, the recording was aimed chiefly at catching the songs which will break with the release of pictures scheduled during the next six months. However, Count Basie, who got into town latter part of July, managed to salt away a blues series of eight sides, which will be released as an album entitled *Blues by Basie*. The Count used his rhythm section, which includes himself on piano, topped off with Buck Clayton's trumpet and Don Byas' tenor sax.

In addition to the octet of blues sides, the entire Basie band knocked out an additional seven sides.

Volume of tunes waxed by other bands here was in keeping with the Basie batch except that most of the bands put their efforts into pop songs which have been guaranteed exploitation by the publishers.

Tuesday 4 August 1942

Count Basie and his Orchestra close at the Orpheum Theatre in Los Angeles.

Wednesday 5 August 1942

Count Basie and his Orchestra open a one-week engagement at the Golden Gate Theatre in San Francisco.

Tuesday 11 August 1942

Count Basie and his Orchestra close at the Golden Gate Theatre in San Francisco.

Wednesday 19 August 1942

Count Basie and his Orchestra open a six-week engagement at the Trianon Ballroom in Southgate, Los Angeles.

Basie vs. Hampton

Lionel Hampton, making his homecoming appearance at the Casa Manana, had what we fear will be a bit of bad luck in having Count Basie at the Trianon during the same period. (Hampton opened at the C.M. August 20, one night after Basie boomed into the Trianon). Basie, as a draw, is hot as fire right now. What may make it tough for Lionel is the fact that both bands appeal more or less to same type of rhythm fans. Hampton is a great performer and has a good band, but isn't the name yet that Basie is. Casa Manana operators shared misgivings over the situation and at last minute were thinking of putting in a "cafe name" to bolster Lionel—if they could find one.

Basie's New Tenor Man Gets Call

Los Angeles—Couchy Roberts, the tenor man secured by Count Basie from Los Angeles just before the band headed west, has already left the band to don the uniform of Uncle Sam, and the Count is again scratching his head over the worrisome problem of how to fill that all-important tenor spot.

Roberts left the band to be inducted during the last week of August shortly after the Count opened at the Trianon. Marvin Johnson, a local boy, was in as a temporary replacement at writing.

The Basie band is hitting a terrific pace at the Trianon, both musically and at the box office, where house records were going down like bowling pins.

Basie and Slack Signed for Pic

Los Angeles—Count Basie and Freddie Slack share the dance band honors in a Columbia picture entitled *Reveille with Beverly*, which is built around the career of Jean Ruth, the Denver radio singer and pianist who blossomed into a big network feature when her early morning musichatter show clicked big with the boys in the service. Production starts this month.

Musical and other production details were still to be lined up as script for the opus was not completed at writing.

Thursday 20 August 1942

Count Basie and his Orchestra broadcast over KFJ-Mutual from the Trianon Ballroom in Southgate.
BUCK CLAYTON, ED LEWIS, AL KILLIAN, HARRY EDISON (trumpets), ROBERT SCOTT, DICKY WELLS, ELI ROBINSON (trombones), EARLE WARREN (alto sax/vocal), CAUGHEY ROBERTS (alto sax), DON BYAS, BUDDY TATE (tenor sax), JACK WASHINGTON (baritone sax), COUNT BASIE (piano), FREDDIE GREEN (guitar), WALTER PAGE (bass), JO JONES (drums)
One O'Clock Jump (theme) / *Diggin' For Dex* / *Basie Blues* / *Airmail Special* / *Rhythm Man* / *Serenade In Blue* (vEW) / *My, What A Fry!* / *One O'Clock Jump* (theme)

Friday 21 August 1942

Count Basie and Catherine Morgan are married in Seattle on his 38th birthday.
Around this time, the band are recording *One O'Clock Jump* in the Columbia Studios for the motion picture *Reveille With Beverly* starring Ann Miller.

Basie's Birthday Bash!

Hollywood—The Count was grinning about his 37th anniversary when this party picture was snapped. Grabbing the cake are Buck Clayton and Joe Jones, flanking Basie in the front row, with manager Maceo Birch, Earl Warren and five-by-five Jimmy Rushing bringing up the rear. The bash was staged on the *Reveille for Beverly* lot.

Remember That Mustache, Girls?

Los Angeles—The next day he shaved off the mustache and joined the air corps, but here Clark Gable was still his romantic self, as he inspects one of Count Basie's new scores.

Above: Count Basie and his Orchestra with Dorothy Dandridge in a still from the Republic movie 'Hit Parade of 1943.'
Right: The band in a still from the Columbia movie 'Reveille With Beverley.'

Late in August, Count Basie and his Orchestra appear in a second movie, a romantic comedy called 'Hit Parade of 1943' for Republic Pictures.
BUCK CLAYTON, ED LEWIS, AL KILLIAN, HARRY EDISON (trumpets), ROBERT SCOTT, DICKY WELLS, ELI ROBINSON (trombones), EARLE WARREN (alto sax/vocal), CAUGHEY ROBERTS (alto sax), DON BYAS, BUDDY TATE (tenor sax), JACK WASHINGTON (baritone sax), COUNT BASIE (piano), FREDDIE GREEN (guitar), WALTER PAGE (bass), JO JONES (drums); DOROTHY DANDRIDGE, JACK WILLIAMS (vocals)
Harlem Sandman

Page Leaves Basie

Walter Page, bass, has left Count Basie following a disagreement with Basie with whom he had been associated for years. He is said to be considering an offer from Lionel Hampton.

At the end of August, Caughey Roberts is drafted, and Walter Page leaves the band. They are both missing when the band return to the Columbia Studios in September to film their sequence for *Reveille With Beverly*. By this time Marvin Johnson is on alto sax and Vernon Alley has joined on bass. Freddie Green is also missing on screen, having been caught without his draft card, and road manager Snodgrass fakes it on guitar.

Tuesday 29 September 1942
Count Basie and his Orchestra broadcast on the AFRS programme 'Command Performance' in Hollywood.
BUCK CLAYTON, ED LEWIS, AL KILLIAN, HARRY EDISON (trumpets), ROBERT SCOTT, DICKY WELLS, ELI ROBINSON (trombones), EARLE WARREN (alto sax/vocal), MARVIN JOHNSON (alto sax), DON BYAS, BUDDY TATE (tenor sax), JACK WASHINGTON (baritone sax), COUNT BASIE (piano), FREDDIE GREEN (guitar), VERNON ALLEY (bass), JO JONES (drums)
Basie Boogie
On the same broadcast, Basie plays with an unlikely group of stars:
TOMMY DORSEY (trombone); LIONEL HAMPTON (vibes); COUNT BASIE (piano); BOB BURNS (bazooka); SPIKE JONES (drums); DINAH SHORE (vocal)
Dinah (vDS)
In the evening Basie and his Orchestra close at the Trianon Ballroom in Southgate, Los Angeles.

Thursday 1 October 1942
Count Basie and his Orchestra begin a tour of four one-nighters in California.

Wednesday 7 October 1942
Count Basie and his Orchestra open a one-week engagement at the Golden Gate Theatre in San Francisco.

ʀᴋᴏ GOLDEN GATE

Looks Like the Count Is Next

New York—Maybe the *Beat* is getting out on that well-known limb again, but look for Count Basie to be commissioned in the army specialist corps in the fashion of Glenn Miller, Abe Lyman, and Kay Kyser.

The Count's immediate plans call for a part in Republic's picture *Hit Parade of 1943*, now that the shooting on Columbia's *Reveille for Beverly* has been completed. If and when Basie goes into the army, his orchestra will be disbanded for the duration.

Tuesday 13 October 1942
Count Basie and his Orchestra close at the Golden Gate Theatre in San Francisco.

Wednesday 14 October 1942
Count Basie and his Orchestra resume their tour of one-nighters in California as they head south for San Diego.

Thursday 15 October 1942
Mike Levin reviews the latest Basie release in *Down Beat*:

Count Basie
Ride On and *It's Sand, Man*
(Columbia)

First side is the Skeets Tolbert tune done here with an Earl Warren vocal. Second is a typical Basie tune with figures that the band has used many, many times before. The title is descriptive of the surface quality of the record. *Ride* has some *Gamblers' Blues* touches, with excellent Buddy Tate tenor, and Warren doing the vocal well.

Tuesday 20 October 1942
Count Basie and his Orchestra open a one-week engagement at the Orpheum Theatre in San Diego.

Monday 26 October 1942
Count Basie and his Orchestra close at the Orpheum Theatre in San Diego.

Wednesday 4 November 1942
Count Basie and his Orchestra begin a series of one-nighters en route to Chicago.

Friday 13 November 1942
Count Basie and his Orchestra open a one-week engagement at the Oriental Theatre in Chicago. Vocalist Thelma Carpenter joins the band. Bassist Vernon Alley leaves and Walter Page returns.

Thursday 19 November 1942
Count Basie and his Orchestra close at the Oriental Theatre in Chicago.

Friday 20 November 1942
Count Basie and his Orchestra open a one-week engagement at the Paradise Theatre in Detroit.

Thursday 26 November 1942
Count Basie and his Orchestra close at the Paradise Theatre in Detroit.

Thursday 3 December 1942
Count Basie and his Orchestra open a one-week engagement at the Adams Theatre in Newark, New Jersey.

Wednesday 9 December 1942
Count Basie and his Orchestra close at the Adams Theatre in Newark, New Jersey.

Friday 11 December 1942
Count Basie and his Orchestra open a one-week engagement at the Royal Theatre in Baltimore.

Basie and Hines Plans Uncertain

New York—Count Basie's army plans were still uncertain up to press time along with those of Earl Hines. Both band-leaders are classed in 3-A but are without wives, and will probably have their status changed as soon as the draft boards get around to their cases.

You can look for them to be in the service within three months, provided, of course, that they are physically fit. Basie is the best bet for duty shortly, inasmuch as his draft board was reported calling him in for a talk two weeks ago.

Thursday 17 December 1942
Count Basie and his Orchestra close at the Royal Theatre in Baltimore.

Tuesday 22 December 1942
Count Basie and his Orchestra broadcast over the NBC Blue Network at 9.30pm in the 'Spotlight Bands' series sponsored by Coca-Cola. The broadcast is from the Switlik Parachute Company in Trenton, New Jersey.

Friday 25 December 1942
Count Basie and his Orchestra open a one-week engagement at the Apollo Theatre in New York City.

Thursday 31 December 1942
Count Basie and his Orchestra close at the Apollo Theatre in New York City.

1943

Tuesday 19 January 1943
Count Basie and his Orchestra broadcast on WMCAs 'Pabst Blue Ribbon Beer Guest Night' programme in New York City.
BUCK CLAYTON, ED LEWIS, AL KILLIAN, HARRY EDISON (trumpets); ROBERT SCOTT, DICKY WELLS, ELI ROBINSON (trombones); EARLE WARREN (alto sax/vocal); MARVIN JOHNSON (alto sax); DON BYAS, BUDDY TATE (tenor sax); JACK WASHINGTON (baritone sax); COUNT BASIE (piano); FREDDIE GREEN (guitar); WALTER PAGE (bass); JO JONES (drums); THELMA CARPENTER, JIMMY RUSHING (vocals)
One O'Clock Jump (theme) / *Every Tub* / *It's Sand, Man!* / *Why Don't You Do Right?* (vTC) / interview / *Basie Boogie* / beer commercial / *Swingin' The Blues* / *Sent For You Yesterday* (vJR) / *KMA [Dance Of The Gremlins]* / *One O'Clock Jump* (theme)

Wednesday 20 January 1943
Count Basie and his Orchestra open a two-night engagement at the Poli Theatre in Waterbury, Connecticut.

Thursday 21 January 1943
Count Basie and his Orchestra close at the Poli Theatre in Waterbury, Connecticut.

Friday 22 January 1943
Count Basie and his Orchestra open a three-night engagement at the Lyric Theatre in Bridgeport, Connecticut.

Sunday 24 January 1943
Count Basie and his Orchestra close at the Lyric Theatre in Bridgeport, Connecticut.

Monday 25 January 1943
Count Basie and his Orchestra open a three-night engagement at the State Theatre in Harrisburg, Pennsylvania.

Wednesday 27 January 1943
Count Basie and his Orchestra close at the State Theatre in Harrisburg, Pennsylvania.

Friday 29 January 1943
Count Basie and his Orchestra open a one-week engagement at the Howard Theatre in Washington, D.C.

Princess Aloha May Get Count

New York—Count Basie denied reports here that he had been married recently to Princess Aloha, a Cleveland girl whose real name is Katherine Morgan. While the Count admitted that he had gone so far as to buy an engagement ring, he insisted that he had not yet done any wedding ring window-shopping and probably wouldn't for some time. Insiders expect that he will marry Miss Morgan within three months.

Ethel Waters and Count Basie's Orchestra in 'Stage Door Canteen.'

Thursday 4 February 1943
Count Basie and his Orchestra close at the Howard Theatre in Washington, D.C.

Monday 8 February 1943
Count Basie and his Orchestra are at the Fox-Movietone Studios in Astoria, Long Island, to film 'Stage Door Canteen' for United Artists with Ethel Waters. Jimmy Powell replaces Marvin Johnson on alto sax and Louis Taylor is added to the trombone section.
BUCK CLAYTON, ED LEWIS, AL KILLIAN, HARRY EDISON (trumpets); ROBERT SCOTT, DICKY WELLS, ELI ROBINSON, LOUIS TAYLOR (trombones); EARLE WARREN (alto sax/vocal); JIMMY POWELL (alto sax); DON BYAS, BUDDY TATE (tenor sax); JACK WASHINGTON (baritone sax); COUNT BASIE (piano); FREDDIE GREEN (guitar); WALTER PAGE (bass); JO JONES (drums); ETHEL WATERS (vocals)
Quicksand (vEW)

Tuesday 9 February 1943
Count Basie and his Orchestra are again at the Fox-Movietone Studios in Astoria, Long Island, filming 'Stage Door Canteen'.

Wednesday 10 February 1943
Count Basie and his Orchestra complete filming at the Fox-Movietone Studios in Astoria, Long Island.

Tuesday 16 February 1943
Count Basie and his Orchestra open a three-night engagement at the Colonial Theatre in Utica, New York.

Thursday 18 February 1943
Count Basie and his Orchestra close at the Colonial Theatre in Utica, New York.

Friday 19 February 1943
Count Basie and his Orchestra open a one-week engagement at the Earle Theatre in Philadelphia.

Thursday 25 February 1943
Count Basie and his Orchestra close at the Earle Theatre in Philadelphia.

Friday 26 February 1943
Count Basie and his Orchestra play the N.A.A.C.P. Birthday Ball at the Golden Gate Ballroom in New York City.

Friday 5 March 1943
Count Basie and his Orchestra open a one-week engagement at the Regal Theatre in Chicago.

Thursday 11 March 1943
Count Basie and his Orchestra close at the Regal Theatre in Chicago.
During the engagement at the Regal Theatre, Basie and the band also play an afternoon concert at the New Trier high school in Wilmette, Indiana.

Basie Is Boffo In Wilmette High Concert
Evanston, Ill.—Count Basie and band completely knocked out Northwestern university and high school students alike in a terrific two-hour swing concert at New Trier high school in Wilmette. The huge bash was last in a series of music presentations at the north shore school this year.

Friday 12 March 1943

Count Basie and his Orchestra open a one-week engagement at the Riverside Theatre in Milwaukee.

Thursday 18 March 1943

Count Basie and his Orchestra close at the Riverside Theatre in Milwaukee.

Friday 19 March 1943

Count Basie and his Orchestra open a one-week engagement at the Paradise Theatre in Detroit.

Thursday 25 March 1943

Count Basie and his Orchestra close at the Paradise Theatre in Detroit.

Friday 26 March 1943

Count Basie and his Orchestra open a one-week engagement at the Palace Theatre in Cleveland, Ohio.

Sunday 28 March 1943

Count Basie and his Orchestra play a concert in aid of the Russian Army at Carnegie Hall in New York City. The entire cast of Café Society Uptown and Downtown also appear.

Count Basie To Play Uncle?

New York—Got an extra watch, chum? If you do, it will serve as an Annie Oakley to a Count Basie Carnegie Hall concert March 28. Purpose of the bash is to dig up watches and money for the tickers for the Russian Army.

Watch experts will be stationed at the hall starting March 25, to exchange wristclocks for ducats, while those without timepieces will fork out from $1.40 to $3.30 for seats. The show will consist of Count Basie's Band and the entire Cafe Society Uptown and Downtown revues.

Thursday 1 April 1943

Count Basie and his Orchestra close at the Palace Theatre in Cleveland, Ohio.

Friday 2 April 1943

Count Basie and his Orchestra open a week-end engagement at the Temple Theatre in Rochester, New York.

Sunday 4 April 1943

Count Basie and his Orchestra close at the Temple Theatre in Rochester, New York.

Wednesday 7 April 1943

Count Basie and his Orchestra broadcast on the Coca-Cola 'Spotlight Bands' programme.

Thursday 8 April 1943

Count Basie and his Orchestra open a one-week engagement at the RKO Theatre in Boston.

Wednesday 14 April 1943

Count Basie and his Orchestra close at the RKO Theatre in Boston.

Friday 23 April 1943

Count Basie and his Orchestra open a one-week engagement at Fay's Theatre in Philadelphia.

Thursday 29 April 1943

Count Basie and his Orchestra close at Fay's Theatre in Philadelphia.

Saturday 1 May 1943

Count Basie and his Orchestra play a dance at the Manhattan Center, 34th Street and 8th Avenue, in New York City.

Gala DANCE This Saturday Evening, May 1st
IN PERSON—ALL EVENING
"The Jump King of Swing"
COUNT BASIE
AND HIS ENTIRE ORCHESTRA
Featuring JAMES RUSHING-"Mr. Five-By-Five Himself"
EARL WARREN—JO JONES
With His Original Company of Artists
As Featured in the Motion Picture "The Hit Parade"
NEW YORK'S LARGEST PROMENADE BALLROOM
MANHATTAN CENTER
34th ST. and 8th AVE., N.Y. Adm. 91c
Doors open from 9 P.M. Until

COUNT BASIE
(Reviewed at Manhattan Center, New York)

Ballads were infrequent on this Basie jump bill-of-fare. When they did turn up, always pleasingly conceived and played, alto man Earl Warren usually sang them. Jimmy Rushing's blues vocals were fun, as always.

The Basie music is as neat as a well-kept golf green, its effect on the ear similar to such a golf green's effect on the eye. There's never a note out of place. The arrangements are marked by a fine sense of proportion: each section—brass, reed, rhythm—is allotted just the right number of measures to result in a well-balanced whole. This same balance is maintained in solos, also, two men from a section (i.e., Don Byas and Buddy Tate, tenors; Harry Edison and Buck Clayton, trumpets) nearly always being featured on each tune.

Basie's instrumentation of four trumpets, four trombones, four rhythm, and five reeds (two altos, two tenors, a baritone) gives balance to the appearance of the band.

There are no clarinets.

The band's intonation is flawless. The muted trumpet work is impeccable. The hat work of the brass is extremely effective, both visually and musically.

Control is the band's most telling quality, and happiness its most consistent effect. Tremendous power is engendered, stemming from Joe Jones' perfectly co-ordinated, momentum-driving drums and Count's piano, and developed fully in every section and finally in ensemble. Because this power is never allowed to go wild, its impact is the more thorough.

This is a forthright band, speaking candidly, in music constructed soundly and simply, the unpretentious musical thoughts the titles, familiar to Basie followers, convey: *One O'Clock Jump, Air Mail Special, Rock-a-Bye Basie, John's Idea, Every Tub, Coming Out Party, Basie Boogie.*

Tuesday 4 May 1943

Count Basie and his Orchestra open a three-night engagement at the Palace Theatre in Columbus, Ohio.

Thursday 6 May 1943

Count Basie and his Orchestra close at the Palace Theatre in Columbus, Ohio.

Friday 7 May 1943

Count Basie and his Orchestra open a one-week engagement at the Colonial Theatre in Fort Wayne, Indiana.

Thursday 13 May 1943

Count Basie and his Orchestra close at the Colonial Theatre in Fort Wayne, Indiana.

New Basie vocalist—Thelma Carpenter

Tuesday 18 May 1943

Count Basie and his Orchestra play a dance at the White City Ballroom in Chicago, before setting out on a tour of one-nighters, including a concert at the Municipal Auditorium in Kansas City. The tour heads west to Hollywood where they are scheduled to make several pictures while playing the Aragon ballroom.

Count Basie Headin' West

New York—Milt Ebbins, personal manager for the bands of Count Basie and Vaughn Monroe left for the west coast to be on hand for the shooting of Monroe's *Meet The People* movie which will start on May 10. Basie's band opens at the Orpheum theater in Los Angeles on May 26 for a week and then moves to the Aragon ballroom for a six-week stay on June 2. After the dance date, the Count will move over to the MGM lot for a new musical movie, tentatively set to be filmed in the middle of July.

Basie, by the way, has a new Columbia recording which should be a natural. The A side, *All Of Me*, has Lynn Sherman handling the vocal, while the flip-over is another oldie, *Time On My Hands*, which could also make the revival hit list easily.

Swingsational
DANCE
—AND—
CABARET
PARTY
With a Parade of
BANDS
COUNT
BASIE

COUNT BASIE

DYETT'S
Dusableites

Vocalists
JIMMY
Rushing
THELMA
Carpenter
Stars Of Stage
Screen & Radio

TUESDAY
MAY 18
White
CITY
Ballroom
63rd & So. Parkway

ADMISSION:
85c ADVANCE
Tax Included
DOOR:
Before 8:30   85c
After 8:30 $1.10

Ebbins Grabbing Films for Basie

Hollywood—Milt Ebbins set the first of several new picture deals for Count Basie by signing the Count for a featured band spot in a big-budget untitled musical at Universal in which studio plans to put the biggest names it can muster.

In the talking stage was a deal to put Basie and his band in MGM's forthcoming edition of *Broadway Melody* in a sequence which will feature Lena Horne.

Wednesday 26 May 1943

Count Basie and his Orchestra open a one-week engagement at the Orpheum Theatre in Los Angeles. The Mills Brothers are also on the bill.

Basie Fans Like New Girl Singer

Los Angeles—Count Basie's loyal followers turned out en masse to give him a big welcome at the Orpheum theater, where the Count played a week's run preliminary to opening June 5 at Harry Schooler's new Aragon at Ocean Park.

Generous hand went to the Count's new girl singer, Thelma Carpenter, who may be recalled as having cut some platters with Coleman Hawkins, Just as he was ready to open at the Aragon Basie lost trumpeter Al Killian (to Charlie Barnet). He plucked Snooky Young from Benny Carter's line-up to fill the hole. Another new face in the band is that of saxman Jimmie Powell, who recently replaced Tab Smith.

NOW! 4 STAGE SHOWS EVERY DAY!
Orpheum
BDWY. NR. 9... · MI. 6272

Tuesday 1 June 1943

Count Basie and his Orchestra close at the Orpheum Theatre in Los Angeles.

Saturday 5 June 1943

Count Basie and his Orchestra open an engagement at the Aragon Ballroom in Ocean Park, California.

Trianon Bars 2 Basie Men, Jimmie Sore

Los Angeles—Refusal of the Trianon's doorman to admit two members of Count Basie's band who visited the nitery on their night off from the Aragon in order to hear Jimmie Lunceford's band brought a sharp protest here from the Negro press and also from Lunceford, who was so incensed over the incident that he attempted to cut his engagement short at the spot.

Lunceford said that he had issued an invitation to the boys to come out and that he understood it would be okay for them to enter even though the Trianon ordinarily does not admit negro patrons. The two Basie men, Snookie Young and Harry Edison, reached the spot just a few minutes before closing time. When the door man refused to admit them, Lunceford was sent for. He registered a strong protest, during which he, to use his own words regarding the incident, "did everything but sock someone in the jaw." But the boys did not get in.

Lunceford stated: "I wanted to quit the job that night, and my boys were 100 per cent behind me, but my contract was iron-bound. There was nothing I could do."

Ed Jameson, manager of the Trianon, which is supposed to be owned by Horace Heidt, declined to offer any comment on the incident. However, he pointed out that the municipality of Southgate, in which the Trianon is located, has a local ordinance which prohibits "mixing of races" in night clubs, ballrooms, and restaurants.

Basie Gets Berth In Picture

HOLLYWOOD, Calif.—Count Basie and his celebrated orchestra current at the Aragon Ballroom are scheduled soon to pitch their musical tepee on the movie stage of Universal Studio pictures corporation. The band will occupy a featured spot in the production 'Man of the Family.'

Donald O'Connor, teen year old screen star is the stellar attraction in 'Man of the Family,' which has Richard Dix and Lillian Gish in powerful grownup supporting roles. Currently Basie and his crew are drawing record breaking crowds at the Aragon Ballroom.

Leaders Stage California KNX Clambake

Los Angeles—Woody Herman, Count Basie, Al Jarvis, Phil Harris, Nat (King) Cole and Freddy Martin huddle around a KNX-CBS microphone for a Sunday morning session with Jarvis on Al's "Record Performance" program, newest of the recorded air-shows on the coast. Jarvis, who gave Martin Block his start in radio, also handles daily "Make Believe Ballroom" stanzas on KFWB in Hollywood. He's one of the most prominent disc-jockeys in the nation and every Sunday, plays host to a flock of maestros as pictured above. KNX Photo.

CLAMBAKE in Hollywood on a recent Sunday morning at KNX-CBS found Count Basie, Freddy Martin, Al Jarvis, Nat (King) Cole, Woody Herman and Phil Harris gathered about to take part in Jarvis' new "Record Performance" program. The show is one of the most popular platter sessions on the Coast.

Monday 7 June 1943

Count Basie and his Orchestra broadcast on the AFRS 'Jubilee' programme in Hollywood. Rose Murphy is also on the show which was probably recorded a few days earlier.

Basie Boogie / Don't Get Around Much Anymore (vTC) / *Dance Of The Gremlins / Baby, Won't You Please Come Home?* (vJR) / *Green / Them There Eyes* (vTC) / *One O'Clock Jump*

Monday 21 June 1943

Count Basie and his Orchestra broadcast on the AFRS 'Jubilee' programme in Hollywood. Butterfly McQueen is also on the show which was probably recorded a few days earlier.

Rhythm Man / Jazz Me Blues / Boogie Woogie Blues (vJR) / *One O'Clock Jump*

Monday 5 July 1943

Count Basie and his Orchestra broadcast on the AFRS 'Jubilee' programme in Hollywood. Singer Ida James is also on the show which was probably recorded a few days earlier.

Air Mail Special / After You've Gone (vIJ) / *St. Louis Blues* (vIJ) / *Cabin In The Sky* (vEW) / *Exactly Like You* (vJR) / *I Won't Say I Will* (vIJ) / *Swing Shift / One O'Clock Jump*

Sunday 11 July 1943

Count Basie and his Orchestra close at the Aragon Ballroom in Ocean Park, California.

Thursday 15 July 1943

Down Beat celebrates its 10th Anniversary and Basie takes a half-page advertisement.

Count...
ME IN ON THOSE ANNIVERSARY GREETINGS!

Count BASIE And His Orchestra

Exclusively on
COLUMBIA RECORDS

Currently on tour, WEST COAST

FEATURED IN MGM'S MUSICAL HIT
"STAGE DOOR CANTEEN"

WILLIAM MORRIS AGENCY, Inc.

Basie Working In Three Pics
Count Kept Busy At Universal With Two Features, Short

Hollywood—Count Basie has drawn a total of three picture assignments at Universal. The Count and his boys will appear in a Donald O'Connor feature entitled *Man of the Family*, for which they have already recorded several numbers; in the Olsen & Johnson starrer, *Crazy House*, and will be featured in a musical featurette to be produced by Will Cowan, who has been doing a series of shorts featuring name bands.

Among the numbers soundtracked by the Basie men for *Man of the Family*—were two of the Count's originals, *Basie Boogie* and *Get It*.

Numbers for Crazy House had not been lined up at writing but it was understood Basie would be featured in the new Don Raye-Gene De Paul ditty *Get On Board Little Chillun*. Vocalist Jimmy Rushing will draw featured vocals.

Sunday 1 August 1943
Count Basie and his Orchestra spend the week in the Universal Studios in Hollywood, recording and filming for three movies.

Choo Choo Swing
featuring Count Basie orchestra, Bobby Brooks and the Delta Rhythm Boys.
Dance Of The Gremlins / Red Bank Boogie / Swingin' The Blues / St. Louis Blues (vBB) / *One O'Clock Jump / Sent For You Yesterday* (vJR) / *Knock Me A Kiss* (vDRB) / *Someone's Rockin' My Dreamboat* (vBB)

Top Man (Man Of The Family)
83 min feature starring Donald O'Connor with the Count Basie orchestra and Bobby Brooks.
Basie Boogie / Wrap Your Troubles In Dreams (vBB)

Crazy House (Funzapoppin')
80 min feature starring Olsen & Johnson with the Count Basie orchestra, Delta Rythm Boys, Glenn Miller Singers and Martha Tilton.
Rigoletto Quartet / Pocketful Of Pennies (vDRB, GMS, JR, MT)

Above: Thelma Carpenter and Jimmy Rushing in 'Crazy House'.

Friday 6 August 1943
Count Basie and his Orchestra complete their work at the Universal Studios in Hollywood.

Friday 13 August 1943
Count Basie and his Orchestra open a one-week engagement at the Orpheum Theatre in Omaha, Nebraska.

Thursday 19 August 1943
Count Basie and his Orchestra close at the Orpheum Theatre in Omaha, Nebraska.

Friday 20 August 1943
Count Basie and his Orchestra open a one-week engagement at the Tower Theatre in Kansas City, Missouri.

Thursday 26 August 1943
Count Basie and his Orchestra close at the Tower Theatre in Kansas City, Missouri.

Friday 27 August 1943
Count Basie and his Orchestra open a one-week engagement at the Orpheum Theatre in Wichita, Kansas.

Thursday 2 September 1943
Count Basie and his Orchestra close at the Orpheum Theatre in Wichita, Kansas.

Monday 6 September 1943
Count Basie and his Orchestra play a one-nighter at the Dreamland Ballroom in Omaha, Nebraska. Preston Love is the temporary replacement for the ailing Earl Warren.

Tuesday 7 September 1943
Count Basie and his Orchestra play a one-nighter in St. Louis, Missouri.

Friday 10 September 1943
Count Basie and his Orchestra open a one-week engagement at the Regal Theatre in Chicago.

Thursday 16 September 1943
Count Basie and his Orchestra close at the Regal Theatre in Chicago.

Laurel Watson, attractive singer once with Don Redman and Roy Eldridge, has replaced Thelma Carpenter with Count Basie. Thelma returned to Kelly's Stable. Earl Warren out of band for a while with bad stomach; Preston Love replaced him in the reeds. Dickie Wells, ace Basie trombone, is in the Army.

Saturday 18 September 1943
James C. Petrillo, AFM president, and Decca's Jack Kapp close an agreement which permits Decca and World Recording to commence recording bands immediately.

Friday 24 September 1943
Count Basie and his Orchestra open a one-week engagement at the Royal Theatre in Baltimore, Maryland.

Thursday 30 September 1943
Count Basie and his Orchestra close at the Royal Theatre in Baltimore, Maryland.

Friday 1 October 1943
Count Basie and his Orchestra open a one-week engagement at the Howard Theatre in Washington, D.C.

Thursday 7 October 1943
Count Basie and his Orchestra close at the Howard Theatre in Washington, D.C.

Barry Ulanov celebrates 60 years of *Metronome* with news of a Basie breakthrough in his editorial:

Count Basie!

Perhaps, if you've ever seen the Count Basie band perform, you've heard one of its trumpeters, Harry Edison, yell forth enthusiastically, "Count Basie!" Well, this month, we're yelling forth, "Count Basie!"

You see, the Count and his fine band are opening at the Hotel Lincoln next month. That's cause for rejoicing, if you like Basie's music as much as we do. But we normally leave critical appreciation to other pages than the editorial. This yelling we're doing here is not because Basie's fine music is coming into the Lincoln. It's simple because the fine music of a colored band is set for that important hotel, with its strategic location and all its air time. It's because the color line has been broken in one more top New York spot.

We're a little proud, personally, because we've been told that our strong editorials on the color line helped bring Basie's booking into the Lincoln. That makes us feel fine. But, more important, it makes quite obvious the fact that protest against bigotry and stupidity can get somewhere. It makes it incumbent upon us, and all who feel as we do, to continue fighting for equal rights for all in the music business, regardless of race or creed or color. We shall continue this vital fight. Will you?

Friday 8 October 1943

Count Basie and his Orchestra open a one-week engagement at the Apollo Theatre in New York City. Don Byas is taken ill and Lester Young agrees to play the week at the Apollo.

Thursday 14 October 1943

Count Basie and his Orchestra close at the Apollo Theatre in New York City. The band then embark on a series of one-nighters in the New York area.

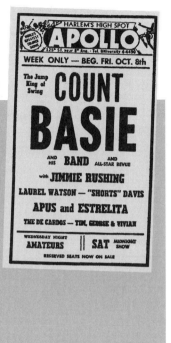

Thursday 21 October 1943

Count Basie and his Orchestra play a dance at the Lost Battalion Hall in Elmhurst, Long Island, New York.

Friday 22 October 1943

Count Basie and his Orchestra open a one-week engagement at the Earle Theatre in Philadelphia.

Thursday 28 October 1943

Count Basie and his Orchestra close at the Earle Theatre in Philadelphia.

Saturday 30 October 1943

Count Basie and his Orchestra play a Hallowe'en dance at the Brooklyn Palace in Brooklyn.

Thursday 4 November 1943

Count Basie and his Orchestra play a dance at the Golden Gate Ballroom in New York City.

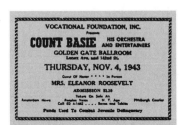

Count Basie For Lincoln

New York—Count Basie will play his first New York hotel booking when he opens at the Lincoln on November 5. Basie, set for eight weeks, is the first colored band to play the Lincoln and at a price reputed to be the highest ever paid by Maria Kramer for any previous attraction. Basie's last New York downtown date was at the Famous Door on 52nd Street.

Friday 5 November 1943

Count Basie and his Orchestra open an eight-week engagement at the Blue Room of the Hotel Lincoln in New York City. Thelma Carpenter is back with the band.

Count Returns To Please Mob
Basie Clicking Steadily at the Hotel Lincoln

New York—Count Basie and his band made their downtown bid recently when they opened an eight-week engagement on the bandstand of the Hotel Lincoln's Blue Room here. The Basie outfit, famous for its *One O'Clock Jump*, has spent much of the last year out on the west coast making movies and on opening night, an unusually large collection of music world celebrities was on hand to dig the Count's pianistics, the pounding rhythm section, the biting brass, and to wonder perhaps whether or not the band had changed any while it had been away.

Overheard hep chatter would indicate that Basie is still in there for most. There are good reasons why. Still intact in the band, during these days when musicians are draft will-of-the-wisps, are most of the Count's original band members, including his now-legendary rhythm section.

On hand for Basie's coming-out party were music big-wigs Duke Ellington, Lena Horne, Red Norvo, Perry Como, Charlie Barnet and Jan Savitt, as well as most of the music publishers and the inevitable trade press.

Thursday 11 November 1943

Buck Clayton is drafted and replaced by Joe Newman.

Don Byas is causing problems with his heavy drinking. At the end of November he pulls a gun during an intermission at the Lincoln Hotel. Basie fires him immediately and sends Jo Jones to find Lester Young.

I WENT ROUND TO THE WHITE ROSE AND GOT LESTER AND LESTER DIDN'T KNOW WHAT I WAS DOING. I BOUGHT HIM A BEER AND TOLD HIM, 'YOU'RE DUE AT WORK TOMORROW NIGHT AT 7 O'CLOCK. YOU COME TO THE LINCOLN HOTEL, ETCETERA. AND THERE HE WAS!

Wednesday 1 December 1943

Lester Young rejoins Count Basie and his Orchestra at the Blue Room of the Lincoln Hotel in New York City. Lester has been working with Dizzy Gillespie's group at the Onyx Club on 52nd Street. Don Byas fills the vacancy with the two tenor players effectively swapping jobs.

Basie appears on the cover of *Down Beat*.

LENA HORNE, COUNT BASIE and THELMA CARPENTER

December 1, 1943

MUSIC NEWS FROM COAST-TO-COAST

20 CENTS
CANADA and FOREIGN 25c

Army Rejects Basie's Boys

New York—Don Byas, tenor, and Harry Edison, trumpet, from the Count Basie band, were called for physical examinations late last month, but both were rejected by the army. Buck Clayton, so far, is the band's only loss to the service, although Buddy Tate is vulnerable.

Monday 6 December 1943

Count Basie and his Orchestra record an AFRS 'Jubilee' programme (No 55) at the NBC Studios in Radio City, New York City.
One O'Clock Jump (theme) / *Jumpin' At The Woodside* / *Baby, Won't You Please Come Home?* (vJR) / *Do Nothin' Till You Hear From Me* (vTC) / *Don't Believe Everything You Dream* (vEW) / *I Found A New Baby* / *One O'Clock Jump* (theme)

Tuesday 7 December 1943

Count Basie and his Orchestra are guests at the People's Victory All Star Ball at the Golden Gate Ballroom in New York City.

Monday 13 December 1943

Count Basie and his Orchestra are guests at a Breakfast Dance at the Renaissance Casino in New York City.

Harlem's 6th Annual Pre-Xmas Bars & Grills
Popularity Contest

BREAKFAST DANCE & SHOW

Mon., Dec. 13th — 11 P. M. Until ?
at RENAISSANCE CASINO
138th St. & 7th Ave.

COUNT BASIE, Guest Artist
and Other Stars of Stage - Radio and Screen
SUBSCRIPTION (Advance) $1.10

Basie Builds Lincoln Biz

New York—Count Basie followed up his celebrity-studded opening at the Hotel Lincoln here by consistently bringing in more customers than the usually inactive Blue Room has seen for some time.

Bringing the Basie crew into her name band room was an experiment on the part of Mrs. Maria Kramer, who owns the Lincoln and several other hotels where name band work is featured. Not only was presenting Negro orchestra on the Lincoln stand without precedent, but the price paid for the band was much higher than that paid in the past to high caliber outfits.

Another indication of Basie's new spurt to popularity is the fact that he was recently called back to the Kate Smith radio show for an encore guest shot and also has been asked to do a return appearance on the *Million Dollar Band* program on New Year's Day.

Bregman Greets His Writers

New York—Jack Bregman, music publisher, is seen here flanked by Buck Clayton, ex-Basie trumpet and arranger now stationed at Camp Shanks, and by the Count himself, at the Hotel Lincoln here. Bregman publishes all of Basie's tunes, as well as those by Clayton, including *Swing Shift*, *It's Sand, Man!*, *Red Bank Boogie*, *Love Jumped Out*, *What's Your Number?*, *Avenue C*, *High Ball*, *Sneaky Pete* and *Khaki Tan*.

1944

Saturday 1 January 1944
Count Basie and his Orchestra close at the Blue Room of the Hotel Lincoln in New York City.

Monday 10 January 1944
Count Basie and his Orchestra record Lang-Worth Transcriptions at the Lincoln Hotel in New York City. AL KILLIAN, ED LEWIS, JOE NEWMAN, HARRY EDISON (trumpets), TED DONNELLY, LOUIS TAYLOR, DICKY WELLS, ELI ROBINSON (trombones), EARLE WARREN (alto sax/vocal), JIMMY POWELL (alto sax), LESTER YOUNG, BUDDY TATE (tenor sax), RUDY RUTHERFORD (baritone sax), COUNT BASIE (piano), FREDDIE GREEN (guitar), RODNEY RICHARDSON (bass), SHADOW WILSON (drums), JIMMY RUSHING, THELMA CARPENTER (vocal)
One O'Clock Jump (theme) / *Rock-a-bye Basie* / *I Couldn't Sleep A Wink Last Night* (vEW) / *Basie Boogie* / *I've Had This Feeling Before* (vEW) / *I Found A New Baby* / *Red Bank Boogie* / *I Sent For You Yesterday* (vJR) / *Do Nothin' Till You Hear From Me* (vTC) / *Don't Believe Everything You Dream* (vEW) / *Swing Shift* / *Dinah* / *Baby Won't You Please Come Home* / *Don't Cry, Baby* (vJR) / *9.20 Special* / *Rockin' The Blues* / *Wiggle Woogie* / *Down For Double*

Thursday 13 January 1944
Count Basie and his Orchestra open a one-week engagement at the Adams Theatre in Newark, New Jersey.

Wednesday 19 January 1944
Count Basie and his Orchestra close at the Adams Theatre in Newark, New Jersey.

Friday 21 January 1944
Count Basie and his Orchestra open a one-week engagement at the Stanley Theatre in Pittsburgh, Pennsylvania.

Thursday 27 January 1944
Count Basie and his Orchestra close at the Stanley Theatre in Pittsburgh, Pennsylvania.

Friday 28 January 1944
Count Basie and his Orchestra open a one-week engagement at the Paradise Theatre in Detroit, Michigan.

Thursday 3 February 1944
Count Basie and his Orchestra close at the Paradise Theatre in Detroit, Michigan.

Friday 4 February 1944
Count Basie and his Orchestra open a one-week engagement at the Riverside Theatre in Milwaukee, Wisconsin.

Sunday 6 February 1944
Count Basie's wife Catherine gives birth to their daughter Diane in Cincinnati.

Thursday 10 February 1944
Count Basie and his Orchestra close at the Riverside Theatre in Milwaukee, Wisconsin.

Saturday 12 February 1944
Count Basie and his Orchestra open a week-end engagement at Castle Farms in Cincinnati, Ohio.

Sunday 13 February 1944
Count Basie and his Orchestra close at Castle Farms in Cincinnati, Ohio.

Friday 25 February 1944
Count Basie and his Orchestra open a one-week engagement at the Apollo Theatre in New York City. Also on the bill are Peg Leg Bates and Shorty Davis.

Thursday 2 March 1944
Count Basie and his Orchestra close at the Apollo Theatre in New York City.

Wednesday 8 March 1944
Count Basie and his Orchestra open a four-week engagement at the Roxy Theatre in New York City. Also on the bill are Carol Bruce, Zero Mostel and the Berry Brothers. The movie presentation is 'The Purple Heart.'

Friday 22 March 1944
Count Basie and his Kansas City Seven record for Harry Lim's Keynote in New York City. Buck Clayton, still in the army but stationed nearby, is brought in for the session which takes place in the early hours after the last show at the Roxy.
BUCK CLAYTON (trumpet); DICKY WELLS (trombone); LESTER YOUNG (tenor sax); COUNT BASIE (piano); FREDDIE GREEN (guitar); RODNEY RICHARDSON (bass); JO JONES (drums)
After Theatre Jump / *Six Cats And A Prince* (2 takes) / *Lester Leaps Again* (BC,DW out) / *Destination K.C.* (2 takes)

Basie May Get More Celluloid

New York—Count Basie returns to the Hotel Lincoln here on April 6 or 13, depending upon the length of his run at the Roxy. Basie played his first Lincoln date last fall and was one of the few bands to draw heavily there for some time. At the end of the hotel booking, the band moves to the west coast, playing theaters en route, and will probably do more picture work.

Saturday 1 April 1944

Count Basie and his Orchestra close at the Roxy Theatre in New York City.

Sunday 2 April 1944

Count Basie and his Orchestra appear at a Salute to Fats Waller Concert at Carnegie Hall in New York City.
Ain't Misbehavin' / I'm Gonna Sit Right Down And Write Myself A Letter (vJR)

Thursday 6 April 1944

Count Basie and his Orchestra open an eight-week engagement at the Blue Room of the Hotel Lincoln in New York City. The band broadcast over CBS from the hotel.
AL KILLIAN, ED LEWIS, JOE NEWMAN, HARRY EDISON (trumpets), TED DONNELLY, LOUIS TAYLOR, DICKY WELLS, ELI ROBINSON (trombones), EARLE WARREN (alto sax/vocal), JIMMY POWELL (alto sax), LESTER YOUNG, BUDDY TATE (tenor sax), RUDY RUTHERFORD (baritone sax), COUNT BASIE (piano), FREDDIE GREEN (guitar), RODNEY RICHARDSON (bass), JO JONES (drums), JIMMY RUSHING, THELMA CARPENTER (vocal)
Swing Shift / I've Had This Feeling Before (vEW) / *Blue Room Jump / One O'Clock Jump* (theme)

Count Basie Signs To Return To NYC Hotel

New York—Count Basie and his band are back at Hotel Lincoln here for their second date. Signed to a deal with the hotel for the next two years, the Basie orch will play further but as yet indefinite return engagements. The Count's keyboard work can be heard every Friday at 8 p.m. (EWT) on Kate Smith's CBS show.

Friday 7 April 1944

Count Basie and his Orchestra broadcast on AFRS 'One Night Stand' from the Blue Room of the Hotel Lincoln in New York City.
One O'Clock Jump (theme) / *Diggin' For Dex / My Ideal* (vTC) / *Blue Lou / Ain't It The Truth? / Take Me Back, Baby* (vJR) / *And So Little Time / Journey To A Star* (vEW) / *Jumpin' At The Woodside / One O'Clock Jump* (theme)

Monday 10 April 1944

Count Basie and his Orchestra broadcast from the Blue Room of the Hotel Lincoln in New York City.
My, What A Fry! / One O'Clock Jump

Friday 14 April 1944

Count Basie and his Orchestra broadcast over WOR-Mutual from the Blue Room of the Hotel Lincoln in New York City.
Bangs / Irresistible You (vEW) / *Ain't But The One / Don't Cry Baby / I've Found A New Baby*
Basie also broadcasts on his regular Friday evening slot on CBS's Kate Smith Show.
King Porter Stomp

Monday 17 April 1944

Count Basie and his Orchestra broadcast on AFRS 'One Night Stand' from the Blue Room of the Hotel Lincoln.
One O'Clock Jump (theme) / *Avenue C / Tess Torch Song* (vTC) / *Jumpin' At The Woodside / I'm Gonna Sit Right Down And Write Myself A Letter* (vJR) / *Rock-a-bye Basie / And So Little Time* (vEW) / *Dance Of The Gremlins / When They Ask About You* (vTC) / *One O'Clock Jump* (theme)

Tuesday 18 April 1944

Earl Warren and his Orchestra (essentially the Count Basie Orchestra with Clyde Hart replacing Basie on piano) record for Savoy at the WOR Studios in New York City.

Friday 21 April 1944

Count Basie broadcasts with a studio band on CBS's Kate Smith Show in New York City.
One O'Clock Jump (theme) / *On A Trolley* (vKS) / *Nagasaki / Suddenly It's Spring* (vKS) / *Kansas City Keys [Basie Boogie]*
Count Basie and his Orchestra broadcast from the Blue Room of the Hotel Lincoln in New York City.
Kansas City Stride / One O'Clock Jump (theme)

Monday 24 April 1944

Count Basie and his Orchestra broadcast on AFRS 'One Night Stand' from the Blue Room of the Hotel Lincoln in New York City.
Hey, Rube! / I Dream Of You (vTC) / *Basie Blues / Irresistible You* (vEW) / *Ain't Misbehavin' / I'm In Love With Someone* (vTC) / *Jumpin' At The Woodside / 9.20 Special*
Later the same night they broadcast over WOR-Mutual from the Blue Room of the Hotel Lincoln.
One O'Clock Jump (theme) / *I've Found A New Baby / Tess' Torch Song* (vTC) / *Jazz Me Blues / I Couldn't Sleep A Wink Last Night* (vEW) / *Blue Lou / My Melancholy Baby* (vJR) / *Avenue C / One O'Clock Jump* (theme)

Friday 28 April 1944

Count Basie broadcasts with a studio band on CBS's Kate Smith Show in New York City.
One O'Clock Jump (theme) / *Rose Room*

Monday 1 May 1944

Count Basie records with Lester Young's Quintet for Savoy at the WOR Studios in New York City. Drummer Shadow Wilson is a temporary replacement for Jo Jones who takes some time off for personal reasons.

LESTER YOUNG (tenor sax); COUNT BASIE (piano); FREDDIE GREEN (guitar); RODNEY RICHARDSON (bass); SHADOW WILSON (drums)

Blue Lester / Ghost Of A Chance (2 takes) / *Indiana* (2 takes) / *Jump, Lester, Jump*

Friday 5 May 1944

Count Basie and his Orchestra record AFRS Transcriptions in New York City.

One O'Clock Jump / I've Found A New Baby / Avenue C / Do Nothin' Till You Hear From Me (vTC) / *Basie Boogie / Harvard Blues* (vJR) / *My Ideal* (vTC) / *Exactly Like You* (vJR) / *Beaver Junction / One O'Clock Jump* (theme)

Wednesday 10 May 1944

Count Basie and his Orchestra broadcast from the Blue Room of the Hotel Lincoln in New York City.

Diggin' For Dex / Ain't It The Truth / Jumpin' At The Woodside / My Ideal (vTC) / *Blue Lou / Take Me Back Baby* (vJR) / *And So Little Time* (vEW) / *Journey To A Star*

Saturday 13 May 1944

Count Basie and his Orchestra broadcast over WOR-Mutual from the Blue Room of the Hotel Lincoln in New York City.

One O'Clock Jump (theme) / *Hey, Rube! / Tush / This Is A Lovely Way To Spend An Evening* (vTC) / *Rock-a-bye Basie / Harvard Blues* (vJR) / *Jazz Me Blues / I Couldn't Sleep A Wink Last Night* (vEW) / *I Never Knew* (vJR) / *One O'Clock Jump* (theme)

Sunday 14 May 1944

Count Basie and his Orchestra broadcast over WOR-Mutual from the Blue Room of the Hotel Lincoln in New York City.

Every Tub

Monday 15 May 1944

Count Basie and his Orchestra broadcast on AFRS 'One Night Stand' from the Blue Room of the Hotel Lincoln in New York City.

One O'Clock Jump (theme) / *Hey, Rube! / Same Little Words* (vTC) / *Let's Jump / Too Much In Love* (vEW) / *There'll Be Some Changes Made* (vJR) / *Time Alone Will Tell* (vEW) / *Avenue C / One O'Clock Jump* (theme)

Wednesday 17 May 1944

Count Basie and his Orchestra broadcast over WOR-Mutual from the Blue Room of the Hotel Lincoln in New York City. Vocalist Freddie Bryant joins in.

I Never Knew / This I Love Above All (vFB) / *Let's Mop It* (vTC) / *I Want A Little Girl* (vJR) / *Dance Of The Gremlins / How Blue The Night* (vTC) / *Too Much In Love* (vEW) / *Blue Room Jump / One O'Clock Jump* (theme)

Saturday 20 May 1944

Count Basie and his Orchestra broadcast over CBS from the Blue Room of the Hotel Lincoln in New York City.

Call Me Darling (vTC) / *Ain't It The Truth*

Monday 22 May 1944

Count Basie and his Orchestra broadcast over CBS from the Blue Room of the Hotel Lincoln in New York City.

It's Sand, Man / I Dream Of You (vTC) / *Circus In Rhythm / Time Alone Will Tell* (vEW) / *I'm In Love With Someone* (vTC) / *Swing Shift / Gee, Baby, Ain't I Good To You?* (vJR) / *Jumpin' At The Woodside / One O'Clock Jump* (theme)

Thursday 25 May 1944

Count Basie and his Orchestra record Lang-Worth Transcriptions at the Lincoln Hotel in New York City. Vocalist Freddie Bryant is added to the session.

Tush / Time Alone Will Tell / Ain't It The Truth? / This I Love Above All (vFB) / *I Dream Of You* (vTC) / *I'm Gonna Sit Right Down And Write Myself A Letter* (vJR)

Saturday 27 May 1944

Count Basie and his Orchestra record for V-Disc in New York City.

Kansas City Stride (2 takes) / *Beaver Junction /Circus In Rhythm / Gee Baby, Ain't I Good To You?* (vJR) / *Aunt Hagar's Country Home* (vEW) / *Basie Strides Again (Along Avenue C) / Call Me Darling* (vTC) / *Playhouse No2 Stomp*

In the evening, Count Basie and his Orchestra broadcast over WOR-Mutual from the Blue Room of the Hotel Lincoln in New York City.

The Jumpin' Jive / Broadway / My Ideal (vTC) / *Circus In Rhythm / Journey To A Star* (vEW) / *Tuesday At Ten / Harvard Blues* (vJR) / *Rock-a-bye Basie / Down For Double*

Sunday 28 May 1944

Count Basie and his Orchestra broadcast from the Blue Room of the Hotel Lincoln in New York City.

Basie Boogie / Avenue C / One O'Clock Jump

Monday 29 May 1944

Count Basie and his Orchestra broadcast over WOR-Mutual from the Blue Room of the Hotel Lincoln in New York City.

One O'Clock Jump (theme) / *Blue Lou / Call Me Darling* (vTC) / *Jazz Me Blues / Harvard Blues* (vJR) / *My, What A Fry! / Time On My Hands* (vEW) / *Avalon / One O'Clock Jump* (theme)

Count Basie Guest Artist At Downbeat Club's Celeb Night

Count Basie was the guest of honor Monday at the Downbeat Club's weekly celebrity party. Coleman Hawkins, whose orchestra is featured nightly at the club, has written a modern composition titled "K.C. Diner" dedicated to the Count, and introduced it Monday. Basie and many of his musicians came from Kansas City and have made famous the Kansas City style of swing.

At the Downbeat Club, such famous K.C. style musicians as Lester Young, Sgt. Buck Clayton, Jo Jones, Dickie Wells, Freddy Green, Harry Edison, Al Killian, Buddy Tate and Earl Warren jammed with Basie.

Tuesday 30 May 1944
Count Basie and his Orchestra record National Guard Transcriptions from the Blue Room of the Hotel Lincoln in New York City.
AL KILLIAN, ED LEWIS, JOE NEWMAN, HARRY EDISON (trumpets), TED DONNELLY, LOUIS TAYLOR, DICKY WELLS, ELI ROBINSON (trombones), EARLE WARREN (alto sax/vocal), JIMMY POWELL (alto sax), LESTER YOUNG, BUDDY TATE (tenor sax), RUDY RUTHERFORD (baritone sax), COUNT BASIE (piano), FREDDIE GREEN (guitar), RODNEY RICHARDSON (bass), JO JONES (drums), JIMMY RUSHING, THELMA CARPENTER (vocal)
There'll Be Some Changes Made (vJR) / *Jumpin' For Maria* / *Blue Lou* / *Avenue C* / *Gee, Baby, Ain't I Good To You?* (vJR) / *Blue Skies* (vJR) / *Jazz Me Blues* / *I Never Knew* (vJR)
Count Basie and his Orchestra broadcast over CBS from the Blue Room of the Hotel Lincoln in New York City.
The Jumpin' Jive / *I'm In Love With Someone* (vTC) / *Kansas City Stride* / *Tess' Torch Song* (vTC) / *There'll Be Some Changes Made* (vJR) / *Let's Jump* / *Time Alone Will Tell* (vEW) / *Jumpin' At The Woodside* / *One O'Clock Jump* (theme)

Wednesday 31 May 1944
Count Basie and his Orchestra close at the Blue Room of the Hotel Lincoln in New York City.

Friday 2 June 1944
Count Basie and his Orchestra open a week-end engagement at the Metropolitan Theatre in Providence, Rhode Island.

Sunday 4 June 1944
Count Basie and his Orchestra close at the Metropolitan Theatre in Providence, Rhode Island.

Monday 5 June 1944
Count Basie and his Orchestra open a three-day engagement at the Plymouth Theatre in Worcester, Massachusetts.

Wednesday 7 June 1944
Count Basie and his Orchestra close at the Plymouth Theatre in Worcester, Massachusetts.

Friday 9 June 1944
Count Basie and his Orchestra open a three-day engagement at the State Theatre in Hartford, Connecticut.

Sunday 11 June 1944
Count Basie and his Orchestra close at the State Theatre in Hartford, Connecticut.

Thursday 15 June 1944
Down Beat reviews a Count Basie Columbia album:

BLUES BY BASIE
Columbia C-101

In this wonderful album the Count really gets a chance to go! His piano is showcased all the way, backed by his deservedly famous rhythm section. 36709 couples Clarence Williams' *Sugar Blues* with Basie's own version of *Bugle Blues*, based primarily on the "Oh Miss" portion of *Bugle Call Rag*. Trumpeter Buck Clayton and tenorman Don Byas sit in on both sides, with marvelous results. 36710 pairs up *Royal Garden Blues*, by Spencer and Clarence Williams, with Leroy Carr's *How Long Blues*. The work of Clayton and Byas on the first should be compared with that of Cootie Williams and George Auld in the Goodman Sextet rendition. Basie has recorded *How Long* twice before, as a piano solo for Decca and as a band number for Okeh. 36711 couples Handy's *St. Louis Blues* with a Basie original called *Cafe Society Blues*. Buck and Byas are outstanding on the former, the Count on the latter. 36712 pairs up *Farewell Blues*, by Mares and Rappolo, with Basie's own *Way Back Blues*. Both are taken as piano solos entirely, as are *Cafe Society* and *How Long*. If this set is any indication of the shape of things to come, we can expect great things from Columbia from now on!

Friday 16 June 1944
Count Basie and his Orchestra open a one-week engagement at the Regal Theatre in Chicago.

Thursday 22 June 1944
Count Basie and his Orchestra close at the Regal Theatre in Chicago.
After the Regal theatre engagement Joe Newman returns to New York to complete residential qualifications for a Local 802 AFM card.

Thursday 30 June 1944
Count Basie and his Orchestra play a dance at the Savoy Ballroom in Chicago.

Earl Warren To Head Own Band

New York—Earl Warren, lead alto with the Count Basie band, plans to leave his present boss to lead his own band in about three months, following a cross-country tour by the Basie band. Warren's popularity has zoomed since the release of his recent Savoy recordings.

Basie's personnel now includes: saxes, Rudy Rutherford, Earl Warren, Les Young, Buddy Tate and Jimmy Powell; trumpets, Ed Lewis, Al Killian, Joe Newman and Harry Edison; trombones, Dickie Wells, Ted Donnelly, Lewis Taylor and Eli Robinson; Jo Jones, drums; Rodney Richardson, bass; Freddie Green, guitar and the leader's piano.

Tuesday 4 July 1944
Count Basie and his Orchestra open a three-day engagement at the Palace Theatre in Columbus, Ohio.

Thursday 6 July 1944
Count Basie and his Orchestra close at the Palace Theatre in Columbus, Ohio.

Friday 7 July 1944
Count Basie and his Orchestra open a one-week engagement at the Palace Theatre in Cleveland, Ohio.

Thursday 13 July 1944
Count Basie and his Orchestra close at the Palace Theatre in Cleveland, Ohio.

Friday 14 July 1944
Count Basie and his Orchestra open a four-day engagement at the Palace Theatre in Youngstown, Ohio.

Monday 17 July 1944
Count Basie and his Orchestra close at the Palace Theatre in Youngstown, Ohio.

Friday 21 July 1944
Count Basie and his Orchestra open a one-week engagement at the Tower Theatre in Kansas City, Missouri.

Thursday 27 July 1944
Count Basie and his Orchestra close at the Tower Theatre in Kansas City, Missouri.

Sunday 30 July 1944
Lester Young, Harry Edison and Jo Jones are scheduled to appear at Norman Granz' second swing concert at the Philharmonic Hall in Los Angeles. The management of the Orpheum Theatre, where Basie is due to open on August 1, threaten a lawsuit if the three men appear and they are withdrawn at the last minute.

Tuesday 1 August 1944
Count Basie and his Orchestra open a two-week engagement at the Orpheum Theatre in Los Angeles, California.

Metronome's Milton Benny reviews the show:

COUNT BASIE
A Fair AcCounting
Orpheum Theater, Los Angeles.

The Jump King played two consecutive weeks at this downtown house in August, and despite three mediocre acts on the same bill managed to provide a fair batch of entertainment throughout the 14 days. Basie has presented better shows on this very stage. But despite minor weaknesses this shaped up more strongly than the Orpheum's ordinary band bills.

An up-tempoed instrumental, un-named, with Les Young and Buddy Tate moving upstage for solo spots, led off. One trumpet was missing, too, and the brass team may have been affected by its absence. Thelma Carpenter got across well with *Do Nothin'* and *More Than You Know* even if the latter ran much too long for vaude purposes. And she looked good in a trim pink gown. The band romped its way through *Basie Boogie* and *9:20 Special*, both numbers garnering spontaneous applause as the mob (a capacity house) recognized them from the records. Basie played his usual refreshing, confident Steinway. Earl Warren's vocal on a pop ballad no one ever heard of before (or probably will again) was sub-par stuff. His brief alto soloings were much stronger musically.

Two dance acts, Short Davis and Patterson & Jackson, appeared run-of-the-mill, and four tunes by the Delta Rhythm Boys weren't much stronger. Long on appearance, weak in originality, the group of four coloured singers made a so-so impresh here. Basie's Kansas City Eight riffing *Royal Garden Blues* started solidly but wound up as a clambake. It, too, ran fully two minutes too long. The boys acted as if they weren't sure of who would play what when. Musically, it was a *faux pas* unworthy of the time and spot it was allowed.

On the whole, however, it was a satisfying exhibition. Production to enhance the band's offering was at a minimum, but Basie kept things together with a modest, personable bit of emseeing. He and his boys can do better, however. Mebbe it was the heat.—BENNY.

Monday 14 August 1944
Count Basie and his Orchestra close at the Orpheum Theatre in Los Angeles, California.

Wednesday 16 August 1944
Count Basie and his Orchestra open a one-week engagement at the Golden Gate Theatre in San Francisco, California.

Tuesday 22 August 1944
Count Basie and his Orchestra close at the Golden Gate Theatre in San Francisco, California.

Thursday 24 August 1944
Count Basie and his Orchestra open a one-week engagement at the Orpheum Theatre in Oakland, California.

Wednesday 30 August 1944
Count Basie and his Orchestra close at the Orpheum Theatre in Oakland, California.

Sunday 3 September 1944
Count Basie and his Orchestra open a two-night engagement at Sweet's Ballroom in Oakland, California.

Monday 4 September 1944
Count Basie and his Orchestra close at Sweet's Ballroom in Oakland, California.

Thursday 7 September 1944
Count Basie and his Orchestra open a six-week engagement at the new Plantation Club in Los Angeles. Celebrities attending the opening include Gloria De Haven, David Rose, Tommy Dorsey and Buddy Rich. Buddy sits in with the band and has a ball.

Above: Basie enjoying himself at the Plantation Club opening. Second left in the back row is actor Rex Ingram, next to him, with back turned, is Buddy Tate. Drummer Buddy Rich can be seen behind Basie.

Monday 11 September 1944
Count Basie and his Orchestra broadcast on the AFRS Jubilee Show at NBC Studio D in Los Angeles. The show was probably recorded a few days earlier.
HARRY EDISON, AL KILLIAN, ED LEWIS (trumpets), DICKY WELLS, ROBERT SCOTT, ELI ROBINSON, LOUIS TAYLOR (trombones), EARLE WARREN, JIMMY POWELL (alto sax), BUDDY TATE, LESTER YOUNG (tenor sax), RUDY RUTHERFORD (baritone sax), COUNT BASIE (piano), FREDDIE GREEN (guitar), RODNEY RICHARDSON (bass), JO JONES (drums), JIMMY RUSHING, THELMA CARPENTER (vocals)
One O'Clock Jump (theme) / *Avenue C* / *More Than You Know* (vTC) / *Basie Boogie* / *Harvard Blues* (vJR) / *I'll Be Seeing You* (vEW) / *Jumpin' At The Woodside* / *One O'Clock Jump* (theme)

Monday 18 September 1944
Count Basie and his Orchestra broadcast on the AFRS Jubilee Show featuring the King Sisters at NBC Studio D in Los Angeles. Illinois Jacquet (tenor sax) guests with the band on *My, What A Fry!* The show was probably recorded a few days earlier.
One O'Clock Jump (theme) / *Let's Jump* / *Gee Baby, Ain't I Good To You?* (vJR) / *Snoqualmie Jo-Jo* (KS) / *Do Nothin' Till You Hear From Me* (vTC) / *My, What A Fry!* / *One O'Clock Jump* (theme)

Wednesday 20 September 1944
An FBI agent visits the Plantation Club and serves a summons on Lester Young and Jo Jones, requiring them to report before the draft board in the morning. Basie brings in Lucky Thompson on tenor sax and drummer Jesse Price agrees to fill in until Shadow Wilson can join. Buddy Rich, of the Tommy Dorsey band, sits in until Price arrives.

Two Basie Sidemen Drafted by Army
Los Angeles—Lester Young and Jo Jones, who were drafted recently, are now stationed at Fort MacArthur, Calif., where they are undergoing their basic training. Jesse Price has replaced Jones at the drums, with Jimmy Keith, formerly with Harlan Leonard, taking over Young's tenor chair.

Draft Grabs Pair From Basie Band
Los Angeles—Count Basie lost heavily via the selective service route as Jo Jones, drums, and Lester Young, tenor, reported for duty to the armed forces. Milt Ebbins, Basie's manager, was hopeful that boys might yet draw 4-F ratings. He said both had entered pleas for further examination of certain physical symptoms which they believed had led to exemptions in other cases.
Jesse Price took over the rhythm spot following short period during which Buddy Rich sat in to ease the band over a tough spot. No permanent replacement for Young was set at this writing. Dave Matthews was among the local saxmen who went in for a night or so to help out.

Monday 25 September 1944
Count Basie and his Orchestra broadcast on the AFRS Jubilee Show at NBC Studio D in Los Angeles. Artie Shaw and Buddy Rich guest with the band.
HARRY EDISON, AL KILLIAN, ED LEWIS, JOE NEWMAN (trumpets), DICKY WELLS, TED DONNELLY, ELI ROBINSON, LOUIS TAYLOR (trombones), ARTIE SHAW (clarinet), EARLE WARREN, JIMMY POWELL (alto sax), BUDDY TATE, LUCKY THOMPSON (tenor sax), RUDY RUTHERFORD (baritone sax), COUNT BASIE (piano), FREDDIE GREEN (guitar), RODNEY RICHARDSON (bass), BUDDY RICH (drums), JIMMY RUSHING, THELMA CARPENTER (vocals)
One O'Clock Jump (theme) / *Rhythm Man* / *I'm Gonna Sit Right Down And Write Myself A Letter* (vJR) / *Oh! Lady Be Good* / *Blues Jam* (Artie Shaw and rhythm section only) / *Embraceable You* (vTC) / *Kansas City Stride* / *One O'Clock Jump* (theme)

Saturday 30 September 1944
Count Basie records an AFRS 'Command Performance' transcription with an all-star group at NBC Studio D in Los Angeles.
ZIGGY ELMAN (trumpet), TOMMY DORSEY (trombone), ARTIE SHAW (clarinet), ILLINOIS JACQUET (tenor sax), LIONEL HAMPTON (vibes), COUNT BASIE (piano), LES PAUL (guitar), ED McKINNEY (bass), BUDDY RICH (drums), JACK BENNY, DEANNA DURBIN (mc's)
Honeysuckle Rose

Monday 2 October 1944
Count Basie and his Orchestra broadcast from the Plantation Club in Los Angeles.
HARRY EDISON, EMMETT BERRY, ED LEWIS, SNOOKY YOUNG (trumpets), DICKY WELLS, TED DONNELLY, ELI ROBINSON, J. J. JOHNSON (trombones), PRESTON LOVE, GEORGE DORSEY (alto sax), BUDDY TATE, ILLINOIS JACQUET (tenor sax), RUDY RUTHERFORD (baritone sax), COUNT BASIE (piano), FREDDIE GREEN (guitar), RODNEY RICHARDSON (bass), SHADOW WILSON, BUDDY RICH (drums), JIMMY RUSHING, THELMA CARPENTER (vocals)
Dinah (dBR) / *Basie Boogie* / *Baby Won't You Please Come Home* (vJR) / *Rhythm Man* / *One O'Clock Jump* (theme) / *Kansas City Stride* (sign-off)

Wednesday 4 October 1944
Count Basie and his Orchestra close at the new Plantation Club in Los Angeles.

Friday 13 October 1944
Count Basie and his Orchestra open a one-week engagement at the Paradise Theatre in Detroit.

Thursday 19 October 1944
Count Basie and his Orchestra close at the Paradise Theatre in Detroit.

Friday 20 October 1944
Count Basie and his Orchestra open a four-day engagement at the Palace Theatre in Akron, Ohio.

Monday 23 October 1944
Count Basie and his Orchestra close at the Palace Theatre in Akron, Ohio.

Tuesday 24 October 1944
Count Basie and his Orchestra play a one-nighter at the Public Auditorium in Cleveland, Ohio.

Wednesday 25 October 1944
Count Basie and his Orchestra play a one-nighter at the Chestnut Street Hall in Harrisburg, Pennsylvania.

Friday 27 October 1944
Count Basie and his Orchestra open a one-week engagement at the Apollo Theatre in New York City.

Monday 30 October 1944
Count Basie and his Orchestra broadcast on NBC's 'For The Record' from NBC Studio 8-H in New York City.
My, What A Fry! / *Harvard Blues* (vJR) / *One O'Clock Jump* (theme)

Thursday 2 November 1944
Count Basie and his Orchestra close at the Apollo Theatre in New York City.
Leonard Feather reviews the show for *Metronome*:

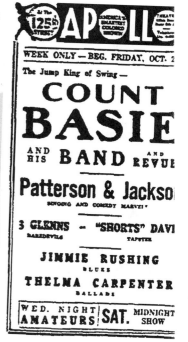

COUNT BASIE Tate Is Great
Apollo, New York.
There was a lot of talk before Basie hit the Apollo to the general effect that the Count's band wouldn't be its old self now that Lester Young and Jo Jones were no longer around. Well, much as one regrets the departure of these two key men to the Army, it didn't seem to me that Basie failed in any way to make his show as exciting musically as ever.

As a matter of fact, the outstanding item in the show, *Royal Garden Blues*, was as thrilling as anything I've heard this band do in years. It featured a Dixieland ensemble first—Harry Edison, Dickie Wells, Buddy Tate and Rudy Rutherford playing semi-jam stuff in front of the rest of the band—and it wound up with a long solo by Rutherford on clarinet, with a fine build-up from the other horns. Rudy has developed into a superlative artist and this was the best thing he's done yet.

In this number and in all the other instrumentals on the show, Buddy Tate's tenor was an impressive feature. With all the tenor solo work exclusively on his shoulders, Buddy handled the job perfectly, providing a welcome reminder that he's among the all-time greats on his instrument.

Jesse Price's drumming seemed solid and effective. Basie's piano tinkled through the humorous, swinging *Basie Boogie*; the whole band swung gently but firmly on *It's Sand, Man*; and Jimmy Rushing and Thelma Carpenter turned in their customary reliable performances.

Basie is proving what Ellington proved; a couple of personnel changes can't stop a great band from staying great.—FEATHER.

Friday 3 November 1944
Count Basie and his Orchestra open a one-week engagement at the Royal Theatre in Baltimore.

Thursday 9 November 1944
Count Basie and his Orchestra close at the Royal Theatre in Baltimore.

Friday 10 November 1944
Count Basie and his Orchestra open a one-week engagement at the Howard Theatre in Washington, D.C.

Thursday 16 November 1944
Count Basie and his Orchestra close at the Howard Theatre in Washington, D.C.

Friday 17 November 1944
Count Basie and his Orchestra open a one-week engagement at the Earle Theatre in Philadelphia.

Thursday 23 November 1944
Count Basie and his Orchestra close at the Earle Theatre in Philadelphia.

Thursday 24 November 1944
Count Basie and his Orchestra begin a two-week vacation, their first in almost two years. When the band reconvenes, Lucky Thompson replaces Illinois Jacquet and Shadow Wilson comes in on drums.

Friday 1 December 1944
Count Basie and his Orchestra open a three-day engagement at the Temple Theatre in Rochester, New York.

Sunday 3 December 1944
Count Basie and his Orchestra close at the Temple Theatre in Rochester, New York.

Monday 4 December 1944
Count Basie and his Orchestra open a three-day engagement at the Stanley Theatre in Utica, New York.

Wednesday 6 December 1944
Count Basie and his Orchestra record for Columbia in New York City.
HARRY EDISON, AL KILLIAN, JOE NEWMAN, AL STEARNS (trumpets), DICKY WELLS, TED DONNELLY, ELI ROBINSON, LOUIS TAYLOR (trombones), EARLE WARREN, JIMMY POWELL (alto sax), BUDDY TATE, LUCKY THOMPSON (tenor sax), RUDY RUTHERFORD (baritone sax), COUNT BASIE (piano), FREDDIE GREEN (guitar), RODNEY RICHARDSON (bass), SHADOW WILSON (drums), JIMMY RUSHING, THELMA CARPENTER (vocals)
Taps Miller / Jimmy's Blues (vJR, 2 takes) / *I Didn't Know About You* (vTC) / *Red Bank Boogie* (2 takes)

Count Basie and his Orchestra close at the Stanley Theatre in Utica, New York.

Thursday 7 December 1944
Count Basie and his Orchestra open a one-week engagement at the RKO Theatre in Boston.

Wednesday 13 December 1944
Count Basie and his Orchestra close at the RKO Theatre in Boston.

Friday 15 December 1944
Count Basie and his Orchestra open a week-end engagement at the State Theatre in Hartford, Connecticut.

Sunday 17 December 1944
Count Basie and his Orchestra close at the State Theatre in Hartford, Connecticut.

Monday 18 December 1944
Count Basie and his Orchestra open an eight-week engagement at the Blue Room of the Hotel Lincoln in New York City. The band broadcast nightly over the CBS and Mutual networks.

COUNT BASIE
(Reviewed at the Hotel Lincoln, New York)
    If the Hotel Lincoln ever finds its name immortalized in the annals of jazz, it will undoubtedly be because the spot once served as a NYC roosting place for Count Basie's band. Except for the Lincoln, local hot fans would only be able to hear Basie on his far-too-rare one-nighters and theatre visits here.
    There've been a couple of important changes in the band since last reviewed in these pages: tenor-man "Lucky" Thompson is in for Lester Young and Shadow Wilson vice Jo Jones. Though neither of the new men has the talent of his predecessor, it's pleasant to be able to say that the substitutions don't rob the ork of its greatness.
    "Lucky" blows a wild horn—a little too wild and undisciplined for my taste—but he's colorful and exciting and should develop to a point where ideas and tone won't be sacrificed to sheer fire and guts. Same is true of Wilson, who beats a helluva drum but lacks the wonderful taste and physical coordination that make Jo Jones one of the all-time great drummers and made the Basie rhythm section the jumpingest ever.
    As always, the most exciting aspect of the band is its hypnotic development of a simple riff to a smashing climax. It's basically a simple formula but no other band has ever been able to duplicate the insistent drive to a repeated crescendo which is the Basie trademark.
    Thelma Carpenter, one of this reviewer's favorites from a long way back gets prettier and sings better all the time.

Friday 22 December 1944
Count Basie appears on CBS's 'Music Till Midnight' radio show starring Mildred Bailey. Basie plays one number with the Paul Baron Orchestra.
I Got Rhythm

Saturday 23 December 1944
Count Basie and his Orchestra broadcast over CBS from the Blue Room of the Hotel Lincoln in New York City.
One O'Clock Jump (theme) / *It's Sand, Man / Blue Room Jump / Kansas City Stride / One O'Clock Jump* (theme)

Wednesday 27 December 1944
Count Basie and his Orchestra broadcast over WOR-Mutual from the Blue Room of the Hotel Lincoln in New York City.
Red Bank Boogie / I'm Making Believe / Taps Miller / Jumpin' At The Woodside

Sunday 31 December 1944
Count Basie and his Orchestra broadcast on the AFRS 'Coastguard' radio programme in New York City.
I'm Confessin' (vJR) / *Red Bank Boogie / Avenue C*

1945

Monday 1 January 1945
Count Basie and his Orchestra broadcast over WOR-Mutual from the Blue Room of the Hotel Lincoln in New York City.
Love Jumped Out / *After A While* (vEW) / *One O'Clock Jump* (theme)

Basie Angling For Fem Chirp

New York—Count Basie is reported dickering with Ella Fitzgerald to take over the vocal spot which will be left vacant when Thelma Carpenter leaves the band to single at the Ruban Bleu here. Ella's price was an obstacle at presstime and Helen Humes, who sang with the Count more than two years ago, was rumored set to rejoin.

Currently at the Hotel Lincoln on an eight-week return booking, Basie is catching up on record-making at Columbia. Singer Jimmy Rushing is cutting a *Blues* album with a band-from-within-the-band and the full ork is expected to do several wax dates before leaving town. Underway is a plan to cut a *Count Basie Presents* album featuring Benny Goodman, Harry James, Gene Krupa and Frank Sinatra, each artist doing two sides with a small Basie band.

On this third stop at the Lincoln, Basie has the disadvantage of losing late air-time, due to owner Maria Kramer's decision to eliminate wires after 1.00 a.m. because she believes that radio audiences fall off at that hour. Basie leaves the Lincoln February 13 for theater dates, goes into the Roxy in April.

Thursday 11 January 1945
Count Basie and his Orchestra record for V-Disc in New York City.
HARRY EDISON, AL KILLIAN, JOE NEWMAN (trumpets), DICKY WELLS, TED DONNELLY, ELI ROBINSON, LOUIS TAYLOR (trombones), EARLE WARREN, JIMMY POWELL (alto sax), BUDDY TATE, LUCKY THOMPSON (tenor sax), RUDY RUTHERFORD (baritone sax), COUNT BASIE (piano), FREDDIE GREEN (guitar), RODNEY RICHARDSON (bass), JOE MARSHALL (drums), JIMMY RUSHING, THELMA CARPENTER (vocals)
Taps Miller / *Playhouse No2 Stomp* / *Just An Old Manuscript* / *On The Upbeat* / *Jimmy's Blues* (vJR) / *Take Me Back Baby* (vJR) / *All Of Me* / *Call Me Darling* (vTC)
After this recording session Thelma Carpenter leaves the band and is replaced by Maxine Johnson.

Basie Nixes Ella To Sign New Chirp

New York—Maxine Johnson is the new singer with Count Basie's band at the Hotel Lincoln, replacing Thelma Carpenter, now singing at the Ruban Bleu club here. A deal which would have had Ella Fitzgerald taking over vocals was nixed because the name chirp wanted a piece of the band.

Rumor says that both Lester Young and Jo Jones are coming out of the service but Basie manager Milt Ebbins says it's not true.

Thursday 25 January 1945
Count Basie and his Orchestra broadcast on the AFRS 'One Night Stand' programme from the Blue Room of the Hotel Lincoln in New York City.
One O'Clock Jump (theme) / *Red Bank Boogie* / *This Heart Of Mine* (vMJ) / *I'm Gonna See My Baby* (vJR) / *Paging Mr Green* / *Sleigh Ride In July* (vMJ)

Wednesday 31 January 1945
Count Basie and his Orchestra broadcast over CBS from the Blue Room of the Hotel Lincoln in New York City.
I Didn't Know About You (vMJ) / *One O'Clock Jump* (theme) / *I'm Fer It, Too* / *Taps Miller* / *Avenue C* / *One O'Clock Jump* (theme)

Thursday 1 February 1945
Count Basie and his Orchestra broadcast on WNEW's 'Second Annual Swing Session' from the Hotel Lincoln in New York City. The presenter is Martin Block.
Interview with Count Basie / *Honeysuckle Rose*

Friday 2 February 1945
Count Basie and his Orchestra broadcast on the AFRS 'One Night Stand' programme from the Blue Room of the Hotel Lincoln in New York City.
Swing Shift / *Solo Flight* / *Wish You Were Waiting For Me* (vMJ) / *Together* (vJR) / *Hey, Rube!*

Sunday 4 February 1945
Count Basie and his Orchestra broadcast on the NBC 'Fitch Bandwagon' programme from the Blue Room of the Hotel Lincoln in New York City.
One O'Clock Jump (theme) / *Aces And Faces* / *Don't Cry, Baby* (vJR) / *Just An Old Manuscript* / *One O'Clock Jump* (theme)

Monday 12 February 1945
Count Basie and his Orchestra are guests of honor at a jam session at the Lincoln Square Center in New York City.

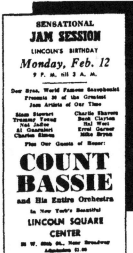

Tuesday 13 February 1945
Count Basie and his Orchestra close at the Hotel Lincoln in New York City.

Earlier in the day, the band record Lang-Worth transcriptions at Columbia's Liederkranz Hall studios in New York City.
Sugar Hill Shuffle / *I Should Care* (vEW) / *Just An Old Manuscript* / *Wish You Were Waiting For Me* (vMJ) / *Harvard Blues* (vJR) / *Please Don't Say No* (vEW) / *I Didn't Know About You* (vMJ) / *I'm Fer It, Too*

Thursday 15 February 1945
Count Basie and his Orchestra open a one-week engagement at the Adams Theatre in Newark, New Jersey.

Saturday 17 February 1945
Count Basie is guest of honor at a jam session featuring Claude Hopkins and his Orchestra at the Lincoln Square Center in New York City.

Wednesday 21 February 1945
Count Basie and his Orchestra close at the Adams Theatre in Newark, New Jersey.

Friday 23 February 1945
Count Basie and his Orchestra open a one-week engagement at the Stanley Theatre in Pittsburgh.

Saturday 24 February 1945
While at the Stanley Theatre in Pittsburgh Count Basie and his Orchestra travel to Dover USAAF Base to broadcast on a Coca-Cola 'Spotlight bands' show. Jimmy Rushing doesn't travel with the band and Basie himself does the vocal on *Harvard Blues*.
Avenue C / Wish You Were Waiting For Me (vMJ) / *Harvard Blues* (vCB) / *Evelina* (vEW)

Monday 26 February 1945
Count Basie and his Orchestra record for Columbia in New York City.
Avenue C (3 takes)
String section and LYNNE SHERMAN (vocal) added:
This Heart Of Mine (vLS) / *That Old Feeling* (vLS, 2 takes)
In the evening Count Basie and his Orchestra play a dance at the Renaissance Casino in New York City.

Thursday 1 March 1945
Count Basie and his Orchestra close at the Stanley Theatre in Pittsburgh.

Down Beat reviews Basie's latest Columbia release:

COUNT BASIE
Red Bank Boogie
I Didn't Know About You
Columbia 36766

The first side, written by Buck Clayton and the Count, amounts to nothing more than another concerto for Basie's light boogie work. The Count sounds just a bit apathetic, and so consequently does his band. Still, it's better stuff than most white bands could furnish. The Basie trumpets and saxes alternate on the Ellington opus, with Thelma Carpenter's vocal sandwiched in the middle none too smoothly. There's much better Kansas City jazz than this, somewhere in the Basie library!

Friday 2 March 1945
Count Basie and his Orchestra open a one-week engagement at the Downtown Theatre in Detroit.

Thursday 8 March 1945
Count Basie and his Orchestra close at the Downtown Theatre in Detroit.

Friday 9 March 1945
Count Basie and his Orchestra open a one-week engagement at the National Theatre in Louisville, Kentucky.

Thursday 15 March 1945
Count Basie and his Orchestra close at the National Theatre in Louisville, Kentucky.

Friday 16 March 1945
Count Basie and his Orchestra open a one-week engagement at the Riverside Theatre in Milwaukee.

Thursday 22 March 1945
Count Basie and his Orchestra close at the Riverside Theatre in Milwaukee.

Friday 23 March 1945
Count Basie and his Orchestra open a one-week engagement at the Regal Theatre in Chicago. Also on the bill are Patterson & Jackson and Pops 'n' Louie. Barry Ulanov reviews the show for *Metronome*:

COUNT BASIE
Maxine's Vaccine
Regal, Chicago

Basie's band has always rocked; it did in this largest of the country's colored theatres. It's always offered fine jazz solos; Lucky Thompson, Buddy Tate, Rudy Rutherford, Harry Edison, Dickie Wells and the Count presented same here. It has not, however, often complemented the delicate piano style, the soft muted brass work also associated with Basie, with singing in the same lovely frame. At this show, a vaccination of that kind of warbling was imposed on the good right arm of the Basie band; I certainly hope it takes.

Maxine Johnson is her name. Tall, attractive, beautifully dressed and with a soft, self-possessed stage presence, this New York night club singer slid throatily through the cadences of *I'm Beginning to See the Light* and *He's Home for a Little While*. She doesn't sing with much heart; but her tones are full, her pitch even, her phrasing intelligent; she delivers a song in a manner that fits exceedingly well with subdued Basie. Properly exploited, this girl will mean a lot to the Count, on records, on stages, in hotel rooms. And she'll make it necessary for Red Bank's most distinguished citizen to play even more in a low down, slow-down groove. Good deal!

Thursday 29 March 1945
Count Basie and his Orchestra close at the Regal Theatre in Chicago.

Sunday 8 April 1945
Count Basie and his Orchestra play a dance at the Savoy Ballroom in Chicago.

Thursday 12 April 1945
Count Basie and his Orchestra open a one-week engagement at the Miller Theatre in Wichita, Kansas.

Wednesday 18 April 1945
Count Basie and his Orchestra close at the Miller Theatre in Wichita, Kansas.

Thursday 19 April 1945
Count Basie and his Orchestra open a two-night engagement at the Coliseum Theatre in Tulsa, Oklahoma.

Friday 20 April 1945
Count Basie and his Orchestra close at the Coliseum Theatre in Tulsa, Oklahoma.

Saturday 21 April 1945
Count Basie and his Orchestra open a two-night engagement at the Auditorium in Kansas City, Missouri.

Sunday 22 April 1945
Count Basie and his Orchestra close at the Auditorium in Kansas City, Missouri.

Monday 23 April 1945
Count Basie and his Orchestra open a one-week engagement at the Kiel Auditorium Opera House in St. Louis, Missouri.

Saturday 28 April 1945
Count Basie and his Orchestra close at the Kiel Auditorium Opera House in St. Louis, Missouri.

Tuesday 1 May 1945
Down Beat reviews Basie's latest Columbia release:

COUNT BASIE
This Heart Of Mine
That Old Feeling
Columbia 36795

So the label reads. Strings were imported to back Lynne Sherman's vocals. Basie could have lost both and turned out some good wax. Instead, with the exception of a clean, biting brass section which is definitely Basie, they sound like stuff a mess of other average bands would record.

Wednesday 2 May 1945
Count Basie and his Orchestra open a four-week engagement at the Roxy Theatre in New York City. The movie presentation is 'Diamond Horseshoe' starring Betty Grable and Dick Haymes.

Monday 14 May 1945
Count Basie and his Orchestra record for V-Disc at NBC Studios 8-H in New York City.
HARRY EDISON, AL KILLIAN, KARL GEORGE, ED LEWIS, BUCK CLAYTON (trumpets), DICKY WELLS, TED DONNELLY, ELI ROBINSON, J. J. JOHNSON (trombones), EARLE WARREN, JIMMY POWELL (alto sax), BUDDY TATE, LUCKY THOMPSON (tenor sax), RUDY RUTHERFORD (baritone sax), COUNT BASIE (piano), FREDDIE GREEN (guitar), RODNEY RICHARDSON (bass), SHADOW WILSON (drums), JIMMY RUSHING, TAPS MILLER (vocals)
High Tide (vTM) / *Sent For You Yesterday* (vJR) / *Jimmy's Boogie Woogie* (vJR) / *Tippin' On The Q.T.* / *San José* / *B-flat Blues* / *Sweet Lorraine* (vEW)

Saturday 26 May 1945
Alto saxist Preston Love begins to sit in with the band as replacement for Earl Warren who has given notice.

Sunday 27 May 1945
Count Basie and his Orchestra play a concert at the Pauline Edwards Theatre at City College, New York City. Also featured are Jimmy Savo and Teddy Wilson.

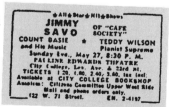

Tuesday 29 May 1945
Count Basie and his Orchestra are held over for another week at the Roxy Theatre in New York City.

Tuesday 5 June 1945

Count Basie and his Orchestra close at the Roxy Theatre in New York City. On the last night at the Roxy, Basie and the band get special permission to appear at the WNEW 'Tribute to Glenn Miller' concert at the nearby Paramount Theatre with Cab Calloway and Pearl Bailey.

One O'Clock Jump (theme) / *B-Flat Blues* / *I'm Gonna See My Baby* (vMJ) / *Duration Blues* (vPB) / *Red Bank Boogie* / Lead-altoist Earl Warren leaves to form his own band. Jimmy Powell also leaves and is replaced by George Dorsey.

Broadway Chatters

Count Basie, the "Jump King of Swing", departed the Roxy Theatre on Tuesday, June 5, after having rolled up the highest gross in the theater's history during a record-breaking five week run at the Roxy was but a few thousand admissions short of reaching $5000,000, and only inclement weather during the last weekend of his stand stopped him from hitting the half million dollar mark.

Wednesday 6 June 1945

Count Basie and his Orchestra play a one-nighter in Johnstown, Pennsylvania.

Friday 8 June 1945

Count Basie and his Orchestra open a one-week engagement at the Howard Theatre in Washington, D.C.

Thursday 14 June 1945

Count Basie and his Orchestra close at the Howard Theatre in Washington, D.C.

Friday 22 June 1945

Count Basie and his Orchestra play a dance at the Golden Gate Ballroom in New York City.

Count Basie and his Orchestra then set out on a series of one-nighters across the States to California. While in Milwaukee Basie discovers Ann Moore singing in a club and asks her to join the band.

Monday 2 July 1945

Count Basie and his Orchestra broadcast on the AFRS Jubilee Show with Lena Horne and Timmie Rogers at Starlight Grove in Los Angeles.

One O'Clock Jump (theme) / *B-Flat Blues* / *Sent For You Yesterday* (vJR) / *Honeysuckle Rose* (vLH) / *Red Bank Boogie* / *Daddy-O* (vTR) / *Jumpin' At The Woodside* / *One O'Clock Jump* (theme)

COUNT BASIE AND HIS ORCHESTRA

JAMES RUSHING
VOCALIST

DANCE !!

Golden Gate Ballroom
142nd St. & Lenox Ave.

FRIDAY
JUNE 22

Adm. $1.35 Tax Incl.
Boxes $3.50. Tables $2.00.

For Reservation:
Woodside Hotel; Lud's Barber
Shop; 166 W. 116th St.

Tuesday 3 July 1945

Count Basie and his Orchestra open a four-week engagement at the Casa Mañana in Los Angeles.

LA Nitery Drops Color Line Ban

Los Angeles—Since the resumption of a Negro band policy at the Casa Manana, owners have gradually dropped discriminatory bars as far as patronage is concerned.

Attendance was more than half colored during Count Basie's recent engagement at the dance spot. Mixed dancing is permitted though there have been few cases noted, probably this is the first time that a major nitery here has operated regularly on a non-discriminatory policy.

Monday 9 July 1945

Count Basie and his Orchestra broadcast on the AFRS Jubilee Show with The King Sisters in Los Angeles.

One O'Clock Jump (theme) / *Basie Boogie* / *What Can I Say, Dear?* (vAM) / *Gotta Be This Or That* / *Andy's Blues*

Monday 15 July 1945

Count Basie and members of his Orchestra broadcast on the Lamplighter Show from the Streets Of Paris Club in Hollywood.

HARRY EDISON, SNOOKY YOUNG (trumpets), DICKY WELLS, TED DONNELLY (trombones), LUCKY THOMPSON (tenor sax), RUDY RUTHERFORD (baritone sax), COUNT BASIE (piano), FREDDIE GREEN (guitar), RODNEY RICHARDSON (bass), SHADOW WILSON (drums), JIMMY RUSHING (vocals)

Royal Garden Blues / *Body And Soul* / *Evenin'* (vJR) / *I Got Rhythm*

Coast Jazz Attracts Musicians

Los Angeles—The jazz sessions put on for the Coast Guard by Ted Yerxa, Daily News columnist and Charlie Emge, *Down Beat* coast editor, at the Streets of Paris nitery on Hollywood blvd. have attracted several name musicians and plenty of local comment. Sessions are aired each Sunday afternoon. Sitting in or digging the music at one recent session were (left to right): Zutty Singleton, Larry Goldner, owner of the club, Frankie Carlson, Matty Matlock, Ted Yerxa and Mrs. Yerxa, Harry Fields, Coast Guard musician, Count Basie and Art Tatum.

Monday 16 July 1945

Count Basie and his Orchestra broadcast on the AFRS Jubilee Show with Martha Lewis in Los Angeles.

One O'Clock Jump (theme) / *Avenue C* / *I Never Knew* (vJR) / *Hey, Rube!* / *I Should Care* (vML) / *My, What A Fry!*

Monday 23 July 1945

Count Basie and his Orchestra broadcast on the AFRS Jubilee Show with June Richmond and the Delta Rhythm Boys in Los Angeles.

One O'Clock Jump (theme) / *Queer Street* / *Are You Living, Old Man?* (vJuneR) / *Old Man River* (vJuneR) / *I'm Beginning To See The Light* (vDRB) / *Hey, John!* (vDRB) / *High Tide*

Monday 30 July 1945

Count Basie and his Orchestra close at the Casa Mañana in Culver City.

Karl George (trumpet), Buddy Tate (tenor sax), J. J. Johnson (trombone), Harry Edison (trumpet) and Jimmy Rushing (vocal) from the Basie band appear at a Philharmonic Jazz Concert featuring the King Cole Trio at the Philharmonic Auditorium in Los Angeles. Also appearing are Barney Kessel (guitar), Charlie Mingus (bass), Georgie Auld (tenor sax) and Buddy Rich (drums).

Count Basie, currently in California, will lose trumpeter Karl George when he comes East. George has given notice and plans to continue working on the Coast. Basie, who just finished at Casa Mañana, has a new girl vocalist, Cora Ann Moore from Milwaukee.

Thursday 2 August 1945

Members of the Count Basie Orchestra record as the Karl George Octet for Melodisc in Los Angeles.

Karl George (trumpet), J. J. Johnson (trombone), Rudy Rutherford (clarinet), Buddy Tate (tenor sax), Bill Doggett (piano), Freddie Green (guitar), John Simmons (bass), Shadow Wilson (drums)

Grand Slam / *Baby It's Up To You* / *Peek-A-Boo* / *How Am I To Know*

Tuesday 7 August 1945

Count Basie and his Orchestra open a one-week engagement at the Orpheum Theatre in Los Angeles.

Wednesday 8 August 1945

Count Basie and his Orchestra record the AFRS Christmas Jubilee Show in Los Angeles. Bing Crosby, Lena Horne and the Delta Rhythm Boys also guest on the show which is compered by Ernie 'Bubbles' Whitman.

Harry Edison, Karl George, Ed Lewis, Snooky Young (trumpets), Dicky Wells, Ted Donnelly, Eli Robinson, J. J. Johnson (trombones), George Dorsey, Preston Love (alto sax), Buddy Tate, Lucky Thompson (tenor sax), Rudy Rutherford (baritone sax), Count Basie (piano), Freddie Green (guitar), Rodney Richardson (bass), Shadow Wilson (drums), Delta Rhythm Boys, Lena Horne, Bing Crosby (vocals)

Jingle Bells (vDRB) / *One O'Clock Jump* (theme) / *Jumpin' At Ten* / *Just A-Settin' And A-Rockin'* (vDRB with rhythm section) / *My Silent Love* (vLH) / *Christmas Jive Routine* (dialogue) / *Gotta Be This Or That* (vBC) / *Jumpin' At The Woodside* / *Silent Night* (vLH)

Monday 13 August 1945

Count Basie and his Orchestra close at the Orpheum Theatre in Los Angeles.

Wednesday 15 August 1945

Count Basie and his Orchestra open a one-week engagement at the Golden Gate Theatre in San Francisco.

Tuesday 21 August 1945

Count Basie and his Orchestra close at the Golden Gate Theatre in San Francisco.

Tuesday 28 August 1945

Count Basie and his Orchestra open a one-week engagement at the T & D Theatre in Oakland.

Saturday 1 September 1945

Down Beat reviews Basie's latest Columbia release:

COUNT BASIE
Taps Miller
Jimmy's Blues
Columbia 36831

Taps is an excellent side, finding the band close to their wonderful kick of five years or so ago. It exhibits plenty of power, with as much of it felt as actually heard. Band is sparked throughout both sides with some wonderful drumming by ShadowWilson, though the rhythm lacks otherwise, the outstanding tone and beat of the old Jones-Page-Green section. There are good tenor, trumpet, trombone solos besides a few bars that the Count takes over for himself. Trumpet, which sounds a good deal like Harry Edison, is outstanding. The guy really blows! *Blues* is all Jimmy Rushing's, well taken care of in his particular Kaycee shout style. Lyrics are typical Negro blues, lowdown and wonderful. It isn't subtle at all, but then Rushing never has been, and his type of blues singing certainly is not. There's fine trombone backing the first part of the vocal. Band comes on nicely.

Monday 3 September 1945

Count Basie and his Orchestra close at the T & D Theatre in Oakland.

Flash! *Trumpeter Joe Newman is rejoining Count Basie. Lucky Thompson, tenor, and Shadow Wilson, drummer, have left the Basie band, and the Count is seeking a new drummer…*

Thursday 6 September 1945

Count Basie and his Orchestra open a four-week engagement at the Club Plantation in Los Angeles.

Monday 10 September 1945

Count Basie and his Orchestra broadcast on the AFRS Jubilee Show in Los Angeles.

One O'Clock Jump (theme) / *Rambo* / *Mean To Me* (vAM) / *Boogie Woogie* (vJR) / *Andy's Blues*

Monday 17 September 1945

Count Basie and his Orchestra broadcast on the AFRS Jubilee Show in Los Angeles.

One O'Clock Jump (theme) / *I've Found A New Baby* / *Blue Skies* (vJR) / *Jivin' Joe Jackson* (vAM) / *Taps Miller* / *One O'Clock Jump* (theme)

Monday 24 September 1945
Count Basie and his Orchestra broadcast on the AFRS Jubilee Show with the Delta Rhythm Boys in Los Angeles. The show was probably recorded a few days earlier.
One O'Clock Jump (theme) / *Rhythm Man* / *Gotta Be This Or That* (vDRB) / *Jazz Me Blues* / *Please Don't Talk About Me When I'm Gone* (vJR) / *It's Sand, Man!*

Monday 1 October 1945
Count Basie and his Orchestra broadcast on the AFRS Jubilee Show with Lena Horne in Los Angeles. The show was probably recorded a few days earlier.
One O'Clock Jump (theme) / *San Jose* / *One For My Baby* (vLH) / *Good For Nothin' Joe* (vLH) / *Tush*

Down Beat reviews Basie's latest Columbia release:

> ### COUNT BASIE
> ### *Feather Merchant*
> ### *Ain't It the Truth*
> #### Columbia 36845
>
> The band has hit a fine stride of late and these sides carry right along. Instrumentalists, sections and rhythm are all great. *Merchant* has lots of the Count's piano, with choruses by trumpet (Harry Edison?) and trombone (Dickie Wells?). There's the typical Basie riff pattern, the usual strong, full-toned rhythm. Great is the way the brass comes in behind the piano, very lightly, almost undistinguishable, to accent the beat. *Truth*, which could make a good jump ballad, again spots trumpet, trombone and piano, with plenty of section patterns. Brass outshines saxes for precision and blend.

Tuesday 2 October 1945
Count Basie and his Orchestra close at the Club Plantation in Los Angeles.

Tuesday 9 October 1945
Count Basie and his Orchestra record for Columbia in Los Angeles.
HARRY EDISON, EMMETT BERRY, ED LEWIS, SNOOKY YOUNG (trumpets), DICKY WELLS, TED DONNELLY, ELI ROBINSON, J. J. JOHNSON (trombones), GEORGE DORSEY, PRESTON LOVE (alto sax), BUDDY TATE, ILLINOIS JACQUET (tenor sax), RUDY RUTHERFORD (baritone sax), COUNT BASIE (piano), FREDDIE GREEN (guitar), RODNEY RICHARDSON (bass), SHADOW WILSON (drums), JIMMY RUSHING, ANN MOORE (vocals)
Blue Skies (vJR) / *Jivin' Joe Jackson* (vAM) / *High Tide* (3 takes) / *Queer Street* (3 takes)

When the band leaves California after a few one-nighters, George Dorsey stays behind. Snooky Young joins the Lionel Hampton band and Joe Newman returns. Dicky Wells is having stomach problems and George Matthews takes his place. The band take the train to Omaha where altoist Jimmy Powell rejoins.

Friday 19 October 1945
Count Basie and his Orchestra open a one-week engagement at the Orpheum Theatre in Omaha, Nebraska.

Thursday 25 October 1945
Count Basie and his Orchestra close at the Orpheum Theatre in Omaha, Nebraska.

Friday 26 October 1945
Count Basie and his Orchestra open a one-week engagement at the Orpheum Theatre in Minneapolis.

Thursday 1 November 1945
Count Basie and his Orchestra close at the Orpheum Theatre in Minneapolis.

Friday 2 November 1945
Count Basie and his Orchestra play a one-nighter at the Arkota Ballroom in Sioux Falls, South Dakota.

Saturday 3 November 1945
Count Basie and his Orchestra play a one-nighter at the Skylon Ballroom in Sioux City, Iowa.

Sunday 4 November 1945
Count Basie and his Orchestra play a one-nighter at the Tromar Ballroom in Des Moines, Iowa.

Monday 5 November 1945
Count Basie and his Orchestra play a one-nighter at the Municipal Auditorium in Kansas City.

Tuesday 6 November 1945
Count Basie and his Orchestra play a one-nighter at the Kiel Auditorium in St. Louis.

Wednesday 7 November 1945
Count Basie and his Orchestra play a one-nighter at the Tomlinson Hall in Indianapolis.

Thursday 8 November 1945
Count Basie and his Orchestra open a one-week engagement at the Colonial Theatre in Dayton, Ohio.

Wednesday 14 November 1945
Count Basie and his Orchestra close at the Colonial Theatre in Dayton, Ohio.

Thursday 15 November 1945
Count Basie and his Orchestra play a one-nighter at the Trianon Ballroom in Toledo, Ohio.

Friday 16 November 1945
Count Basie and his Orchestra open a one-week engagement at the Paradise Theatre in Detroit.

Thursday 22 November 1945
Count Basie and his Orchestra close at the Paradise Theatre in Detroit.

Friday 23 November 1945
Count Basie and his Orchestra open a two-night engagement at Club Queensway in Toronto, Canada.

Saturday 24 November 1945
Count Basie and his Orchestra close at Club Queensway in Toronto, Canada.

Sunday 25 November 1945
Count Basie and his Orchestra play a one-nighter in Buffalo, New York.

Monday 26 November 1945
Count Basie and his Orchestra play a one-nighter in Kitchener, Ontario, Canada.

Friday 30 November 1945
Count Basie and his Orchestra open a one-week engagement at the Earle Theatre in Philadelphia.

Thursday 6 December 1945
Count Basie and his Orchestra close at the Earle Theatre in Philadelphia.

After the week in Philadelphia the band play a string of one-nighters into New England.

Friday 14 December 1945
Count Basie and his Orchestra open a one-week engagement at the State Theatre in Hartford, Connecticut.

Thursday 20 December 1945
Count Basie and his Orchestra close at the State Theatre in Hartford, Connecticut.

Friday 21 December 1945
Count Basie and his Orchestra open a week-end engagement at the RKO Boston Theatre in Boston.

Sunday 23 December 1945
Count Basie and his Orchestra close at the RKO Boston Theatre in Boston.

Paige Re-counts
Walter Page, Kansas City bassist who was with Count Basie during the band's first years of success, is rejoining the Count. Emerging from two years spent in his home town, Page worked recently with Hot Lips Page's current big band.

Others expected back in the Basie band are Jack Washington and Jo Jones, both returning to their old jobs after sojourns in the Army. Buck Clayton, also due out of the Army soon, informed METRONOME that he plans to form his own band.

While in New York, Basie signed up a new singer, Bob Bailey, discovered by John Hammond in an Alabama college, about whom Basie and managers are currently blowing their tops. He joins the band in February after its vacation.

Friday 28 December 1945
Count Basie and his Orchestra open a one-week engagement at the Apollo Theatre in New York City.

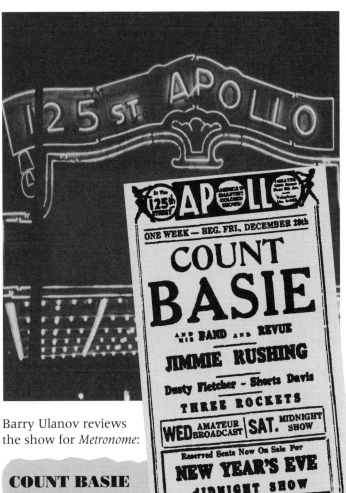

Barry Ulanov reviews the show for *Metronome*:

COUNT BASIE
The Case
For Base
Apollo, New York.

There was only one exciting new number in this show, *High Tide*, but throughout its sprawling length, the wonderful combination of rhythmic drive and good taste and languorous wit which motivates every Basie performance was in evidence. The band, as usual, boasted one good soloist after another: trumpeter Harry Edison, tenors Illinois Jacquet and Buddy Tate, clarinetist Rudy Rutherford, trombonist George Matthews. The rhythm section, sparked by Shadow Wilson's impeccable drumming, imbued everything with a beat that can only be described as uplifting (and I don't mean morally). New singer Ann Moore was impressive in her spot. Rushing was his usual ebullient self. And then there was *High Tide*.

Clarinet, trumpet and trombone start the *Tide* rolling. Follows the ensemble and the catchiest verbalized riff of the year: "I ain't mad at you, and you ain't mad at me, that's all." Back to band, to the opening trio and out. Great. Now if Basie will add *Queer Street* to his shows, I will be happy to catch all of them, all over.

Monday 31 December 1945
Count Basie and his Orchestra broadcast on AFRS 'Parade of the Bands' in New York City.
One O'Clock Jump

1946

Metronome reviews Count Basie's latest Columbia release:

Count Basie
Queer Street A–
Jivin' Joe Jackson B

A provocative introduction and good original scoring distinguish *Queer Street* which gathers added power from a trumpet solo by Harry Edison and Lucky Thompson's kinetic tenor. The band jumps impressively through Jimmy Mundy's instrumental, too. *Jackson* is all Ann Moore's, and the new Basie singer deserves the breathing space: she gets a fine beat, displays an uncommon feeling for jazz phrasing and that sensitively balanced vibrato which, in combination, add up to vocal distinction in this craft. If there were more to the novelty song than there is, this side would be a great one. (Columbia 36889)

Thursday 3 January 1946
Count Basie and his Orchestra close at the Apollo Theatre in New York City.

Wednesday 9 January 1946
Count Basie and his Orchestra record for Columbia in New York City.
HARRY EDISON, EMMETT BERRY, ED LEWIS, SNOOKY YOUNG (trumpets), GEORGE MATTHEWS, TED DONNELLY, ELI ROBINSON, J. J. JOHNSON (trombones), GEORGE DORSEY, PRESTON LOVE (alto sax), BUDDY TATE, ILLINOIS JACQUET (tenor sax), RUDY RUTHERFORD (baritone sax), COUNT BASIE (piano), FREDDIE GREEN (guitar), RODNEY RICHARDSON (bass), SHADOW WILSON (drums), JIMMY RUSHING (vocals)
Patience And Fortitude (vJR, 3 takes) / *The Mad Boogie* (4 takes)

Thursday 10 January 1946
Count Basie and his Orchestra open a one-week engagement at the Adams Theatre in Newark, New Jersey.

Wednesday 16 January 1946
Count Basie and his Orchestra close at the Adams Theatre in Newark, New Jersey.

Thursday 17 January 1946
Count Basie and his Orchestra open a one-week engagement at the Palace Theatre in Cleveland, Ohio.

Wednesday 23 January 1946
Count Basie and his Orchestra close at the Palace Theatre in Cleveland, Ohio.

Friday 25 January 1946
Count Basie and his Orchestra open a one-week engagement at the Royal Theatre in Baltimore. Drummer Jo Jones returns to the band after his discharge from the Army.

Thursday 31 January 1946
Count Basie and his Orchestra close at the Royal Theatre in Baltimore.

Wednesday 6 February 1946
Count Basie and his Orchestra record for Columbia at Liederkranz Hall in New York City.
HARRY EDISON, EMMETT BERRY, ED LEWIS, JOE NEWMAN (trumpets), GEORGE MATTHEWS, TED DONNELLY, ELI ROBINSON, J. J. JOHNSON (trombones), GEORGE DORSEY, PRESTON LOVE (alto sax), BUDDY TATE, ILLINOIS JACQUET (tenor sax), RUDY RUTHERFORD (baritone sax), COUNT BASIE (piano), FREDDIE GREEN (guitar), RODNEY RICHARDSON (bass), JO JONES (drums), JIMMY RUSHING (vocals)
Lazy Lady Blues (vJR, 3 takes) / *Rambo* (3 takes) / *Stay Cool* (3 takes) / *The King* (3 takes)

Count Basie is taking the first two weeks of February off, and begins a one-nighter tour of the Midwest in mid-February, followed by dates at the Regal Theatre in Chicago and the Paradise in Detroit. The Count is preparing for concerts in Boston, New York and Philadelphia, and a possible appearance at the Hollywood Bowl. He's readying a three-part jazz suite, tentatively titled *Royal Suite*, made up of boogie-woogie, blues and jump sections. George Matthews is temporarily replacing Dickie Wells on trombone, the latter on vacation. Jack Washington is returning to the band on baritone, Rudy Rutherford switching to 2nd alto replacing Jimmy Powell. Jo Jones is expected to return in mid-February, the time when vocalist Bob Bailey joins the band. Band may go into Hotel Lincoln or Cafe Zanzibar in the spring.

COUNT . . .
Count Basie, during a two-week vacation in New York, appeared on nine top commercial radio shows, which netted him more than $10,000; his hosts included Fred Allen, Jack Smith, Perry Como, Jo Stafford, and Kate Smith, the latter signing the Count for five guest shots during his Roxy run in May...

Monday 11 March 1946
Count Basie and his Orchestra open a one-week engagement at the Tune Town Ballroom in St. Louis, Missouri.

Saturday 16 March 1946
Count Basie and his Orchestra close at the Tune Town Ballroom in St. Louis, Missouri.

Jo Jones With Basie
Chicago—Jo Jones, just out of the army, set up his drums with Count Basie at the Tune Town ballroom earlier this month. Basie comes into the Regal theater here first of April.

Monday 18 March 1946
Count Basie and his Orchestra play a one-nighter at the Palace Gardens in St. Louis, Missouri.

Tuesday 19 March 1946
Count Basie and his Orchestra play a one-nighter at the Madison Square Rink in Louisville, Kentucky.

Wednesday 20 March 1946
Count Basie and his Orchestra play a one-nighter at the Ballroom in Lexington, Kentucky.

Friday 22 March 1946
Count Basie and his Orchestra play a one-nighter at the University of Indiana in Bloomington.

Saturday 23 March 1946
Count Basie and his Orchestra play a one-nighter at the Sunset Terrace in Indianapolis.

Sunday 24 March 1946
Count Basie and his Orchestra play a one-nighter at the Auditorium in Gary, Indiana.

Count Basie's Band To Receive $12,500 A Week At The Roxy

Count Basie, the "Jump King of Swing", will be paid the record high figure of $12,500 a week during his engagement at the Roxy Theater in April, it has been disclosed here.

The Count's deal with the Roxy marks an increase of $2,500 over the $10,000 a week price he was paid in his last booking at that deluxe Manhattan theater last May when he grossed a total of almost a half-million dollars in a record-breaking five-week stand.

Basie is set for three weeks at the Roxy, starting early in April, with the theater taking an option on his services for an additional two weeks. He played a four week run there in 1944 and five weeks last year.

Currently one of the hottest attractions at theater box offices throughout the country, the "Jump King" rose to new musical heights during 1945 as he rolled up some of the biggest grosses of all time.

Tuesday 26 March 1946
Count Basie and his Orchestra open a three-night engagement at the Palace Theatre in Youngstown, Ohio.

Thursday 28 March 1946
Count Basie and his Orchestra close at the Palace Theatre in Youngstown, Ohio.

Friday 29 March 1946
Count Basie and his Orchestra open a one-week engagement at the Paradise Theatre in Detroit.

Thursday 4 April 1946
Count Basie and his Orchestra close at the Paradise Theatre in Detroit.

Friday 5 April 1946
Count Basie and his Orchestra open a one-week engagement at the Regal Theatre in Chicago.

Thursday 11 April 1946
Count Basie and his Orchestra close at the Regal Theatre in Chicago.

Friday 12 April 1946
Count Basie and his Orchestra open a three-night engagement at the Palace Theatre in Canton, Ohio.

Sunday 14 April 1946
Count Basie and his Orchestra close at the Palace Theatre in Canton, Ohio.

Monday 15 April 1946
Count Basie and his Orchestra open a three-night engagement at the Palace Theatre in Columbus, Ohio.

Wednesday 17 April 1946
Count Basie and his Orchestra close at the Palace Theatre in Columbus, Ohio.

Thursday 18 April 1946
Count Basie and his Orchestra play a one-nighter in Pittsburgh, Pa.

Saturday 20 April 1946
Count Basie and his Orchestra play a one-nighter at the Armory in Orange, New Jersey.

Sunday 21 April 1946
Count Basie and his Orchestra play a one-nighter in Holyoke, Massachusetts.

Wednesday 24 April 1946
Count Basie and his Orchestra play a one-nighter in Portland, Maine.

Thursday 25 April 1946
Count Basie and his Orchestra play a one-nighter in Lowell, Massachusetts.

Friday 26 April 1946
Count Basie and his Orchestra play a one-nighter in Providence, Rhode Island.

Saturday 27 April 1946
Count Basie and his Orchestra play a one-nighter in Manchester, New Hampshire.

Monday 29 April 1946
Count Basie and his Orchestra play a one-nighter in Trenton, New Jersey.

Tuesday 30 April 1946
Count Basie and his Orchestra play a one-nighter in Mahoney City, Pennsylvania.

Friday 17 May 1946
Count Basie and his Orchestra open a one-week engagement at the Apollo Theatre in New York City.

Thursday 23 May 1946
Count Basie and his Orchestra close at the Apollo Theatre in New York City.

Friday 24 May 1946
Count Basie and his Orchestra open a three-week engagement at the Roxy Theatre in New York City. Also on the bill are The Peters Sisters and Gene Sheldon. The movie presentation is 'Do You Love Me' starring Maureen O'Hara, Dick Haymes, and Harry James.

The show is reviewed by *Metronome*:

COUNT BASIE
Balaban Kills Cats
Roxy, New York.

Basie's back, but the Roxy's got him. Once again the band that wrote such a brilliant page in the recent history of jazz finds itself hampered by the mammoth proportions of Broadway's big Balaban and Katz showhouse, weighted down by the usual, pompous production numbers and relegated to an almost supporting role during most of the show's running time.

Opening with two evergreens from the Basie book, *Every Tub* and *Out the Window*, the band had just about settled into its rightful groove when the bandstand was rolled back and there began the parade of typical showhouse talent, for which the Count's men had to supply dismal background accompaniment; only behind one chorus dance routine did the band give off any of the spark that music fans attach to the name of Basie, and that was a breakneck tempo version of *Rhythm Mad*.

The opening pair put the spotlight on Illinois Jacquet for his now-standard six or seven choruses of high register, frantic tenor, while Buddy Tate had to be content with a mere eight bars. Emmett Berry was down front for a brief solo on the opener, but the wonderful Harry Edison trumpet might just as well have stood in bed for all the opportunities it received. The rhythm section, now back at its pre-war position with Jo Jones and Walter Page returned, came in for a share of attention, Jo getting the spotlight for the inevitable long drum solo. After several pretty stupid production numbers, Jimmy Rushing was rushed on for a fast chorus of *Blue Skies*, and the Count closed the bake with a Hammond organ version of *Basie Boogie* and a community sing (yet!)

The Peters Sisters, comic Herb Shelton and Basie's fine young singer by the name of Bob Bailey rounded out the rest of this Roxy bill. The Peters gals are show stoppers in every sense of the word, Bailey the possessor of a robust, sure voice.

Blushing Cop Catches Basie Show—For Free

New York—The other day a blushing copper sat quietly through Count Basie's stage show at the Roxy. They had met that afternoon when the Count, chatting with his press agent, Jim McCarthy, on Broadway and 51st street, whipped a notebook from his pocket to make notations of several appointments. The ever-alert copper put the sleeve on the Count, declaring, "You bookies are getting nervier every day."

McCarthy intervened, explaining that Basie was merely making notes and not taking horse bets or numbers.

The officer threatened to run them both in. Then he looked through the notebook.

"O-o-ops," he said, "I'm sorry!"

He accepted two free tickets.

Wham!
Taps Miller
PRESENTS
EVERY MONDAY

GUEST NIGHT OF STARS

JUNE 17, 1946

COUNT BASIE

THE JUMP KING OF SWING

AT

845 **Club** 845

845 Prospect Ave.
Bronx, N.Y.

Monday 17 June 1946

Count Basie is a special guest star at Club 845 in the Bronx, New York City.

Wednesday 26 June 1946

Count Basie and his Orchestra close at the Roxy Theatre in New York City.

Monday 1 July 1946

Down Beat reviews Count Basie's latest Columbia release.

Count Basie
** *High Tide*
** *Lazy Lady Blues*

Tide opens with a muted trumpet-clary figure that gets over unfortunately because of over-miking of the clary. Last quarter goes from the famed Basie rhythm section into a solo bit for Rudy Rutherford's clary, ensemble, and out. *Blues* has a couple of choruses of trombone with some unusual ideas. The lyrics sung by Jimmy Rushing build up to the big climax when Rush sings "Too tired to lay her body down and die' and stops right after the infinitive. (*Columbia 36990*)

Wednesday 10 July 1946

Count Basie and his Orchestra play a one-nighter at the Paradise Theatre in Detroit.

Thursday 11 July 1946

Count Basie and his Orchestra play a one-nighter in Dayton, Ohio.

Friday 12 July 1946

Count Basie and his Orchestra open a one-week engagement at Castle Farm in Cincinnati, Ohio.

Thursday 18 July 1946

Count Basie and his Orchestra close at Castle Farm in Cincinnati, Ohio.

Friday 19 July 1946

Count Basie and his Orchestra play a one-nighter in Akron, Ohio.

Saturday 20 July 1946

Count Basie and his Orchestra play a one-nighter in Huntington, West Virginia.

Thursday 25 July 1946

Count Basie and his Orchestra open a three-week engagement at the Aquarium in New York City.

Below: Count Basie and his Orchestra on stage at the Aquarium Restaurant. Basie introduces special guest Hazel Scott.

Friday 26 July 1946

Count Basie and his Orchestra broadcast on AFRS 'One Night Stand' from the Aquarium in New York City.
HARRY EDISON, EMMETT BERRY, ED LEWIS, SNOOKY YOUNG, JOE NEWMAN (trumpets), GEORGE MATTHEWS, TED DONNELLY, ELI ROBINSON, J. J. JOHNSON (trombones), RUDY RUTHERFORD, PRESTON LOVE (alto sax), BUDDY TATE, ILLINOIS JACQUET (tenor sax), JACK WASHINGTON (baritone sax), COUNT BASIE (piano), FREDDIE GREEN (guitar), WALTER PAGE (bass), JO JONES (drums), BOB BAILEY, ANN MOORE, JIMMY RUSHING (vocals)
One O'Clock Jump (theme) / *Jazz Me Blues* / *I'm Just A Lucky So-And-So* (vAM) / *San Jose* / *Adventure* (vBB) / *Red Bank Boogie* / *Take Me Back, Baby* (vJR) / *Queer Street* / *Mean To Me* (vAM) / *Every Tub*

Sunday 28 July 1946

Count Basie and his Orchestra broadcast from the Aquarium in New York City.
High Tide / *I Ain't Mad At You* / *One O'Clock Jump* (theme)

Tuesday 30 July 1946

Count Basie and his Orchestra broadcast from the Aquarium in New York City.
Blue House / *No Name*

Wednesday 31 July 1946

Count Basie and his Orchestra record for Columbia at Liederkranz Hall in New York City.
HARRY EDISON, EMMETT BERRY, ED LEWIS, SNOOKY YOUNG, JOE NEWMAN (trumpets), GEORGE MATTHEWS, TED DONNELLY, ELI ROBINSON, J. J. JOHNSON (trombones), RUDY RUTHERFORD, PRESTON LOVE (alto sax), BUDDY TATE, ILLINOIS JACQUET (tenor sax), JACK WASHINGTON (baritone sax), COUNT BASIE (piano), FREDDIE GREEN (guitar), WALTER PAGE (bass), JO JONES (drums), BOB BAILEY (vocals)
Hob Nail Boogie (3 takes) / *Danny Boy* (vBB) / *Mutton Leg* (4 takes) / *Stay On It*
J. J. Johnson leaves and is replaced by Bill Johnson.

August 1946

Metronome reviews Basie's latest Columbia release:

Count Basie
Lazy Lady Blues A–
High Tide A–
   Lazy is remarkable for its 24 bars of George Matthews' trombone. George has been around a long time (L. Armstrong, W. Bryant in the 30's) but never revealed this Morton-Wells-Dorsey talent before. Jimmy Rushing follows him with two typical blues choruses with nice backgrounds. *High Tide* features trumpet, tenor and clarinet in a neat riff, plus 4-1-beat handclapping by the band, a nice release in diminisheds, and a sequence of fine solos, tenor, trombone, Rudy Rutherford's swell clarinet, and the same old malarkey from the Count. Those who know the full-length version will regret the exclusion here of the second or vocal movement (*I Ain't Mad At Chew*). However, what's left is good fun and pleasant music. (Columbia 36990)

Friday 2 August 1946

Count Basie and his Orchestra broadcast on AFRS 'One Night Stand from the Aquarium in New York City.
HARRY EDISON, EMMETT BERRY, ED LEWIS, SNOOKY YOUNG (trumpets), GEORGE MATTHEWS, TED DONNELLY, ELI ROBINSON, BILL JOHNSON (trombones), RUDY RUTHERFORD, PRESTON LOVE (alto sax), BUDDY TATE, ILLINOIS JACQUET (tenor sax), JACK WASHINGTON (baritone sax), COUNT BASIE (piano), FREDDIE GREEN (guitar), WALTER PAGE (bass), JO JONES (drums), JIMMY RUSHING, ANN MOORE (vocals)
One O'Clock Jump (theme) / *My, What A Fry!* / *Down For Double* / *I Don't Know Why* (vAM) / *9:20 Special* / *Blue Skies* (vJR) / *Jumpin' At The Woodside* / *One O'Clock Jump* (theme)

Friday 9 August 1946

Count Basie and his Orchestra record for Columbia in New York City.
Wild Bill's Boogie (6 takes) / *Fla-Ga-La-Pa* (vAM) / *Don't Ever Let Me Be Yours* (vBB) / *Goodbye, Baby* (vJR, 3 takes)
Count Basie and his Orchestra broadcast on AFRS 'One Night Stand from the Aquarium in New York City.
One O'Clock Jump (theme) / *I'm Fer It Too* / *The Mad Boogie* / *Symphony* (vBB) / *9:20 Special* / *Blue Skies* (vJR) / *Jumpin' Jim* (vHE) / *One O'Clock Jump* (theme)

Monday 12 August 1946

Count Basie guests with the Benny Goodman Orchestra on the NBC 'Benny Goodman Music Festival' radio show in New York City.
The Mad Boogie / *One O'Clock Jump*

Wednesday 14 August 1946

Count Basie and his Orchestra close at the Aquarium in New York City. Illinois Jacquet and Joe Newman leave the band. Jacquet's replacement is Paul Gonsalves.

Basie Band Personnel Gets Shaky

New York—There was an undercurrent of action in the Count Basie band as the crew left the Aquarium here last week—Trumpeter Snooky Young reportedly left the band, Illinois Jacquet, ceiling-hitting tenorist, was eyeing the concert circuit, and blues-chanter Jimmy Rushing was mulling his often-thought-of desire to form his own band.

Jacquet, who has worked with Norman Granz as a guest soloist during the Basie band's stem turn, may turn the concert idea into a steady thing with Granz acting as his personal manager.

Basie Opens Own Pub Firm

New York—Following negotiations for the last six months, Count Basie opened his own music publishing company, Sterling music corporation, a firm that will be a subsidiary company of Burke-Van Heusen. He broke off with Bregman, Vocco and Conn after a relationship of more than seven years.

Sterling will publish all Basie originals, material by members of his band and his arrangers. Count and his manager, Milt Ebbins, are toying with the idea of expanding to publication of outside material.

Mutton Leg, Wild Bill's Boogie, Hob Nail Boogie, Stay With It and *Get Goin' Blues* are first numbers to be pubbed by Sterling, with a new recording, *The King*, also set.

JO JONES...
sparks COUNT BASIE'S *Rhythm Section*
with his new post-war
GRETSCH BROADKASTER OUTFIT

A terrific rhythm man with a tremendous drive, Jo Jones and his GRETSCH Broadkasters have, for many years, set the beat for Count Basie and his high-riding band.

DEALERS are now getting good deliveries on our new post-war equipment, so ask your Gretsch Dealer to show you the world's "Tops in Drums", or write us today for the name of the Gretsch Dealer in your town.

The FRED. GRETSCH Mfg. Co.
Musical Instrument Makers Since 1883
218 So. Wabash Avenue, Chicago 4, Ill.   60 Broadway, Brooklyn 11, N.Y.

Friday 16 August 1946

Count Basie and his Orchestra open a four-week engagement at the Band Box in Chicago.

Monday 9 September 1946

Down Beat reviews Count Basie's latest Columbia release.

Count Basie
*** *Blue Skies*
*** *The King*

Second side of *Blue* in recent weeks on Columbia, Goodman having done it with an Art Lund vocal. Famed Basie rhythm section slows down a trifle after the intro. My only kick is that this side is a cross between the rough-house swing Count used to play and the more complex approaches coming into fashion. Maybe Count can straddle the fence successfully, but things like confusing balance don't help him here. *King*, dedicated to BG, is a fast phrase tune with brass solos against the Basie reeds. Good trombone section before the Basie piano. Count can and should play more ideas than he does here. He's established his ability to play with pretty tone already. Last part of the record runs wild with tenor sax (Buddy Tate?) romping for three choruses. Don't think this a bad disc because of the above; but because it is Basie, there should be the best. (*Columbia 37070*)

Thursday 12 September 1946

Count Basie and his Orchestra close at the Band Box in Chicago.

Monday 16 September 1946

Count Basie and his Orchestra play a dance at the Savoy Ballroom in Chicago.

Thursday 19 September 1946

Count Basie and his Orchestra open a one-week engagement at the Orpheum Theatre in Minneapolis.

Wednesday 25 September 1946

Count Basie and his Orchestra close at the Orpheum Theatre in Minneapolis.

Friday 27 September 1946

Count Basie and his Orchestra open a one-week engagement at the Orpheum Theatre in Omaha, Nebraska.

Thursday 3 October 1946

Count Basie and his Orchestra close at the Orpheum Theatre in Omaha, Nebraska.

Friday 4 October 1946

Count Basie and his Orchestra play a one-nighter at the Rollerdrome in Denver, Colorado.

Monday 7 October 1946

Count Basie and his Orchestra open a one-week engagement at the Rainbow Rendezvous in Salt Lake City.

Saturday 12 October 1946

Count Basie and his Orchestra close at the Rainbow Rendezvous in Salt Lake City.

Tuesday 15 October 1946

Count Basie and his Orchestra open a one-week engagement at the Lincoln Theatre in Los Angeles.

DANCE
MONDAY, SEPTEMBER 16th
COUNT BASIE
AND HIS ORCHESTRA
JAMES RUSHING
VOCALIST
DANCING 9 P.M. to 1:30 A.M.
SAVOY
South Parkway at 47th St.

LINCOLN THEATRE
CENTRAL AT 23RD   Michigan 6275

West Coast for Basie Crew Until Early '47

Los Angeles—Count Basie, currently on the boards of the Lincoln theater here, is on the first leg of his annual Californian tour that will keep him on the coast until early 1947. Band's next stop is the Golden Gate theater in San Francisco, opening Oct. 23 for a week.

Despite other reports, there has been only one change in the Basie personnel. That was tenor saxist Paul Gonsalves, a Providence, R.I. boy, into Illinois Jacquet's chair, the latter going on tour with the Norman Granz concert unit. Gonsalves will share hot tenor spots with Buddy Tate.

The Basie band personnel is as follows:

Emmett Berry, Harry Edison, Ed Lewis and Snooky Young, trumpets; Ted Donnelly, Bill Johnson, George Matthews and Eli Robinson, trombones; Preston Love, Rudy Rutherford, Jack Washington, Buddy Tate and Paul Gonsalves, saxes; Jo Jones, drums; Walter Page, bass; Freddie Green, guitar and Basie, piano. Ann Moore, Bob Bailey and Jimmy Rushing are featured vocalists.

Above: A gathering of celebrities at the Turban Room in Los Angeles. Louis Armstrong, in town to film 'New Orleans' stands at left. Count Basie, with Mrs Basie seated directly in front of him, is flanked by dancer Harold Nicholas and trumpeter Harry Edison. Actress Dorothy Dandridge is second left in the front row.

Monday 21 October 1946
Count Basie and his Orchestra close at the Lincoln Theatre in Los Angeles.

Wednesday 23 October 1946
Count Basie and his Orchestra open a one-week engagement at the Golden Gate Theatre in San Francisco.

Tuesday 29 October 1946
Count Basie and his Orchestra close at the Golden Gate Theatre in San Francisco.

Monday 4 November 1946
Down Beat reviews Count Basie's latest Columbia release.

Count Basie
*** *Muttonleg*
*** *Fla-Ga-La-Pa*

Muttonleg, taken fast, sounds like the old *Every Tub*. For once Count is playing rhythm with both hands. Solos by Buddy Tate (who still plays a little like Herschel Evans), Rudy Rutherford, Emmett Berry, and Illinois Jacquet carry out the most frantic side from Count in moons. Jackie even squeals on the end to keep everybody happy. *Pa*, the tale of the guy who met her in Florida, kissed her in Georgia, married her in Louisiana, and settled in Pennsylvania is sung capably by Ann Moore, but the song for my dough still belongs to Timmie Rogers. (*Columbia 37093*)

Tuesday 5 November 1946
Count Basie and his Orchestra open a one-week engagement at the Million Dollar Theatre in Los Angeles.

Monday 11 November 1946
Count Basie and his Orchestra close at the Million Dollar Theatre in Los Angeles.

Basie For Europe

New York—Count Basie is scheduling a tour of Continental Europe for next spring. Labor restrictions will prevent him from playing England. Bookings are through the London office of the William Morris agency.

December 1946
Metronome reviews Basie's latest Columbia release:

Count Basie
Mutton Leg ★
Fla-Ga-La-Pa

Mutton Leg, one of the best Basie biscuits in years, is a new version of *Every Tub*, cut some eight years ago by Count on Decca, with the following changes: a counter-riff to the original melody in the first chorus, a much faster tempo and a bigger and better Basie band. Solos are by Buddy Tate, tenor, Rudy Rutherford, clarinet, Emmett Berry, trumpet; then Illinois Jacquet takes over and blows like mad, with the band building up each of his choruses to a tremendous climax in which his freak high notes are forgivable to Deuce Feather, but not to Deuce Simon. Brass section is tremendous. Overleaf, a vocal novelty, is well enough done by Ann Moore and has some dainty Basie. (Columbia 37093)

Count Basie signs with RCA-Victor

Basie Gets Air From Avodon

New York—Count Basie returns to the airlanes Dec. 10 when the band goes into Los Angeles' Avodon ballroom for a four-week engagement. Shots will be over ABC and Mutual.

Basie is currently on a one-nighter and theater tour down the Pacific coast.

During his stay at the Avodon, the Count is skedded to make a pair of musical shorts for Columbia.

Tuesday 10 December 1946
Count Basie and his Orchestra open a four-week engagement at the Avodon Ballroom in Los Angeles.

1947

Wednesday 1 January 1947

Count Basie and his Orchestra broadcast over ABC from the Avodon Ballroom in Los Angeles.

HARRY EDISON, EMMETT BERRY, ED LEWIS, SNOOKY YOUNG (trumpets), GEORGE MATTHEWS, TED DONNELLY, ELI ROBINSON, BILL JOHNSON (trombones), RUDY RUTHERFORD, PRESTON LOVE (alto sax), BUDDY TATE, PAUL GONSALVES (tenor sax), JACK WASHINGTON (baritone sax), COUNT BASIE (piano), FREDDIE GREEN (guitar), WALTER PAGE (bass), JO JONES (drums), JIMMY RUSHING, ANN MOORE (vocals)

Futile Frustration / Wild Bill Boogie / My, What A Fry! / Hob Nail Boogie / High Tide / Body And Soul / One O'Clock Jump (theme)

Friday 3 January 1947

Count Basie and his Orchestra make their first recording for Victor in Los Angeles.

HARRY EDISON, EMMETT BERRY, ED LEWIS, SNOOKY YOUNG (trumpets), GEORGE MATTHEWS, TED DONNELLY, ELI ROBINSON, BILL JOHNSON (trombones), RUDY RUTHERFORD, PRESTON LOVE (alto sax), BUDDY TATE, PAUL GONSALVES (tenor sax), JACK WASHINGTON (baritone sax), COUNT BASIE (piano), FREDDIE GREEN (guitar), WALTER PAGE (bass), JO JONES (drums), JIMMY RUSHING, ANN MOORE (vocals)

Bill's Mill / Me And The Blues (vAM) / *Free Eats* (vHE,BJ, ens) / *Brand New Wagon* (vJR) / *Open The Door, Richard* (vHE,BJ, ens with rhythm section only)

Monday 6 January 1947

Count Basie and his Orchestra close at the Avodon Ballroom in Los Angeles. Basie celebrates the 11th anniversary of forming his big band.

Basie Cuts Victor Sides

Hollywood—Count Basie's first waxings under his new Victor pact were *Bill's Mill*, and original by Basie, and *Open The Door, Richard*, novelty popularized by Jack McVea's version, currently selling so fast that one retail dealer here reported that disc was paying rent on establishment.

Basie Eastward

New York—The Count Basie band, following a successful run at the west coast's Avodon ballroom, treks eastward on a series of one-nighters before starting a theater tour in Detroit Jan. 31 at the Paradise.

Friday 31 January 1947

Count Basie and his Orchestra open a one-week engagement at the Paradise Theatre in Detroit.

Thursday 6 February 1947

Count Basie and his Orchestra close at the Paradise Theatre in Detroit.

Tuesday 11 February 1947

Count Basie and his Orchestra open a one-week engagement at the Tune Town Ballroom in St. Louis, Missouri.

Sunday 16 February 1947

Count Basie and his Orchestra close at the Tune Town Ballroom in St. Louis, Missouri.

Friday 21 February 1947

Count Basie and his Orchestra open a one-week engagement at the Regal Theatre in Chicago.

Thursday 27 February 1947

Count Basie and his Orchestra close at the Regal Theatre in Chicago.

Thursday 13 March 1947

Count Basie and his Orchestra record for Victor in New York City.

HARRY EDISON, EMMETT BERRY, ED LEWIS, SNOOKY YOUNG (trumpets), GEORGE MATTHEWS, TED DONNELLY, ELI ROBINSON, BILL JOHNSON (trombones), RUDY RUTHERFORD, PRESTON LOVE (alto sax), BUDDY TATE, PAUL GONSALVES (tenor sax), JACK WASHINGTON (baritone sax), COUNT BASIE (piano), FREDDIE GREEN (guitar), WALTER PAGE (bass), JO JONES (drums), BOB BAILEY, ANN BAKER (vocals)

One O'Clock Boogie / Meet Me At No Special Place (vAB) / *I'm Drowning In Your Deep Blue Eyes* (vBB) / *Futile Frustration*

Count Basie's Theater Route

New York—The Count Basie band, which opens Friday, March 14, for a week at the Apollo theater, Harlem, follows with an eastern theater tour that will take the band through Washington, Baltimore, Philadelphia and Boston.

Present plans may take the pianist and his crew into Chicago sometime in May for a four-week date at the Rhumboogie. Basie is blueprinting a European trip later in the summer, possibly July.

Friday 14 March 1947

Count Basie and his Orchestra open a one-week engagement at the Apollo Theatre in New York City.

Saturday 15 March 1947

Count Basie is among the guests at a Lionel Hampton Concert (11.30pm) at Carnegie Hall in New York City. Other guests include Ella Fitzgerald, Dizzy Gillespie, the Ink Spots, Billy Eckstine and Cootie Williams.

Thursday 20 March 1947

Count Basie and his Orchestra close at the Apollo Theatre in New York City.

Monday 24 March 1947

Count Basie and members of his band appear at a Blue Monday Night Jam Session at Smalls Paradise in New York City. Also featured are Rex Stewart, Max Roach, George Jenkins and the Starliners.

April 1947

Metronome reviews Count Basie's latest Victor releases:

> ## Count Basie
> *Open The Door, Richard* B–
> *Me and the Blues* C+
> *Free Eats* B
> *Bill's Mill* B
>
> Although the Basie band isn't as well recorded as it was at Columbia, it jumps a great deal more for Victor. *Free* would be a great side if it weren't for some clumsy, inarticulate unison singing by the band. Aside from that, the band plays lightly, with the muted brass jumping like mad. *Bill's Mill* isn't far behind, featuring a pretty tenor by Paul Gonsalves and two fine muted trumpet solos by Emmett Berry and Harry Edison. The Count's piano is tasty on both sides. Harry Edison is fairly amusing on *Richard*, while Anne Moore's vocal is not, on *Me*. (Victor 20-2127/48)

Friday 4 April 1947

Count Basie and his Orchestra open a one-week engagement at the Howard Theatre in Washington, D.C.

Saturday 5 April 1947

Count Basie records with the New York Stars for V-Disc at the WNEW Studios in New York City.
Roy Eldridge (trumpet) Illinois Jacquet (tenor sax), Count Basie (piano), Freddie Green (guitar), Red Callender (bass), Buddy Rich (drums)
Oh! Lady Be Good / Jammin' On A V-Disc

Thursday 10 April 1947

Count Basie and his Orchestra close at the Howard Theatre in Washington, D.C.

Friday 11 April 1947

Count Basie and his Orchestra open a one-week engagement at the Earle Theatre in Philadelphia.

Philadelphia—Voted the best Negro disc jockey by the RCA-Victor distributors of eastern Pennsylvania, Ramon Bruce, right, receives an award presented by Count Basie. Miss Dolly Banks, WHAT program chief, looks on.

Thursday 17 April 1947
Count Basie and his Orchestra close at the Earle Theatre in Philadelphia.

Basie Inks With BVC For Tunes

New York—After a week at the Earle theater in Philadelphia, the Count Basie band twisted south for a four-week tour of one-nighters opening Monday (21) at the USO auditorium, Norfolk, Va.

Basie recently signed a three-year writer's binder with Bregman, Vocco and Conn publishing firm, a deal that will bring the pianist an advance royalty of approximately $10,000 annually. *Bill's Mill, Free Eats, One O'Clock Boogie* and *Futile Frustration* are the first of Basie's tunes to be pubbed by BVC, which has been handling his originals since 1939, although no contract has been in effect the last few years.

Monday 21 April 1947
Count Basie and his Orchestra play a one-nighter at the USO Auditorium in Norfolk, Virginia.

Tuesday 22 April 1947
Count Basie and his Orchestra play a one-nighter at the City Armory in Danville, Virginia.

Wednesday 23 April 1947
Count Basie and his Orchestra play a one-nighter in Greensboro, North Carolina.

Thursday 24 April 1947
Count Basie and his Orchestra play a one-nighter at the City Armory in Charlotte, North Carolina.

Friday 25 April 1947
Count Basie and his Orchestra play a one-nighter at the City Auditorium in Asheville, North Carolina.

Saturday 26 April 1947
Count Basie and his Orchestra play a one-nighter at the City Auditorium in Kingsport, Tennessee.

Monday 28 April 1947
Count Basie and his Orchestra play a one-nighter at the Township Auditorium in Columbia, South Carolina.

Tuesday 29 April 1947
Count Basie and his Orchestra play a one-nighter at the County Hall in Charleston, South Carolina.

Wednesday 30 April 1947
Count Basie and his Orchestra play a one-nighter in Macon, Georgia.

Thursday 1 May 1947
Count Basie and his Orchestra play a one-nighter at the Municipal Auditorium in Atlanta, Georgia.

Friday 2 May 1947
Count Basie and his Orchestra play a one-nighter at the Municipal Auditorium in Birmingham, Alabama.

Saturday 3 May 1947
Count Basie and his Orchestra play a one-nighter at the Propeller Club in Tuskegee, Alabama.

Monday 5 May 1947
Count Basie and his Orchestra play a one-nighter in Jacksonville, Florida.

Tuesday 6 May 1947
Count Basie and his Orchestra play a one-nighter at the Apollo Auditorium in Tampa, Florida.

Wednesday 7 May 1947
Count Basie and his Orchestra play a one-nighter in Orlando, Florida.

Thursday 8 May 1947
Count Basie and his Orchestra play a one-nighter in St. Petersburg, Florida.

Friday 9 May 1947
Count Basie and his Orchestra play a one-nighter in Bartow, Florida.

Sunday 11 May 1947
Count Basie and his Orchestra play a one-nighter at the Liberty City Amusement Park in Miami, Florida.

Monday 12 May 1947
Count Basie and his Orchestra play a one-nighter in Palatka, Florida.

Tuesday 20 May 1947
Count Basie and members of his Orchestra record for Victor in New York City.
EMMETT BERRY (trumpet); GEORGE MATTHEWS (trombone); CHARLIE PRICE (alto sax); PAUL GONSALVES (tenor sax); JACK WASHINGTON (baritone sax); COUNT BASIE (piano/organ); FREDDIE GREEN (guitar); WALTER PAGE (bass); JO JONES (drums)
Swingin' The Blues (JW, GM out) / *St. Louis Boogie* / *Basie's Basement* (org CB) / *Backstage At Stuff's* / *My Buddy*

Wednesday 21 May 1947
Count Basie and a small group record for Victor in New York.
PAUL GONSALVES (tenor sax); JACK WASHINGTON (baritone sax); COUNT BASIE (piano/organ); FREDDIE GREEN (guitar); WALTER PAGE (bass); JO JONES (drums)
Shine On Harvest Moon (PG, JW out) / *Lopin'* (PG out) / *I Never Knew* (JW out) / *Sugar* (JW out)

Thursday 22 May 1947

Count Basie and his Orchestra record for Victor in New York City.

HARRY EDISON, EMMETT BERRY, ED LEWIS, SNOOKY YOUNG (trumpets), GEORGE MATTHEWS, TED DONNELLY, ELI ROBINSON, BILL JOHNSON (trombones), CHARLIE PRICE, PRESTON LOVE (alto sax), BUDDY TATE, PAUL GONSALVES (tenor sax), JACK WASHINGTON (baritone sax), COUNT BASIE (piano), FREDDIE GREEN (guitar), WALTER PAGE (bass), JO JONES (drums), JIMMY RUSHING, TAPS MILLER (vocals)

The Jungle King (vJR) / *Take A Little Off The Top* (HE, TD + rhythm) / *I Ain't Mad At You* (vTM) / *After You've Gone* (vJR) / *House Rent Boogie* (vTM) / *South*

Monday 26 May 1947

Count Basie and his Orchestra open a three-night engagement at the Stanley Theatre in Utica, New York.

Wednesday 28 May 1947

Count Basie and his Orchestra close at the Stanley Theatre in Utica, New York.

Friday 30 May 1947

Count Basie and his Orchestra play a one-nighter at the Pershing Ballroom in Chicago.

Wednesday 4 June 1947

Count Basie and his Orchestra open a one-week engagement at the W. C. Handy Theatre in Memphis.

Down Beat reviews Count Basie's latest Victor release:

HANK MOORE-Proudly Presents
"The Jump King of Swing"
COUNT BASIE
AND HIS FAMOUS ORCHESTRA
With Vocalists
JAMES RUSHING — BOB BAILEY & ANN BAKER
FRIDAY, MAY 30th
At The Beautiful
PERSHING BALLROOM
64th and Cottage Grove
EARLY BIRD PRICES 8 TO 9
Advance Tickets On Sale At Grand Hotel, 51st & So. Parkway

Count Basie
** *One O'Clock Boogie*
** *Meet Me No Special Place*

Boogie was written by Basie, arranger Jim Mundy, and manager Milt Ebbins—which just shows you how much effort it takes to get some extra choruses of *One O'Clock Jump* on wax. Eli Oberstein should be ashamed of the balance here—it has the telephone booth quality of the old recording days. There are spots where the vaunted Basie rhythm section can't seem to keep the brass moving, and the whole side lacks genuine enthusiasm. Regardless of the commercial possibilities, you can't expect musicians to record the same figures all the time and have them achieve anything musical in the process. *Place* is vocaled by Ann Baker. (*Victor 20-2262*)

Tuesday 10 June 1947

Count Basie and his Orchestra close at the W. C. Handy Theatre in Memphis.

Summer bookings are very thin and Basie gives his band the option of taking a long summer summer engagement at the Paradise Club in Atlantic City at reduced wages. They all agree.

Count Basie To Open Engagement in N. J.

Count Basie, the "Jump King of Swing", will be honored by a delegation of leading citizens of his home town of Red Bank, N. J., when he returns to his native state of New Jersey on June 27 to open a summer-long engagement at the smart Club Paradise in Atlantic City.

Basie's engagement in the resort city will mark his first extended stay in his native state since he has had a band, as well as being the first time an Atlantic City nitery has brought in a big name Negro band for the entire season.

Tentative plans call for the Count to be the guest of honor at a testimonial dinner at Red Bank on Thursday, June 26th, the affair to be sponsored by the New Jersey community's Chamber of Commerce as "Count Basie Day" in a tribute to Red Bank's most famous native son.

A special "Count Basie Handicap" will be run at the Mammoth Park race track as an added bonus for the Count, and a similar event is planned for the Atlantic City track.

An all-star sepia revue, produced by Joe "Ziggy" Johnson, will support the Count and his band in their engagement at the Club Paradise, which is sparing no effort to present the most lavish cabaret entertainment in Atlantic City's night life history.

Thursday 26 June 1947

Count Basie is guest of honor at a testimonial dinner in Red Bank, New Jersey.

Friday 27 June 1947

Count Basie and his Orchestra open a summer residency at Club Paradise in Atlantic City, New Jersey.

Friday 11 July 1947

Dan Bied visits Club Paradise in Atlantic City and reports in his book, *Jazz Memories*:

The first time I had seen Basie's band was at the Paradise Club, which resembled a prohibition era roadhouse, at 220 North Illinois Avenue in Atlantic City. It was a dark room, with a low ceiling and small tables surrounding a stage and dance floor. Everything was bathed in white, amber, yellow and blue spotlights during the show.

The club's waiters were well-attired, though it wasn't a posh sort of place. There was a camera girl, showing off nifty legs in a short skirt, taking souvenir photos with a big, heavy Speed Graphic.

The floor show featured two black comedians, Stump and Stumpy. Their routine included a zany satire on "Duel In the Sun," a popular movie, in which one of them whipped out a water pistol and shot his partner between the eyes. Their act was a howl, with my pal and I lubricated with drinks from the bar.

I did, however, think well enough to jot down the names of the band members, provided by Basie's road manager. Edison, Wells, Tate, Washington, Green and Page were there. So were trumpeters Snooky Young, Emmett Berry and Ed Lewis; trombonists Ted Donnelly, Bill Johnson and George Matthews; altoists Charlie Price and Preston Love; tenorman Paul Gonsalves; and drummer Jimmy Crawford, who had propelled Jimmy Lunceford's great band from 1928 to 1943 and was "sitting in" briefly with Basie.

There were three vocalists. Rushing performed such standards of his as "Harvard Blues" and "Jimmy's Blues," a number featuring the robust trombone of Matthews. Bob Bailey crooned "Danny Boy" during the floor show. Ann Baker was featured on "Meet Me At No Special Place," one of Basie's more popular RCA discs at that time.

Other numbers played by the impeccable, swinging band that night included "Rose Room," "Mutton Leg," "South," "Free Eats," "Basie Boogie," "Swinging The Blues," "Bill's Mill," "Jalousie" and an opus called "Paradise Squat" that was, I figured, named in honor of the club.

I recall Gonsalves doing a long, scorching solo on "Mutton Leg" and a group from the band singing "Free Eats," a tune I had on a 78-rpm disc. "Jalousie" was the same arrangement played by Harry James and it was done note for note as the Music Makers did it, with Edison doing the trumpet solo.

Above: The Basie Band on stage at the Paradise Club. The drummer is Jimmy Crawford, subbing for Jo Jones.

Late July:

DON'T SAY FISH—Count Basie was surrounded by his fans shortly after he was fished out of the Atlantic Ocean. On a fishing trip the Count fell into the drink when he tried to pull a "big one" in too fast. A non-swimmer, he was saved by Harold Abrams, manager of the Club Paradise.

Basie Goes Fishing, But Is Fished Out

ATLANTIC CITY, N. J.—Count Basie, the recognized "Jump King of Swing," did very little swinging, but plenty of jumping here last week when he turned out to be the biggest haul of a week-end deep-sea fishing trip.

The story as told by Basie's road manager Murray Bloom, is funny now, even to the piano maestro. However as the real drama unfolded several miles from shore in the rough Atlantic there was no comedy attached.

As it goes the Count hooked one of those big ones the boys usually take pictures of and tell tall winter tales about. Leaning away over the side to insure capture, he slipped none too gracefully into the big drink. A much worse swimmer than he is a musician, the Count just jumped. Realizing the seriousness of the situation and the plight his attraction was in, Harold Abrams, manager of the Club Paradise which brought the son of Red Bank here, went into action and the ocean.

FLOATING HOME

An expert swimmer, Abrams easily kept the maestro afloat until other members of the party tossed them a much needed lifeline. Hauled to safety, the first thing Basie wanted to know was, "What happened to my fish?" He was further concerned over his fishing rod and the fact that the weight of the fish on it would surely have established a new record.

Back on the bandstand at the Paradise that same night he started working on a new tune. The title isn't born yet, but you can bet it will have plenty of salt in it and just might be called "Jumpin' in the Atlantic Ocean."

Thursday 7 August 1947

Count Basie and his Orchestra close at Club Paradise in Atlantic City, New Jersey.

Basie To Strand

New York—Count Basie, a Roxy theater stand-by until the giant theater abandoned its name band policy, opens at the Strand Aug. 22 for two, possibly three weeks. To make the date, Basie had to get out of the last portion of his contract with the Club Paradise, Atlantic City.

Thursday 21 August 1947

Count Basie celebrates his 43rd birthday at a party backstage at the Strand Theatre in New York City.

Friday 22 August 1947

Count Basie and his Orchestra open a one-week engagement at the Strand Theatre in New York City. Pearl Bailey shares the bill and the movie presentation is 'Deep Valley' starring Ida Lupino, Dane Clark, and Wayne Morris.

Thursday 4 September 1947

Count Basie and his Orchestra close at the Strand Theatre in New York City.

Friday 5 September 1947

Count Basie and his Orchestra open a one-week engagement at the Paradise Theatre in Detroit.

Thursday 11 September 1947

Count Basie and his Orchestra close at the Paradise Theatre in Detroit.

The band then play one-nighters in Ohio, Illinois, Indiana, Wisconsin, Iowa and Missouri on the way back to New York.

Friday 19 September 1947

Count Basie and his Orchestra open a one-week engagement at the Apollo Theatre in New York City.

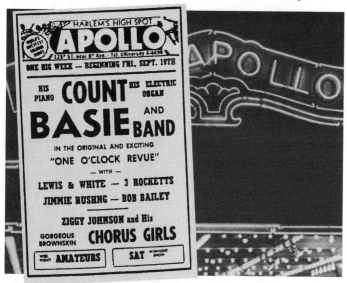

Thursday 25 September 1947

Count Basie and his Orchestra close at the Apollo Theatre in New York City.

Friday 26 September 1947

Count Basie and his Orchestra open a one-week engagement at the Royal Theatre in Baltimore.

Thursday 2 October 1947

Count Basie and his Orchestra close at the Royal Theatre in Baltimore.

Friday 10 October 1947

Count Basie and his Orchestra open a one-week engagement at the Paradise Theatre in Detroit.

Thursday 16 October 1947

Count Basie and his Orchestra close at the Paradise Theatre in Detroit.

Saturday 18 October 1947

Count Basie and his Orchestra play a dance at the Savoy Ballroom in Chicago.

Sunday 19 October 1947

Count Basie and his Orchestra record for Victor in Chicago. HARRY EDISON, EMMETT BERRY, ED LEWIS, SNOOKY YOUNG (trumpets), DICKIE WELLS, TED DONNELLY, GEORGE SIMON, BILL JOHNSON (trombones), CHARLIE PRICE, PRESTON LOVE (alto sax), BUDDY TATE, PAUL GONSALVES (tenor sax), JACK WASHINGTON (baritone sax), COUNT BASIE (piano), FREDDIE GREEN (guitar), WALTER PAGE (bass), JO JONES (drums), JIMMY RUSHING, BOB BAILEY (vocals)
Don't You Want A Man Like Me (vJR) / *Blue And Sentimental* (vBB) / *7th Avenue Express* / *Mr Robert's Roost*

Monday 20 October 1947

Count Basie and his Orchestra open a two-week engagement at the Rainbow Rendezvous in Salt Lake City.

Saturday 1 November 1947

Count Basie and his Orchestra close at the Rainbow Rendezvous in Salt Lake City.

Tuesday 4 November 1947

Count Basie and his Orchestra open a one-week engagement at the Million Dollar Theatre in Los Angeles.

Monday 10 November 1947

Count Basie and his Orchestra close at the Million Dollar Theatre in Los Angeles.

Sunday 12 November 1947

Count Basie and his Orchestra appear at a Gene Norman 'Just Jazz' concert (AFRS Jubilee No245 transcription) at the Civic Auditorium in Pasadena. Ella Mae Morse also stars. HARRY EDISON, EMMETT BERRY, ED LEWIS, SNOOKY YOUNG (trumpets), DICKIE WELLS, TED DONNELLY, GEORGE MATTHEWS, BILL JOHNSON (trombones), CHARLIE PRICE, PRESTON LOVE (alto sax), BUDDY TATE, PAUL GONSALVES (tenor sax), JACK WASHINGTON (baritone sax), COUNT BASIE (piano), FREDDIE GREEN (guitar), WALTER PAGE (bass), JO JONES (drums)
One O'Clock Jump (theme) / *Jimmy's Idea* / *Buzz Me* (vEMM) / *Futile Frustration* / *Stay On It* / *Rusty Dusty Blues* (vJR) / *Sent For You Yesterday* (vJR) / *9.20 Special* / *On The Sunny Side Of The Street* (vEMM) / *Wild Bill's Boogie* / *One O'Clock Jump* (theme)

The band spend the next three weeks playing one-night dance dates in California, Oregon and Washington.

December 1947

Metronome reviews Count Basie's latest Victor release:

Count Basie
Futile Frustration B
Brand New Wagon C+
 Jimmy Mundy's frantic arrangement puts Basie back on the credit side of the ledger. This opus is a fine attempt which just misses fire in its fragmentary form. Band plays the Sauterish instrumental quite well, but it too just doesn't seem to hit home. Reverse side is a slow blues shouted by Mr. Rushing with nice trumpet fill-ins. The Count doesn't count on piano. (Victor 20-2529)

Tuesday 2 December 1947

Count Basie and his Orchestra open a three-week engagement at the Meadowbrook Gardens in Culver City, California.

Monday 8 December 1947

Count Basie and his Orchestra record for Victor in Los Angeles.

HARRY EDISON, EMMETT BERRY, ED LEWIS, SNOOKY YOUNG (trumpets), DICKIE WELLS, TED DONNELLY, GEORGE MATTHEWS, BILL JOHNSON (trombones), CHARLIE PRICE, PRESTON LOVE (alto sax), BUDDY TATE, PAUL GONSALVES (tenor sax), JACK WASHINGTON (baritone sax), COUNT BASIE (piano), FREDDIE GREEN (guitar), WALTER PAGE (bass), JO JONES (drums), JIMMY RUSHING (vocals)

Sophisticated Swing / *Guest In A Nest* (2 takes) / *Your Red Wagon* (vJR) / *Money Is Honey* (vJR)

Tuesday 9 December 1947

Count Basie and his Orchestra record for Victor in Los Angeles.

HARRY EDISON, EMMETT BERRY, ED LEWIS, SNOOKY YOUNG (trumpets), DICKIE WELLS, TED DONNELLY, GEORGE MATTHEWS, BILL JOHNSON (trombones), CHARLIE PRICE, PRESTON LOVE (alto sax), BUDDY TATE, PAUL GONSALVES (tenor sax), JACK WASHINGTON (baritone sax), COUNT BASIE (piano), FREDDIE GREEN (guitar), WALTER PAGE (bass), JO JONES (drums), JEANNE TAYLOR (vocals)

Just A Minute / *Baby, Don't Be Mad At Me* (vJT) / *I've Only Myself To Blame* (vJT, 2 takes)

Friday 12 December 1947

Count Basie and his Orchestra record for Victor in Los Angeles.

HARRY EDISON, EMMETT BERRY, ED LEWIS, SNOOKY YOUNG (trumpets), GEORGE WASHINGTON, TED DONNELLY, GEORGE MATTHEWS, BILL JOHNSON (trombones), CHARLIE PRICE, PRESTON LOVE (alto sax), BUDDY TATE, PAUL GONSALVES (tenor sax), JACK WASHINGTON (baritone sax), COUNT BASIE (piano), FREDDIE GREEN (guitar), WALTER PAGE (bass), JO JONES (drums), JIMMY RUSHING, JEANNE TAYLOR (vocals)

Robbins' Nest (2 takes) / *Hey, Pretty Baby* (vJR) / *It's Monday Every Day* (vJT, 2 takes) / *Bye Bye Baby* (vJR, 2 takes) / *Ready, Set, Go* (vJT)

Around this time, business falls off dramatically at the Meadowbrook and Basie is forced to agree to pay cuts, working on Friday, Saturday and Sunday nights only.

Friday 26 December 1947

Earl Warren returns to the band at the Meadowbrook, replacing Preston Love.

New York—Earl Warren has rejoined Count Basie, taking over the lead alto chair of Preston Love, and Gerald Wilson has replaced Snookie Young in the trumpet section.

Taylor New Basie Thrush

Hollywood—Count Basie has himself a new singer, name of Jeanne Taylor. She made several sides with the band here before the ban clamped down.

Sunday 28 December 1947

Count Basie and his Orchestra close at the Meadowbrook Gardens in Culver City, California.

1948

Count Basie and his Orchestra begin the year with a series of one-nighters and theatre dates taking them across the country to Chicago.

Friday 6 February 1948

Count Basie and his Orchestra open a one-week engagement at the Regal Theatre in Chicago.

Thursday 12 February 1948

Count Basie and his Orchestra close at the Regal Theatre in Chicago.

Friday 13 February 1948

Count Basie and his Orchestra play a senior prom at the University of Minnesota, alternating with the Sam Donahue Band.

Friday 20 February 1948

Count Basie and his Orchestra open a one-week engagement at the Howard Theatre in Washington, D.C.

Wednesday 25 February 1948

Down Beat reviews Count Basie's latest Victor release:

> ### Count Basie
> ** *Blue and Sentimental*
> ** *Don't You Want a Man Like Me*
> The Basie band, which made the original, starring Herschel Evans, over ten years ago, doing **Blue** as a ballad with Bob Bailey singing the vocal. The tenor by Paul Gonsalves is workmanlike, hardly up to the sterling choruses of the late Evans. (**Victor 20-2602**)

Thursday 26 February 1948

Count Basie and his Orchestra close at the Howard Theatre in Washington, D.C.

Thursday 4 March 1948

Count Basie and his Orchestra open a one-week engagement at the Adams Theatre in Newark, New Jersey.

Wednesday 10 March 1948

Count Basie and his Orchestra close at the Adams Theatre in Newark, New Jersey.

Basie Delays Europe Tour

New York—Count Basie has decided to "play America first." Turning down a deal that would guarantee him $15,000 per week for a European tour, the Count is working on his **Count Basie Cavalcade**, a jazz concert with which he will play the key cities in the States. Milt Ebbins, Basie's personal manager, states that the **Cavalcade** may then go in for European engagements, starting around September.

Friday 12 March 1948

Count Basie and his Orchestra open a one-week engagement at the Apollo Theatre in New York City.

New York—There's a count coming on. In this case it happens to be Count Basie, flirting with another kind of count as he tapers off with heavyweight fighter Al Hooseman, whose ring career the band leader is sponsoring.

Thursday 18 March 1948

Count Basie and his Orchestra close at the Apollo Theatre in New York City.

Monday 22 March 1948

Count Basie and his Orchestra open a three-night engagement at the Palace Theatre in Columbus, Ohio.

Wednesday 24 March 1948

Count Basie and his Orchestra close at the Palace Theatre in Columbus, Ohio.

Friday 26 March 1948

Count Basie and his Orchestra open a one-week engagement at the Paradise Theatre in Detroit.

Thursday 1 April 1948

Count Basie and his Orchestra close at the Paradise Theatre in Detroit.

Basie Cavalcade To Tee Off With Carnegie Concert

New York—Count Basie starts his **Cavalcade** at Carnegie Hall with a midnight bash Saturday night, April 24, after which he will take the musical show on a swing around 30 or 40 cities.

For the local extravaganza, the Count is endeavoring to get several of his alumni to "sit in" for the evening. If successful, this will mean his show will be augmented by such personalities as Lester Young, Buck Clayton, Helen Humes and a few others.

Another Suite

The highlight of the concert, both at Carnegie and on the road, will be a composition on which he is currently working, **The Royal Suite**, which will be played in three movements.

Personnel for the Basie bash will include Harry Edison, Ed Lewis, Clark Terry, Emmett Berry and Gerald Wilson, trumpets; Dickie Wells, George Matthews, Ted Donnelly and Billy Johnson, trombones; Buddy Tate and Paul Gonsalves, tenors; Earl Warren and Charles Price, altos; Jack Washington, baritone; Shadow Wilson, drums; Freddie Green, guitar; Eugene Wright, bass; Jimmy Rushing and Bob Bailey, vocals.

Count Basie And Orchestra To Appear In Carnegie Hall Concert, April 24

Count Basie, the "Jump King of Swing," will present something new in the way of jazz concerts when he takes to the stage of Carnegie Hall on Saturday, April 24.

The Count has steered clear of concert presentations for the past several years in order to prepare the material that would do full justice to his celebrated orchestra and soloists. The Basie concert at Carnegie will not be the standard program of a big jazz band concert, but will serve as a compact "Cavalcade" of the greatest Basie music of the past twelve years.

Basie will have a special spot in the program for the featured soloists of his orchestra. These instrumentalists include tenor saxophonists Paul Gonzales and Buddy Tate, alto saxophonist Earle Warren, trumpeters Harry Edison and Clark Terry, trombonists Dicky Wells and George Matthews, and the band's incomparable "All-American Rhythm Section."

The climax of the concert will be the first performance of Basie's own "Royal Suite" in three movements, blues, boogie-woogie and jump rhythm. The "Royal Suite" will highlight the Count's piano artistry and the band's star instrumentalists.

Vocal honors in the Basie concert will go to "The Man Who Sings The Blues", Jimmy Rushing, who will be heard in many of his most famous blues selections, backed by the entire orchestra.

To round out the concert, many of the notable alumni of the Basie band are expected to join as guest soloists. These will include such instrumentalists as Illinois Jacquet, Lester Young, Buck Clayton and others who first tasted musical fame as members of the Basie band during the past twelve years.

Saturday 24 April 1948

Count Basie and his Orchestra play a midnight 'One-Nite Stand' concert at Carnegie Hall in New York City. Woody Herman, Hot Lips Page, Buck Clayton and Billie Holiday make guest appearances. During the Saturday afternoon rehearsal, Earle Warren collapses with pleurisy and is rushed to hospital.

'One-Nite Stand' Concerts Netted Names, Prestige, $

New York—The "One-Nite Stand" series of Saturday midnight concerts conducted since last fall by Ernie Anderson and disc jockey Fred Robbins, was brought to a close with Count Basie, his orchestra and several guest performers on the dais. Stands were split between Town Hall and Carnegie, the latter getting the main play as the season drew near its close.

Anderson, satisfied with the overall financial picture of the '47-'48 collection, notably the packed houses drawn by Stan Kenton, Ella Fitzgerald–Illinois Jacquet and Billie Holiday, will resume next fall. In all probability, Carnegie will be used more than Town Hall.

The Hall, with a primary purpose of serving as an educational element, does not lend itself completely to the freedom demanded for proper presentation of jazz concerts. Dancing on the stage, even by performers, is taboo. The management frowns on comedy. Smoking is prohibited and an announcement is made prior to each performance that should any one member of the audience light up, the performance immediately will be terminated and the patrons turned out into the cold, cold streets.

From the promotor's point of view, however, the Hall is a better proposition in that he can realize more profit and, except when Carnegie is sold out, have a more compact crowd, thus insuring a better performance from the folks on stage.

Carnegie's Attributes

Carnegie is a huge place, is acoustically ideal, and encourages relaxation particularly at the bar it keeps in operation before, during and after concerts. It also allows performers whatever freedom they desire to best display their talents, even though it later regretted letting Hampton put in stairs to the stage.

The Basie bash proved a good closer with the guests giving it the proper flavoring of aulde lang syne. Though several more were expected, those who did show gave a good account of themselves. Woody Herman sang a fast ad lib chorus of the blues; Billie Holiday, by now a very familiar figure at Carnegie, did a pair of tunes; Jimmy Rushing did about ten minutes of blues, and "Hot Lips" Page, Buck Clayton and Leo Parker sat in on the final number of the evening.

Warren Ill

The Count was seriously handicapped by the loss of Earl Warren who collapsed from pleurisy at rehearsal the afternoon of the concert and was rushed to a hospital. His absence was felt in the selection of tunes used and in the premiere presentation of Basie's **Royal Suite**.

The Suite is a modern composition broken into six parts—the **King, Queen, Jack, Ten, Black Rose, Ace**. The **King**, apparently a boisterous soul, opens in up tempo that, for a while, gave the **Suite** no distinction from the jump tunes that had preseded the opus. The **Queen**, a more reserved type, changed things, however, with muted brass throughout. Then the **Jack**, a sly soul, came on in the person of George Matthews playing what might appropriately be described as dirty trombone. The **Ten**, which might mean the Count's fingers, featured those digits at the keyboard. The **Black Rose** was slow, not unlike the **Queen** in many respects, and the **Ace** came in to give the entire classic the proper rapid fire climax.

Publishers On Hand

Jack Bregman, who publishes the Basie originals, was on hand to close the deal of publishing the **Suite**.

After the Carnegie Hall concert Count Basie and his Orchestra set off on a tour of 30 one-nighters through Virginia, West Virginia, North Carolina, South Carolina, Tennessee, Alabama, Georgia, Mississippi and Florida, followed by a tour of midwest.

Wednesday 5 May 1948

Down Beat reviews Count Basie's latest Victor release:

Count Basie
*** *Guest In The Nest*
** *Money Is Honey*

The Count joins the list of those paying homage to jock Fred Robbins with this Basie-type riff manuscript. There's plenty of biting ensemble, a better-than-recently sax blend and good trumpet and tenor. **Honey** is a holler by Jimmy Rushing with short relief from trumpet and tenor. (**Victor 20-2771**)

Sunday 9 May 1948

Count Basie and his Orchestra play a concert at the Civic Opera House in Chicago.

Wednesday 19 May 1948

Down Beat reviews Count Basie's latest Victor album:

Count Basie

Backstage at Stuff's
My Buddy
Shine On Harvest Moon
St. Louis Boogie
Basie's Basement
I Never Knew
Swingin' The Blues

Album rating—***

Basie boosters will rejoice at the issuance of something brand spanking new in the way of a Basie album that isn't a re-hash of old sides. This is all small band, intimate stuff for the most part and though there is a fair portion of ensemble and a few horn solos, the emphasis is on the Count's uncomplicated piano style. All the odd-name tunes other than the standards are on the conventional 12 bar blues theme, which proves that the Count is a man of simple tastes, but also robs the album of a somewhat needed spark of originality. What there is in the way of solos is far above average, particularly the tenor rides, which are mostly melody line affairs, sotto tone in direct contrast to the more boisterous kind of reed that is all too common now. Nothing in here that hasn't been done by the Count before, but it's done particularly well. (**Victor album P-200**)

Monday 24 May 1948

Count Basie and his Orchestra open a one-week engagement at the Town Casino in Buffalo, New York.

Sunday 30 May 1948

Count Basie and his Orchestra close at the Town Casino in Buffalo, New York.

Plans Anniversary

New York—Count Basie has leased Carnegie Hall for a concert Saturday night, October 9, by way of marking the celebration of his 15th anniversary as a band leader. Present plans call for a program made up of a cavalcade of Basie compositions and hits with which his band has been associated and a performing visit by some of the Count's alumni, similar to but more elaborate than the program presented by the pianist-maestro last month.

Wednesday 2 June 1948

Down Beat reviews Count Basie's Decca album of reissues:

Count Basie

Boogie Woogie	*Hey Lawdy Mama*
How Long, How Long Blues	*The Fives*
The Dirty Dozens	*Oh! Red*
When the Sun Goes Down	*Dupree Blues*

Album rating—**

As a relief from the big band swing and small band bop of today these reissues of old Basie-piano-plus-rhythm sides make passable time passers but for serious listening you would have to be a long time Basie devotee to get much out of them. One of the album's main drawbacks is that anyone who has collected jazz for any time at all is bound to find several of these in his collection already. Irving Kolodin, in his well written comments anent the album says correctly that the Basie band derived its style from the Count's piano which is "dry, percussive and intensely rhythmic." By current standards his oversimplified piano **is** dry with its terribly commonplace blues patterns, much too frequent use of trills and sometimes sloppy execution. Even though they are well recorded sides and very representative of a period in which the Count played an important part they should have let them lay. (**Decca Album No. 152**)

Wednesday 16 June 1948

Down Beat reviews Count Basie's latest Victor release:

Count Basie

*** *It's Monday Every Day*
** *I've Only Myself To Blame*

Victor is certainly trying hard to make a commercial dance band out of the Count's, but it just isn't taking. Both of these are Jeanne Taylor vocals in front of reedy backgrounds and although a tenor peeks through like an oasis in the desert on **Blame** he has strict orders to stay on the melody—or else. After all if you want melody you can turn on Vaughn Monroe. Now there is a melody band. (**Victor 20-2850**)

Friday 18 June 1948

Count Basie and his Orchestra open a one-week engagement at the Riverside Theatre in Milwaukee.

Thursday 24 June 1948

Count Basie and his Orchestra close at the Riverside Theatre in Milwaukee.

Friday 2 July 1948

Count Basie and his Orchestra open a two-week engagement at Club Paradise in Atlantic City, New Jersey.

Thursday 15 July 1948

Count Basie and his Orchestra close at Club Paradise in Atlantic City, New Jersey.

Friday 16 July 1948

Count Basie and his Orchestra open a six-week engagement at the Strand Theatre in New York City. Billie Holiday shares the billing along with Stump & Stumpy and the Two Zephyrs. The movie presentation is Key Largo starring Humphrey Bogart. They play 5 shows a day, 7 days a week, for the next six weeks. During this engagement, Jo Jones leaves and is replaced by Gus Johnson.

Thursday 26 August 1948

Count Basie and his Orchestra close at the Strand Theatre in New York City.
With bookings scarce Basie is forced to disband but when an engagement at the Royal Roost comes up he quickly reorganizes.

Sunday 29 August 1948

Count Basie makes his television debut as guest star on 'Toast of the Town," a variety show emceed by Ed Sullivan on CBS in New York City. Basie appears as a solo pianist, without his band, accompanied by Ray Block's studio orchestra.

Thursday 9 September 1948

Count Basie and his Orchestra open a three-week engagement at the Royal Roost in New York City. Also on the bill are Dinah Washington and the Tadd Dameron Band.

OPENING TONITE
MONTE KAY presents
COUNT BASIE
& HIS GREAT *New* ORCHESTRA
EXTRA!
DINAH WASHINGTON
MILES DAVIS QUINTET
featuring MAX ROACH
The Metropolitan Bopera House
ROYAL ROOST
B'way at 47th St., (Opp. Strand Thea.)
90¢ CI 8-9559 90¢
ADMISSION

Basie Trims Before 'Roosting'

New York—The changed personnel of the Count Basie band as it opened at the Royal Roost here recently, included, left to right among the saxes: Paul Gonzales, tenor; Earl Warren, alto; Bernie Peacock, alto; Jack Washington, baritone; Wardell Gray, tenor. Trumpets were Clark Terry, Jimmy Nottingham, Harry Edison; trombones—George Matthews, Bill Johnson, Ted Donnelly, Dickie Wells. Shadow Wilson is the drummer.

COUNT BASIE ADDS 5 NEW MEMBERS TO BAND

Count Basie, the "Jump King of Swing," who has smashed every new attendance record in his current engagement at the Royal Roost nitery on Broadway, also smashed to smithereens the many rumors to the effect that he was coming up with a completely new band.

Contrary to unfounded reports that had been making the rounds of the music trade for several weeks, the Count came into the Roost with but five new faces in his outfit, two of whom, Earle Warren and Shadow Wilson, were merely returnees to the Basie fold.

Jimmy Rushing, whose blues-shouting has been a fixture with the band for more than 12 years remains at the head of the basie vocal corps, with singing saxophone star Earle Warren handling the ballad vocals.

Newcomers to the Basie band are Wardell Gray, exciting tenorman, high note trumpeter Jimmy Nottingham, and Cookie Palmer on the string bass. Gray was most recently with the Benny Goodman Sextet, while Nottingham is an alumnus of the Lionel Hampton and Charlie Barnet crews. Gray replaces the veteran Buddy Tate and will divide the hot tenor sax with Paul Gonsalves. Nottingham takes over the first trumpet chair of Ed Lewis, Palmer supplants Gene Wright in the Basie rhythm section on string bass.

The Basie band's complete personnel is as follows: Clark Terry, Emmett Berry, Jimmy Nottingham and "Sweets" Edison, trumpets; Dickie Wells, George Matthews, Bill Johnson and Ted Donnelly, trombones; Paul Gonsalves and Wardell Gray, tenor saxes; Earle Warren and Bernie Peacock, alto saxes; Jack Washington, baritone sax; Shadow Wilson, drums; Freddie Green, guitar; Cookie Palmer, bass.

Saturday 11 September 1948

Count Basie and his Orchestra broadcast over WMGM from the Royal Roost in New York City.
CLARK TERRY, EMMETT BERRY, JIMMY NOTTINGHAM, HARRY 'SWEETS' EDISON (trumpets); DICKIE WELLS, GEORGE MATTHEWS, BILL JOHNSON, TED DONNELLY (trombones); PAUL GONSALVES, WARDELL GRAY (tenor sax); EARLE WARREN (vocal/alto sax); BERNIE PEACOCK (alto sax); JACK WASHINGTON (baritone sax); COUNT BASIE (piano); FREDDIE GREEN (guitar); SINGLETON 'COOKIE' PALMER (bass); SHADOW WILSON (drums); JIMMY RUSHING (vocal)
DINAH WASHINGTON (vocal) is accompanied by pianist Beryl Booker and the Count Basie Orchestra
Futile Frustration / X-1 / Am I Asking Too Much? (vDW) / *Evil Gal Blues* (vDW) / *Good Bait / Moon Nocturne* (vEW) / *I Wanna Cry* (vDW) / *Paradise Squat / Blue Skies* (vJR) / *The King / Little Dog / Robbins' Nest / Blue Skies* (vJR) / *Far Cry*

Tuesday 14 September 1948

Count Basie and his Orchestra broadcast from the Royal Roost in New York City.
CLARK TERRY, EMMETT BERRY, JIMMY NOTTINGHAM, HARRY 'SWEETS' EDISON (trumpets); DICKIE WELLS, GEORGE MATTHEWS, BILL JOHNSON, TED DONNELLY (trombones); PAUL GONSALVES, WARDELL GRAY (tenor sax); EARLE WARREN, BERNIE PEACOCK (alto sax); JACK WASHINGTON (baritone sax); COUNT BASIE (piano); FREDDIE GREEN (guitar); SINGLETON 'COOKIE' PALMER (bass); SHADOW WILSON (drums)
X-1 / Spasmodic / The King / Good Bait / Far Cry

Thursday 16 September 1948

Singer Anita O'Day replaces Dinah Washington on the bill at the Royal Roost in New York City.

Friday 17 September 1948

Count Basie plays one number with a Benny Goodman group on Ted Husing's WMGM radio show in New York City.
BENNY GOODMAN (clarinet); WARDELL GRAY (tenor sax); COUNT BASIE (piano); BILLY BAUER (guitar); CLYDE LOMBARDI (bass); MEL ZELNICK (drums)
WMGM Jump (Bedlam)

Saturday 18 September 1948

Count Basie and his Orchestra broadcast over WMGM from the Royal Roost in New York City.
The Peacock / Swedish Pastry / Maybe You'll Be There / X-1 / Jimmy's Blues (vJR) / *San Jose / The King / One O'Clock Jump* (theme)

Saturday 25 September 1948

Count Basie and his Orchestra broadcast over WMGM from the Royal Roost in New York City.
CLARK TERRY (trumpet/vocal); EMMETT BERRY, JIMMY NOTTINGHAM, HARRY 'SWEETS' EDISON (trumpets); DICKIE WELLS, GEORGE MATTHEWS, BILL JOHNSON, TED DONNELLY (trombones); PAUL GONSALVES, WARDELL GRAY (tenor sax); EARLE WARREN, BERNIE PEACOCK (alto sax); JACK WASHINGTON (baritone sax); COUNT BASIE (piano); FREDDIE GREEN (guitar); SINGLETON 'COOKIE' PALMER (bass); SHADOW WILSON (drums); JIMMY RUSHING (vocal)
ANITA O'DAY (vocal) is accompanied by pianist Lou Stein and the Count Basie Orchestra
Spasmodic / Robbins' Nest / High Tide (vCT) / *San Jose / Hi Ho, Trailus Boot Whip* (vAO'D) / *That's That* (vAO'D) / *The King / Good Bait / Little Dog / The Peacock / Moon Nocturne* (vEW) / *Ain't It The Truth / Lazy Lady Blues* (vJR) / *Malaguena* (vAO'D)

Wednesday 29 September 1948

Count Basie and his Orchestra close at the Royal Roost in New York City.

Monday 4 October 1948

Count Basie and his Orchestra open a one-week engagement at the Three Rivers Inn in Syracuse, New York.

Sunday 10 October 1948

Count Basie and his Orchestra close at the Three Rivers Inn in Syracuse, New York.

Basie Jump Ends Syracuse Season

Syracuse—New York state's central city closed out a colorful summer season this month with banner names and lots of jump.

Biggest parade of entertainment names appeared at the Three Rivers inn, a recently remodeled club north of the city. Closing October 10, the final week, was Count Basie and his newly renovated group. He had been preceded in the spot by a list of stellars, including the Three Suns, Tony Pastor, Cab Calloway, Louis Armstrong, and Roy Eldridge.

Friday 22 October 1948

Count Basie and his Orchestra open a one-week engagement at the Paradise Theatre in Detroit.

Thursday 28 October 1948

Count Basie and his Orchestra close at the Paradise Theatre in Detroit.

Saturday 6 November 1948

Count Basie and his Orchestra play a one-nighter at the Armory in Gary, Indiana.

Monday 8 November 1948

Count Basie and his Orchestra play a one-nighter in Omaha, Nebraska.

Wednesday 10 November 1948

Count Basie and his Orchestra play a one-nighter at the Auditorium in Kansas City, Missouri.

Friday 12 November 1948

Count Basie and his Orchestra play a one-nighter at the Coliseum in Tulsa, Oklahoma.

Saturday 13 November 1948

Count Basie and his Orchestra play a one-nighter in Oklahoma City.

Sunday 14 November 1948

Count Basie and his Orchestra play a one-nighter in Fort Worth, Texas.

Monday 15 November 1948

Count Basie and his Orchestra play a one-nighter in Dallas, Texas.

Wednesday 17 November 1948

Down Beat reviews Count Basie's latest Victor release:

Count Basie
** *Just a Minute*
** *Bye, Bye Baby*

The Count and Dickie Wells wrote *Minute* which is a crisp, bright riff manuscript of the old Basie school. Muted trumpets with echoing trams take the opening lead followed by a Websterish tenor and tram bridge and an out chorus that merely duplicates No. 1.

Rushing hasn't changed his blues shout style by one inch since his old K. C. days, and he barrels through *Baby* with his accustomed vigor and enthusiasm. This is better than they have been doing by the Count. (**Victor 20-3051**)

Monday 13 December 1948

Count Basie and his Orchestra open a two-week engagement at the Click in Philadelphia.

Sunday 26 December 1948

Count Basie and his Orchestra close at the Click in Philadelphia.

Monday 27 December 1948

Count Basie and his Orchestra, with Buddy Rich on drums, appear on 'The Eddie Condon Floor Show' for WPIX-TV in New York City.

CLARK TERRY, EMMETT BERRY, JIMMY NOTTINGHAM, HARRY 'SWEETS' EDISON (trumpets); DICKIE WELLS, GEORGE MATTHEWS, BILL JOHNSON, TED DONNELLY (trombones); PAUL GONSALVES, WARDELL GRAY (tenor saxes); EARLE WARREN, BERNIE PEACOCK (alto saxes); JACK WASHINGTON (baritone sax); COUNT BASIE (piano), FREDDIE GREEN (guitar), RODNEY RICHARDSON (bass), BUDDY RICH (drums)

The King

COUNT BASIE (piano), RODNEY RICHARDSON (bass), BUDDY RICH (drums), BILLY ECKSTINE (vocal)

Caravan (vBE)

Count Basie Orchestra:

I Got Rhythm / Sent For You Yesterday (vJimmy Rushing) / *Paradise Squat*

JIMMY JONES (piano), RODNEY RICHARDSON (bass), SARAH VAUGHAN (vocal)

I'm Glad There Is You (vSV)

JIMMY JONES (piano), RODNEY RICHARDSON (bass), BUDDY RICH (drums), SARAH VAUGHAN, BILLY ECKSTINE (vocal)

Everything I Have Is Yours (vBE, SV)

Count Basie Orchestra:

The Blues (One O'Clock Jump)

Friday 31 December 1948

Count Basie and his Orchestra open a one-week engagement at the Apollo Theatre in New York City. Pearl Bailey shares top billing.

Thursday 6 January 1949

Count Basie and his Orchestra close at the Apollo Theatre in New York City.

Friday 7 January 1949

Count Basie and his Orchestra and Pearl Bailey open a one-week engagement at the Howard Theatre in Washington, D.C.

Thursday 13 January 1949

Count Basie and his Orchestra close at the Howard Theatre in Washington, D.C.

Friday 14 January 1949

Count Basie and his Orchestra and Pearl Bailey open a one-week engagement at the Royal Theatre in Baltimore.

Thursday 20 January 1949

Count Basie and his Orchestra close at the Royal Theatre in Baltimore.

Count Basie Blames Snarl In Contracts

Count Basie, the "Jump King of Swing," may disband his orchestra following the completion of his booking at the Royal Theatre in Baltimore on Jan. 20 because of a snarl in his contract negotiations at the William Morris Agency, it was revealed here this week.

Bands Affected

Basie's difficulties have arisen out of the fact that the William Morris Agency recently announced the curtailment of its band department and would release from existing contracts only leaders who agreed to shift to the General Artists Corporation, another agency with whom the Morris office reportedly had made an agreement to shift its name-band properties. In addition to Basie, these bands include Duke Ellington, Charlie Spivak, Buddy Rich, Claude Thornhill, Bobby Byrne, Hal McIntyre and others.

Rejects Switch

Several of these bands already have signed with General Artists after having been granted releases by William Morris. On the other hand, there have been several hold-outs, including Basie, who have rejected the switch in booking offices and consequently have been refused a release from the William Morris Agency.

Basie, who is one of the most desirable band properties in the business, has been approached with lucrative contract offers from several other agencies, which he is unable to accept because his William Morris contract still has almost a year to run, and he must remain technically under contract to that agency.

Basie has no booking commitments following Jan. 20, and at that time he may disband his orchestra and take his booking agency difficulties to the American Federation of Musicians for a ruling rather than attempt to continue under existing conditions.

Thursday 24 February 1949

Count Basie and his Orchestra open a one-week engagement at the Cotton Club (previously the Florentine Gardens) in Los Angeles.

Basie Switches To GAC From Morris

New York—Count Basie was added to the string of William Morris band attractions to switch to General Artists corporation, signing an exclusive agency management contract with GAC.

The office took over immediately and books the band for all dates following its Florentine Gardens, Hollywood, engagement.

Basie Reopens Coast Florentine

Hollywood—The lights were turned on again in February in the old Florentine Gardens—now the Cotton club—with a big new show and under new operation. Opening show was headlined by Count Basie, five acts including Marie Bryant, and a line of 12 girls.

A William Morris booking brought Basie into the spot, where he was said to get a guarantee of $3,500 weekly in addition to a cut of the admissions. Club policy calls for no cover but $1 a person admission.

Cotton Club is now being handled by Hal Stanley, who got a clean bill of operations from the unions which shuttered the Florentine when former ops fell behind in salaries.

Wednesday 2 March 1949

Count Basie and his Orchestra close at the Cotton Club in Los Angeles.

Monday 11 April 1949

Count Basie and his Orchestra record for Victor in Los Angeles.

CLARK TERRY (trumpet/vocal); EMMETT BERRY, JIMMY NOTTINGHAM, HARRY 'SWEETS' EDISON, GERALD WILSON (trumpets); DICKIE WELLS, GEORGE MATTHEWS, MELBA LISTON, TED DONNELLY (trombones); EARLE WARREN, CHARLIE PRICE (alto sax); PAUL GONSALVES, BILL PARKER (tenor sax); JACK WASHINGTON (baritone sax); COUNT BASIE (piano); FREDDIE GREEN (guitar); SINGLETON 'COOKIE' PALMER (bass); GEORGE 'BUTCH' BALLARD (drums); BOBBY TROUP (vocal)

Brand New Doll (vBT, 2 takes) / *Cheek To Cheek* (2 takes) / *Just An Old Manuscript*(2 takes) / *Katy* (2 takes)

Count Basie and his Orchestra open a one-week engagement at the Barbary Coast in San Francisco.

Just Like The Good Old Days In San Francisco
By RALPH GLEASON

San Francisco—Live bands have come back to the stage here. Now it's just like it used to be in the good old days, with a 25 cent admission charge before 1 p.m. and everything. Ellis Levey, operator of the Edgewater Beach ballroom, took over the Tivoli theater and opened with Count Basie, plus a vaudeville show which included the Edwards sisters and Lewis and White (quite possibly the two funniest guys around these days).

With the low admission price as a come-on, crowds were good throughout the Count's week. Levey is dickering with other name talent for appearances at the spot, including the King Cole Trio and Lionel Hampton.

Basie's band has had several recent changes. Butch Ballard, bop drummer previously with Cootie Williams, replaced Shadow Wilson on drums when the latter left to join Woody Herman. Butch hadn't had time to learn the book when they played Frisco, but gave every indication of a good future with the band. Steady, precise, and fast, he bops like mad and gives a very modern sound to the rhythm section.

Willie Parker, who used to be with Cootie and also with George Hudson's band in St. Louis, replaced Buddy Tate on tenor. Parker, like all the others of that name, is a bopster. Singleton Palmer, also from the Hudson band, is now on bass, Walter Page remaining in New York.

Nottingham Gone

Jimmy Nottingham, who played the one-niters preceding the Tivoli engagement with the band, went back to L.A., and the trumpet section now consists of Clark Terry, Gerald Wilson, Emmett Berry, and Harry Edison.

The trombone section lines up as follows: Bill Matthews, Dickie Wells, and Ted Donnelley. Paul Gonsalves is featured on tenor, and Earl Warren, much more active than he used to be, sparks the sax section and sings the ballads. Jack Washington on baritone and Charles Price on alto fill out the sax section.

Freddy Greene, the only surviving member of that famous trio of Page, Jones, and Greene is on guitar. Jimmy Rushing, no slimmer, still is singing the blues.

Sunday 17 April 1949

Count Basie and his Orchestra close at the Barbary Coast in San Francisco.

Make It 'Tex' Basie If It Means More Money

Portland, Ore.—Count Basie says business is bad. So bad that "our band would readily adopt the four-string geetar and nasal twang if it meant getting a little more of that loot."

Basie does not dislike bop, even though his band does play little of it. As the Count says, "This is 1949. Next year won't be 1942.

"Anything that's new can't be all bad. Some of the musicians playing bop may be pleasing themselves first and the people second, but for that matter, that's what I'm doing every time I play the organ in a stage show. I'm still learning to play Hammond, and every time I play it, it's with *my* [er] in mind first."

Amazed

[ ] Basie recorded four sides in L.A. [fo]r Victor, and, incidentally, was [am]azed when shown his *Piano [Rh]ythms* album as it was pressed [on] 45 rpm discs. The Count had [ne]ver seen the album, or any of [his] much-discussed slow-speed [ma]tters.

[ ]uartet of RCA etchings includ-

[ ]ed *Brand New Dolly*, *Cheek To Cheek*, an instrumental; *Katy*, a Gerald Wilson original, featuring trumpeter Clark Terry and trombonist George Matthews, and *Old Manuscript*, a Don Redman original.

Basie intended to do a few guest TV shots in NYC, in June, using a small unit and playing organ. He displayed pride over his newest acquisition, drummer Butch Ballard.

—Ted Hallock

Robbins Publishing Jazz Book Series

New York—Series of books on jazz are to be published by Jack Robbins. First in the group is *Inside Be-bop*, by Leonard Feather, now on the stands.

It will be followed by *Inside Jazz*, as told to Feather by Louis Armstrong; *Meet Mr. Ellington*, a series of pieces on the Duke; and some method books on bop.

Basie and the band also play in Portland, Oregon, where Basie is interviewed by Ted Hallock, before heading east on the one-nighter trail.

Friday 20 May 1949

Count Basie and his Orchestra open a one-week engagement at the State Theatre in Cincinnati, Ohio.

Down Beat reviews a Count Basie reissue:

Count Basie
*** *Exactly Like You*
*** *Jumpin' at the Woodside*
Two re-released sides from the halcyon days of the Basie mob, when Lester and Herschel were blowing the tenor chairs and there was the free float of a rhythm section convinced it was the best in the country. Strange how once musicians lose that conviction, their playing deteriorates. (**Coral 60037**)

Chopsticks?

Portland, Ore.—Two hardy perennials, Bill Basie and his traditional plaid shirt and checked jacket, and *Beat* correspondent Ted Hallock, right in there. Drummer Hallock interviewed the Count recently on his *Start The Music* program here, which is aired 2-4 p.m. weekdays on KPOJ.

Thursday 26 May 1949
Count Basie and his Orchestra close at the State Theatre in Cincinnati, Ohio.

Friday 17 June 1949
Down Beat reviews Count Basie's latest Victor release:

> **Count Basie**
> *** *Cheek To Cheek*
> ** *Brand New Dolly*
> This is something! Basie trying to play a Lunceford bounce, modified by bop interjections and Les Brown brass ensembles. Rhythm section moves easily under Basie's usual piano solo. I still can't get over that ensemble brass, though. You can win money on the first section it isn't Basie. He backs the muted trumpet on celeste too! Even Russ Morgan-style trombone in the release! This is really fishing for the buck! *Dolly* is a novelty. (**Victor 20-2439**)

Sunday 19 June 1949
Count Basie appears as a guest on WPIX-TV's 'Eddie Condon Floor Show' in New York City.
COUNT BASIE (organ); EDDIE CONDON (guitar); JACK LESBERG (bass); GEORGE WETTLING (drums)
Untitled / Blues In E-Flat

Monday 20 June 1949
Count Basie and his Orchestra open a three-night engagement at the Palace Theatre in Youngstown, Ohio.

Wednesday 22 June 1949
Count Basie and his Orchestra close at the Palace Theatre in Youngstown, Ohio.

Wednesday 29 June 1949
Count Basie and his Orchestra record for Victor in New York City.
CLARK TERRY (trumpet/vocal); EMMETT BERRY, JIMMY NOTTINGHAM, HARRY 'SWEETS' EDISON, GERALD WILSON (trumpets); DICKIE WELLS, GEORGE MATTHEWS TED DONNELLY (trombones); EARLE WARREN, CHARLIE PRICE (alto sax); PAUL GONSALVES, BILL PARKER (tenor sax); JACK WASHINGTON (baritone sax); COUNT BASIE (piano); FREDDIE GREEN (guitar); SINGLETON 'COOKIE' PALMER (bass); GEORGE 'BUTCH' BALLARD (drums); JIMMY RUSHING (vocal)
She's A Wine-O (vJR) / Did You Ever See Jackie Robinson Hit That Ball? / Shoutin' Blues / After You've Gone (vJR)

Friday 1 July 1949
Count Basie and his Orchestra open a one-week engagement at the Apollo Theatre in New York City.

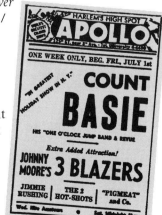

Thursday 7 July 1949
Count Basie and his Orchestra close at the Apollo Theatre in New York City.

Friday 22 July 1949
Count Basie and his Orchestra record for Victor in New York City.
CLARK TERRY (trumpet/vocal); EMMETT BERRY, JIMMY NOTTINGHAM, HARRY 'SWEETS' EDISON, GERALD WILSON (trumpets); DICKIE WELLS, GEORGE MATTHEWS TED DONNELLY (trombones); EARLE WARREN, CHARLIE PRICE (alto sax); PAUL GONSALVES, BILL PARKER (tenor sax); JACK WASHINGTON (baritone sax); COUNT BASIE (piano); FREDDIE GREEN (guitar); SINGLETON 'COOKIE' PALMER (bass); GEORGE 'BUTCH' BALLARD (drums); JIMMY RUSHING (vocal)
Wonderful Thing / The Slider / Mine Too / Walking Slow Behind You (vJR)

Basie In Bop City

New York—For his stint at Bop City starting Aug 4, Count Basie is using the following lineup: trumpets—Emmett Berry, Harry Edison, Jim Nottingham, and Clark Terry; trombones—Dickie Wells, George Matthews, and Theodore Donnelly; saxes—Earl Warren and Charles Price, altos; Paul Gonsalves and Willie Parker, tenors; rhythm—Singleton Palmer, bass; Freddy Green, guitar; Butch Ballard, drums, and Jimmy Rushing on vocals.

Thursday 4 August 1949
Count Basie and his Orchestra open a three-week engagement at Bop City in New York City.

Friday 5 August 1949
Count Basie and his Orchestra record for Victor in New York City.
CLARK TERRY (trumpet/vocal); EMMETT BERRY, JIMMY NOTTINGHAM, HARRY 'SWEETS' EDISON, GERALD WILSON (trumpets); DICKIE WELLS, GEORGE MATTHEWS TED DONNELLY (trombones); EARLE WARREN, CHARLIE PRICE (alto sax); PAUL GONSALVES, BILL PARKER, JIMMY TAYLOR (tenor sax); JACK WASHINGTON (baritone sax); COUNT BASIE (piano); FREDDIE GREEN (guitar); SINGLETON 'COOKIE' PALMER (bass); GEORGE 'BUTCH' BALLARD (drums); BILLY VALENTINE (vocal)
The Slider / Normania / Rocky Mountain Blues (vJR)

Wednesday 24 August 1949
Count Basie and his Orchestra close at Bop City in New York City.

Friday 26 August 1949
Count Basie appears on the cover of *Down Beat*.

Count Basie and his Orchestra open a one-week engagement at the Earle Theatre in Philadelphia.

NYC Rushes Jazz Return

DOWN BEAT

August 26, 1949

Finds Great New Singer

Prize List Grows In Contest

Microgroove Speed War Nears End

On The Cover
Sarah, Diz, Count

25 cents

Thursday 1 September 1949
Count Basie and his Orchestra close at the Earle Theatre in Philadelphia.

Friday 2 September 1949
Count Basie and his Orchestra open a one-week engagement at the Howard Theatre in Washington, D.C.

Thursday 8 September 1949
Count Basie and his Orchestra close at the Howard Theatre in Washington, D.C.

Thursday 22 September 1949
Count Basie and his Orchestra close at the Regal Theatre in Chicago.

Friday 23 September 1949
Down Beat reviews Count Basie's latest Victor release:

Count Basie

*** *Shoutin' Blues*
** *Did You See Jackie Robinson Hit That Ball?*

Shoutin' is the best side Basie has dished up for a while. However, it's one of the weirdest melanges you've heard. Superimposed on the Basie tradition of sax riff repeated, broken up with brass figures and piano tinklings, are bop figures and harmonic approaches. Man, I'll be schizoid, yet! However, the band does sound a little happier in its work than it has recently. Flopover is by Buddy Johnson, about a man who well deserves the accolades coming his way. The song isn't much, has a trumpet solo much like Eldridge in his better days. **(Victor 20-2513)**

Thursday 23 October 1949
Count Basie records with the Harry Sosnick Orchestra in New York City.
Red Bank Boogie / Basie Boogie

Thursday 24 November 1949
Count Basie and his Orchestra open a three-night engagement at the Riviera in St. Louis, Missouri.

Saturday 26 November 1949
Count Basie and his Orchestra close at the Riviera in St. Louis, Missouri.

Monday 5 December 1949
Count Basie and his Orchestra open a one-week engagement at the Blue Note in Chicago.

Sunday 11 December 1949
Count Basie and his Orchestra close at the Blue Note in Chicago.

Wednesday 21 December 1949
Count Basie and his Orchestra open a three-night engagement at the New Orleans Club in New Orleans.

Friday 23 December 1949
Count Basie and his Orchestra close at the New Orleans Club in New Orleans.

1950

Sunday 8 January 1950
Count Basie breaks up his big band.

BASIE DISBANDS

Friday 16 September 1949
Count Basie and his Orchestra open a one-week engagement at the Regal Theatre in Chicago.

INDEX

Abadias 14
Abrams, Harold 99
Aces And Faces 81
Ad-Lib Blues 43
Adventure 92
After A While 81
After Theatre Jump 73
After You've Gone 14, 68, 109
Ain't But The One 74
Ain't It The Truth? 60, 74–75, 86, 106
Ain't Misbehavin' 74
Airmail Special 51, 54, 60, 68
Alexander, Willard 10, 38, 44–45
Allen, Henry 'Red' 49
Alley, Vernon 62–63
All Of Me 54, 67, 81
All Or Nothing At All 44, 46
Always 13
Am I Asking Too Much? 105
Ammons, Albert 49
Andre, Vernon 45
And So Little Time 74–75
And The Angels Sing 28
Andy's Blues 84–85
Apollo Theatre, NYC 12–13, 15, 18, 20, 28, 35, 38–39, 43, 46, 49, 55–56, 64, 71, 73, 79, 87, 90, 95–96, 100, 102, 107, 109
April In My Heart 23
Are You Living, Old Man? 85
Armstrong, Louis 94, 106
Arthur, Zinn 18
A Sailboat In The Moonlight 13–14
As Long As I Live 44
As Long As I Love You (Jeannette) 6
A Study In Brown 14–15
Auld, George 44, 76, 85
Aunt Hagar's Country Home 75
Avalon 75
Avenue C 72, 74–75, 78, 80–82, 84
'Ay Now 56
Baby, Don't Be Mad At Me 101
Baby, Don't Tell On Me 28–29, 36, 54
Baby Girl 13–14
Baby It's Up To You 85
Baby, Won't You Please Come Home? 68, 72–73, 79
Backstage At Stuff's 97, 103
Bailey, Bob 87–88, 90, 92–93, 95, 98, 100, 102
Bailey, Buster 12, 14
Bailey, Mildred 80
Bailey, Pearl 84, 99, 107
Baker, Ann 95, 98
Ballard, George 'Butch' 108–109
Band Box Shuffle 5
Barefield, Eddie 8, 9
Barnet, Charlie 38, 49, 56, 67, 71, 105
Baron, Paul 80
Bascomb, Paul 45–46
Basie Blues 58, 60, 74
Basie Boogie 50–51, 54, 62, 64, 68–69, 73–75, 77–79, 84, 90, 98, 110
Basie, Diane (daughter) 73
Basie, Harvey Lee (father) 4
Basie, Lilly Ann (mother) 4, 54
Basie's Basement 97, 103
Basie Special 49
Basie Strides Again (Along Avenue C) 75
Basin Street Blues 18
Bates, Peg Leg 73
Bauer, Billy 106
Beaver Junction 75
Beau Brummel 46
Beneke, Tex 46, 55
Benny, Jack 79
Benny, Milton 77
Benny's Bugle 44
Berigan, Bunny 11, 39, 49
Bernstein, Artie 12, 44, 46
Berry, Chu 26
Berry, Emmett 79, 86, 88, 90, 92–98, 100–102, 105–109
Berry, Leroy 5, 6, 9
Between The Devil And The Deep Blue Sea 33
B-flat Blues 83–84
Bied, Dan 98
Big Chief De Sota 11
Bill's Mill 95–98
Blake, Jerry 58
Blame It On My Last Affair 26, 29
Block, Martin 21, 44–45, 81
Block, Ray 105
Bloom, Murray 99
Blow Top 38, 41
Blue And Sentimental 21, 100, 102
Blue Ball 13
Blue Jazz 60
Blue Lester 75
Blue Lou 11, 54, 74–75
Blue Room Jump 74–75, 80
Blue Shadows And White Gardenias 56
Blues I Like To Hear 29
Blues In E-Flat 109
Blues In The Dark 16
Blues (I Still Think Of Her) 36, 45
Blues Jam 78
Blue House 92
Blue Skies 85–86, 90, 92–93, 105
Body And Soul 84, 95
Bolero At The Savoy 29
Boogie Woogie 10, 12–14, 18, 23, 30, 85, 104
Boogie Woogie Blues 68
Boogie Woogie Boys 35
Boo-Hoo 12, 13
Booker, Beryl 105
Boot It 5
Born To Love 13
Bostic, Earl 45
Bouncin' Round 6
Bowen, Bill 39
Bradley, Will 49, 54
Brand New Dolly 109
Brand New Wagon 95, 100
Break A Day Shufflle 6
Bregman, Jack 72, 103
Broadway 44, 54, 75
Brooks, Bobby 69
Brooks, Dudley 41
Brown, Johnny 59
Brown, Les 109
Brown, Pete 39
Bruce, Ramon 96
Brunis, George 29
Bryant, Freddie 75
Bryant, Marie 107
Bugle Blues 13, 60, 76
Bugle Call Rag 14, 46, 54, 76
Burke, Sonny 51, 57
Burns, Bob 62
But Definitely 10, 11
Butterbeans & Susie 15
Buzz Me 100
Byas, Don 46, 48–54, 56, 58–62, 64–66, 71–72, 76
Bye Bye Baby 101, 106
Byrne, Bobby 107
Cabin In The Sky 68
Cabin Of Dreams 14
Café Society Blues 60, 76
Callender, Red 96
Call Me Darling 75, 81
Calloway, Blanche 7
Calloway, Cab 60, 84, 106
Can't Help Lovin' Dat Man 15
Caravan 107
Carlson, Frankie 84
Carnegie Hall, NYC 24, 35, 49, 66, 74, 102–103
Carney, Harry 11
Carpenter, Thelma 63–64, 67, 69–74, 76–82
Carr, Leroy 76
Carrington, Jerome 10
Carter, Benny 23, 38, 46, 55–56, 67
Casey, Al 23
Charlie's Dream 43
Cheek To Cheek 109
Cherokee 26, 30
Choo Choo Swing (movie) 69
Christian, Charlie 43–44, 46
Christopher Columbus 10
Circus In Rhythm 75
Clap Hands, Here Comes Charlie 31
Clarke, Kenny 50
Clayton, Buck 10–17, 21, 23, 25–31, 33, 35–36, 38, 40–41, 43–46, 48–54, 56–62, 64–66, 71–73, 75–76, 82–83, 87, 102–103
Cless, Rod 29
Cole, Cozy 12, 15
Cole, Nat 'King' 68, 85, 108
Collins, Shad 25–31, 33
Coming-Out Party 54
Condon, Eddie 11, 106, 109
Confessin' 10
Countless Blues 23
Cox, Ida 35
Crawford, Jimmy 98–99
Crazy House (movie) 68–69
Crosby, Bing 85
Crosby, Bob 30
Cuffee, Ed 46, 48, 50, 50–51
Daddy-O 84
Dameron, Tadd 105
Dance Of The Gremlins [KMA] 64, 68–69, 74–75
Dancing Derby 11
Dandridge, Dorothy 62, 94
Danny Boy 92, 98
Dark Rapture 23
Darn That Dream 36
Dear Old Southland 10–13, 55
Deep In The Blues 46
De Haven, Gloria 78
Delta Rhythm Boys 69, 77, 85–86
Destination K.C. 73
Dexter, Dave 49, 51, 55
Dickenson, Vic 36, 38, 41, 44–46
Dickie's Dream 31, 33
Did You Ever See Jackie Robinson Hit That Ball? 109–110
Diggin' For Dex 50–51, 53–54, 60, 74–75
Dinah 11, 13, 15, 62, 73, 79
Doggett, Bill 85
Doggin' Around 14, 21
Donahue, Sam 45, 51
Donnelly, Ted 73–74, 76–81, 83–86, 88, 92–93, 95, 98, 100–102, 105–109
Do Nothin' Till You Hear From Me 72–73, 75, 77–78
Don't Believe Everything You Dream 72–73
Don't Cry, Baby 73–74, 81
Don't Ever Let Me Be Yours 92
Don't Get Around Much Anymore 68
Don't Worry 'Bout Me 28–29
Don't You Miss Your Baby? 14
Don't You Want A Man Like Me 100, 102
Dorsey, George 79, 84–86, 88
Dorsey, Tommy 39, 46, 62, 78–79
Douglas, Freddy 4
Down, Down, Down 50, 54
Down For Double 54, 57, 73, 75, 92
Do You Wanna Jump, Children? 23
Draftin' Blues 44, 46
Dreamboat 13
Drop Me Off At Harlem 10
Dupree Blues 25, 104
Duration Blues 84
Durbin, Deanna 79
Durham, Eddie 5–6, 9, 13–17, 21, 23, 51
Easy Does It 36
Easy Living 12, 14, 18
Easy To Love 10
Ebbins, Milt 44–45, 51, 54, 67, 78, 81, 98, 102
Ebony Rhapsody 10, 36
Eckstine, Billy 96, 107
Edison, Harry 17, 21, 23, 25–26, 28–31, 33, 35–36, 38, 40–41, 44–46, 48, 50–54, 56, 58–62, 67–65, 70, 72–88, 90, 92–96, 98, 100–102, 105–109
Eldridge, Joe 39
Eldridge, Roy 39, 55, 70, 96, 106
Ellington, Duke 10–11, 52, 60, 71, 107
Elman, Ziggy 46, 79
Elmer's Tune 54
Embraceable You 78
Emge, Charlie 84
Energetic Stomp 14
Evans, Herschel 11–17, 21, 23, 25–27, 29, 31, 52, 94
Evelina 82
Evenin' 10, 11, 14, 41, 75, 84
Everybody's Laughin' 23
Every Day Blues 5
Everything I Have Is Yours 107
Every Tub 17–18, 53, 64, 75, 90, 92, 94
Evil Blues 26
Evil Gal Blues 105
Exactly Like You 12, 68, 75, 108
Famous Door, 52nd St., NYC 22–23, 31
Fancy Meeting You 50–51
Far Cry 105
Fare Thee Honey, Fare Thee Well 25, 33
Farewell Blues 18, 60, 76
Feather, Leonard 79
Feather Merchant 54, 86
Feedin' The Bean 48
Fields, Harry 84
Fiesta In Blue 53
Fitzgerald, Ella 11, 16, 81, 96, 103
Five O'Clock Whistle 44
Fla-Ga-La-Pa 92, 94
Flamingo 54
Foolin' Myself 12
For Sentimental Reasons 11
For The Good Of The Country 56, 60
Frazier, George 51
Free Eats 95–98
Freeman, Slim 9
Futile Frustration 95, 97, 100, 105
Gable, Clark 61
Garrison, Josephine 9
Gee, Baby, Ain't I Good To You? 75, 78
George, Karl 16, 83, 85
Georgianna 16
Get Goin' 6
Get It 68
Get On Board, Little Chillun 69
Getting Some Fun Out Of Life 14
Ghost Of A Chance 75
Gibson, Margie 52
Gillespie, Dizzy 72, 96
Goin' To Chicago 27, 48, 54
Goldberg, Doc 55
Goldner, Larry 84
Gone With What Wind 38, 41, 44, 49
Gonsalves, Paul 92–93, 95–98, 100–102, 105–109
Good Bait 105–106
Goodbye, Baby 92
Good For Nothin' Joe 86
Goodman, Benny 9, 11–12, 16, 35, 38, 40–41, 43–46, 55–56, 58, 81, 92–93, 105–106
Good Morning Blues 13–15, 18, 44, 59
Gotta Be This Or That 84–86
Grable, Betty 83
Grand Slam 85
Granz, Norman 77, 92–93
Gray, Wardell 105–107
Green 68
Green, Freddie 11–17, 21, 23, 25–31, 33, 35–36, 38–39, 41, 43–46, 48, 50, 52–56, 58–62, 64–65, 73–81, 83–86, 88, 92–93, 95–98, 100–102, 105–109
Greer, Sonny 4
Guest In A Nest 101, 103
Hall, Edmond 13
Hallock, Ted 108
Hammond, John 9–12, 15, 35, 51, 87
Ham'n'Eggs 33
Hampton, Lionel 48, 58, 61–62, 79, 86, 96, 105, 108
H And J 48, 51, 54
Hanighen, Bernie 13
Happy Feet 10, 13
Harlem Sandman 62
Harlem Shout 10
Harris, Phil 68
Hart, Clyde 74
Harvard Blues 54, 75, 78–79, 81–82, 98
Have You Any Castles, Baby? 14
Hawkins, Coleman 31, 36, 38–39, 46, 48, 52, 67, 75
Hayes, Edgar 24
Hayes, Thamon 5, 6, 8
Haymes, Dick 83, 90
He Ain't Got Rhythm 11, 14
Heard, J.C. 39
Heaven Help This Heart Of Mine 14
Heidt, Horace 67
Henderson, Fletcher 9
Henry, Lou 4
Here Comes Marjorie 6
Here It Is Tomorrow Again 23
Herman, Woody 11, 68, 103, 108
He's Funny That Way 14
He's Home For A Little While 82
Hey, John! 85
Hey Lawdy Mama 23, 104
Hey, Pretty Baby 101
Hey, Rube! 74–75, 81, 84
Hicks, Billy 13
Hicks, Bobby 14
Higginbotham, J.C. 46, 49, 55–56
High Ball 72
High Tide 83, 85–87, 91–92, 95, 106
Hi Ho, Trailus Boot Whip 106
Hill, Elton 38
Hill, Jimmy 4
Hines, Earl 40, 64
Hit Parade of 1943 (movie) 62–63
Hob Nail Boogie 92, 95
Hodges, Johnny 12
Hoefer, George 59
Holiday, Billie 11–16, 18, 23, 31, 35, 39, 49, 103–104
Hollywood Jump 33
Honeysuckle Rose 11, 14, 44, 79, 81, 84
Hopkins, Claude 82
Horne, Lena 49, 67, 71–72, 84–86
Hot Coffee 10
House Hop 10, 13
Houseman, Al 102
How Am I To Know 85
Howard Theatre, Washington DC 29, 35, 58, 64–65, 70, 79–80, 84, 96, 101–102, 107, 110
How Blue The Night 75
How Could You? 14
How Long Blues? 23, 30, 60, 76
Hudson, George 108
Huff Puff 10
Humes, Helen 22–23, 25–26, 28–31, 33, 36, 41, 44–46, 49–50, 81, 102
Hunt, George 10–13
Husing, Ted 106
I Ain't Got Nobody 11, 14, 18, 27
I Ain't Mad At You 92
I Can't Believe That You're In Love With Me 31
I Can't Get Started 13–15, 18, 23
I Couldn't Sleep A Wink Last Night 73–75
I Cried For You 11, 14
I Didn't Know About You 80–82
I Do Mean You 48, 54
I Don't Know If I'm Coming Or Going 14
I Don't Know Why 92
I Dream Of You 74–75
If I Could Be With You (One Hour Tonight) 28, 30, 36
If I Didn't Care 28
I Found A New Baby 12–14, 18, 72–75, 85
I Found You In The Rain 54
If We Never Meet Again 11
If You Ever Should Leave 14
I Got Rhythm 11, 13–14, 36, 56, 80, 84, 107
I Guess I'll Have To Dream The Rest 53
I Keep Remembering 14
I Left My Baby 33
I'll Always Be In Love 10
I'll Always Be In Love With You 13–14
I'll Be Seeing You 78
I'll Forget 46
I'll Get By 12
I'll Never Be The Same 12
I'll Never Fail You 23
Imagination 9
I'm Always In Love With You 10
I'm Beginning To See The Light 82, 85
I'm Confessin' 80
I'm Drowning In Your Deep Blue Eyes 95
I'm Fer It, Too 81
I'm Glad There Is You 107
I'm Gonna Move To The Outskirts Of Town 58, 60
I'm Gonna See My Baby 81, 84
I'm Gonna Sit Right Down And Write Myself A Letter 74–75, 78
I'm In Love With Someone 74–76
I'm Just A Lucky So-And-So 92
I'm Making Believe 80
I'm Not Complainin' 46
I'm Tired Of Waiting For You 50
I'm Pulling Through 39
I Must Have That Man 11, 13–14
Indiana 75
Indifference Blues 51
I Never Knew 36, 43, 75, 84, 97, 103
Ingram, Rex 78
Ink Spots 96
Inman, Bob 11, 13, 18
Irresistible You 74
I Should Care 81, 84
I Struck A Match In The Dark 54
I Surrender Dear 10–11, 13
It Counts A Lot 45
It's De-Lovely 10
It's Monday Every Day 101, 104
It's Sand, Man 60, 63–64, 72, 75, 79–80, 86
It's Square But It Rocks 46
It's The Same Old South 45
It's Torture 41, 44
I've Got A Date With A Dream 23
I've Got My Eye On You 13
I've Had This Feeling Before 73–74
I've Only Myself To Blame 101, 104
I Wanna Be Around My Baby All The Time 6
I Wanna Cry 105
I Want A Little Girl 23, 41, 44, 54, 75
I Wish I Could Be Blue 6
I Won't Say I Will 68
Jacquet, Illinois 78–80, 86–88, 90, 92–94, 96, 102–103
Jaeger, Harry 44
Jalousie 98
James, Harry 23, 46, 55, 81, 90, 98
James, Ida 68
Jameson, Ed 67
Jammin' On A V-Disc 96
Jam Session 13
Jangled Nerves 10
Jarvis, Al 68
Jazz Me Blues 68, 74–75, 86, 92
Jenkins, George 96
Jenney, Jack 39
Jimmy's Blues 80–81, 85, 98, 106
Jimmy's Boogie Woogie 83
Jimmy's Idea 100
Jingle Bells 85
Jive At Five 26
Jivin' Joe Jackson 85–86, 88
Jivin' The Keys 14
John's Idea 13, 15
Johnson, Bill 92–93, 95, 98, 100–102, 105–107
Johnson, Buddy 110
Johnson, Gus 104
Johnson, James P. 4, 35
Johnson, J.J. 79, 83, 85–86, 88, 92
Johnson, Joe 'Ziggy' 98
Johnson, Margaret 'Queenie' 23
Johnson, Marvin 61–62, 64–65
Johnson, Maxine 50, 81–82
Johnson, Pete 10, 49
Johnson, Puss 31
Jones, Jimmy 107
Jones, Jo 9–17, 21, 23, 25–31, 33, 35–36, 38, 40–41, 43–46, 48–50, 52–54, 56, 58–62, 64–66, 71, 73–81, 87–88, 90, 92–93, 95, 97–101, 104
Jones, Spike 62
Journey To A Star 74–75
Jump For Me 28, 31
Jumpin' At Ten 85
Jumpin' At The Woodside 23, 53, 59, 72, 74–76, 78, 80, 84–85, 92, 108
Jump, Lester, Jump 75
Jump The Blues Away 46
Just A Minute 101, 106
Just An Old Manuscript 81
Just A-Settin' And A-Rockin' 85
Kansas City Keys [Basie Boogie] 74
Kansas City Stride 74–76, 78–80
Kapp, Dave 10
Kapp, Jack 70
Kardos, Gene 18
K.C.Diner 75
Keith, Jimmy 78
Kenton, Stan 103
Kersey, Ken 49
Kessel, Barney 85
Keyes, Joe 9, 11
Khaki Tan 72
Killian, Al 36, 38, 41, 44–46, 48, 50, 52–54, 56, 58–62, 64–65, 67, 73–78, 80–81, 83
King Joe 53
King Porter Stomp 12–13, 18, 74
King Sisters 84
Kirby, John 39, 49, 56
Kirk, Andy 10
KMA [Dance Of The Gremlins] 64
Knock Me A Kiss 69
Kolodin, Irving 104
Kramer, Maria 71–72, 81
Krippen, Katie 4
Krupa, Gene 39, 55–57, 81
Kyser, Kay 63
Lafayette 9
Laughing At Life 39
Lazy Lady Blues 88, 91–92, 106
Lee, George 5, 9

INDEX

Leonard, Harlan 5, 6, 10, 58, 78
Lesberg, Jack 109
Lester Leaps Again 73
Lester Leaps In 31, 33
Lester's Dream 43
Let Me Dream 14
Let Me See 36, 51
Let's Call The Whole Thing Off 14
Let's Jump 75–76, 78
Let's Make Hey! While The Moon Shines 36, 40
Let's Mop It 75
Levine, Henry 49
Lewis, Ed 5–6, 12–17, 21, 23, 25–28, 28–31, 33, 36, 38, 41, 44–46, 48, 50, 52–54, 56, 58–62, 64–65, 73–74, 76–79, 83, 85–86, 88, 92–93, 95, 98, 100–102, 105
Lewis, Martha 84
Lim, Harry 73
Limehouse Blues 10, 11
Listen My Children, And You Shall Hear 13
Liston, Melba 108
Little Dog 105–106
Live And Love Tonight 27
Liza Lee 6
Loch Lomond 16
Loew's State Theatre, NYC 37
Lombardi, Clyde 106
London Bridge Is Falling Down 23
Lonesome Miss Pretty 29
Long, Avon 20
Lopin' 97
Louise 13, 14
Louisiana 36
Louis, Joe 53
Love Is In The Air Tonight 14
Love Jumped Out 44, 52–53, 72, 81
Love Me Or Leave Me 27, 54
Love, Preston 69, 70, 79, 83, 85–86, 88, 92–93, 95, 98, 100–101
Lovetts, Baby 58
Lunceford, Jimmie 13, 41, 67, 98
Lyman, Abe 63
McCarthy, Jim 56, 91
McDaniel, Hattie 55
McGarity, Lou 55
McIntyre, Hal 107
McKinley, Ray 49
McKinney, Ed 7
McQueen, Butterfly 68
McTear, Claude 9
McVea, Jack 95
McWashington, Willie 5, 6, 9
Mack's Rhythm 6
Magnolias In The Moonlight 11
Malaguena 106
Mama Don't Want No Peas An' Rice An' Coconut Oil 21
Man Of The Family (movie) 68–69
Margie 11
Marie 18
Marsala, Joe 39
Marshall, Joe 81
Martin, Freddy 68
Martin, Skippy 49
Mary Had A Little Lamb 11–12
Mary Lee 5
Matlock, Matty 84
Matthews, Dave 78
Matthews, George 86–88, 92–93, 95, 97–98, 100–103, 105–109
Maybe You'll Be There 106
Mayflower 13
Me And The Blues 95–96
Mean To Me 12, 85, 92
Meet Me At No Special Place 95, 98
Melody In F 18
Me, Myself And I 13, 14
Mezzrow, Mezz 11
Milenberg Joys 9, 14
Miller, Glenn 63, 69, 84
Miller, Taps 83, 98
Millinder, Lucky 17, 38
Mills Brothers 67
Mills, Irving 11
Mine Too 109
Mingus, Charlie 85
Minor, Dan 9–17, 21, 23, 25–31, 33, 36, 38, 41, 43–46, 48, 50
Miss Thing 28, 30
Mr Robert's Roost 106
Mondello, Toots 46, 55
Money Is Honey 101, 103
Monroe, Vaughn 67, 104
Moonlight Serenade 31
Moon Nocturne 53–55, 105–106
Moore, Ann 84–88, 92–96
Moore, Bobby 12–13, 15
More Than You Know 54, 57, 77–78
Morgan, Catherine 8, 61, 64, 73
Morgan, Russ 109
Morris, William 38, 44–46, 60, 94, 107
Morse, Ella Mae 100
Morton, Benny 13–17, 21, 23, 25–26, 28–31, 33, 36
Mostel, Zero 73
Moten, Bennie 5, 6, 7, 8, 9
Moten, Buster 5, 6, 10
Moten Swing 9–15, 41, 54
Moten Twist 14

Mundy, Jimmy
Murphy, Rose 68
Music Makers 46
Musso, Vido 15, 55
Mutton Leg 92, 94, 9...
My Blue Heaven 11
My Buddy 97, 103
My First Thrill 11, 13
My Heart Belongs To Daddy
My Ideal 74–75
My Man 15–16
My Melancholy Baby 53, 74
My Old Flame 53, 57
My Silent Love 85
My Wanderin' Man 44
My, What A Fry! 60, 74–75, 78–79, 8...
Nagasaki 11, 74
Nemo, Henry 56
Never In A Million Years 13
Newman, Joe 71, 73–74, 76–78, 80–81, 85–86, 88, 92
New Moten Stomp 6
New Orleans 9
Newton, Frankie 11, 38
New Vine Street Blues 5
Nice Work If You Can Get It 15, 18
Nicholas, Harold 94
Night And Day 35
9.20 Special 48, 52–54, 73–74, 77, 92, 100
Nobody Knows 29, 35
No Name 9
Norman, Gene 100
Normania 109
Norvo, Red 71
Nottingham, Jimmy 105–109
Now That I Need You 6
Now Will You Be Good? 17
Oakley, Helen 11
Oberstein, Eli 98
O'Day, Anita 105–106
Oh! Eddie 6
Oh! Lady Be Good 10–11, 14, 26, 31, 78, 96
Oh! Red 25, 33, 104
Old Fashioned Love 12, 14
Old Man River 85
Olsen & Johnson 68–69
On A Trolley 74
One For My Baby 86
One Never Knows, Does One? 18
One O'Clock Boogie 95, 97–98
One O'Clock Jump 13–15, 18, 36, 40, 46, 49, 53–54, 56, 59–60, 64, 68–69, 71–76, 78–81, 84–87, 92, 95, 100, 106–107
One, Two, Three O'Leary 50–51, 54
On The Sunny Side Of The Street 100
On The Upbeat 81
Open The Door, Richard 95–96
Organ Grinder's Swing 10, 11
Our Love Was Meant To Be 13–14
Out The Window 14, 18, 59, 90
Page, Hot Lips 5, 6, 9, 10, 45, 87, 103
Page, Vernon 5
Page, Walter 5, 8–17, 21, 23, 25–31, 33, 35–36, 38–39, 41, 43–46, 48, 50, 52–54, 56, 58–65, 87, 90, 92–93, 95, 97–98, 100–101, 108
Paging Mr Green 81
Pagin' The Devil 23
Palmer, Singleton 'Cookie' 105–106, 108–109
Panassie Stomp 23
Panther Room, Hotel Sherman, Chi 29–30
Paradise Squat 98, 105, 107
Paramount Theatre, NYC 24
Parker, Bill 108–109
Parker, Leo 103
Pastor, Tony 106
Patience And Fortitude 88
Pattison, Pat 29
Paul, Les 79
Peacock, Bernie 105–107
Peek-A-Boo 85
Pennies From Heaven 11, 13
Perfiidia 14
Petrillo, James 44–45, 60, 70
Platterbrains 54
Playhouse No2 Stomp 75, 81
Please Don't Say No 81
Please Don't Talk About Me When I'm Gone 86
Pocketful Of Pennies 69
Pound Cake 29
Powell, Jimmy 65, 67, 73–74, 76–78, 80–81, 83–84, 86, 88
Powell, Specs 49
Price, Charlie 97–98, 100–102, 108–109
Price, Jesse 9, 78–79
Prince Of Wails 9, 13, 14
Pripps, Eddie 29
Professor Hot Stuff 6
Queer Street 85–88, 92
Quicksand 65
Rambo 85, 88
Ready, Set, Go 101
Red Bank Boogie 69, 72–73, 80–82, 84, 92, 110
Redman, Don 18, 70
Red Wagon 25
Regal Theatre, Chicago 10, 39–40, 51, 57, 65, 70, 76, 82, 88–89, 95, 101, 110
Reuss, Allan 12, 15
Reveille With Beverly (movie) 62–63

R...
Ros...
Rose...
Rosela...
Rose Ro...
Royal Fl...
Royal Gar...
Royal Suite...
Rumba Negr...
Rushing, Jim...
33, 35–36, ...
58–60, 64, 6...
90–93, 95, 98,...
Rusty Dusty Blues
Rutherford, Rudy
St. Louis Blues 13, 6...
St. Louis Boogie 97, 1...
Same Little Words 75
Sampson, Edgar 23
San José 83, 86, 92, 106
Sanford, Birtie 30
Savitt, Jan 71
Savo, Jimmy 83
Savoy Ballroom, NYC 6, 12–13, 16, 18, 21, 23, 25, 32, 45, 55, 58
Savoy Ballroom, Chicago 27, 34, 41, 49, 59, 77, 83, 93, 100
Say It With A Kiss 23
Scott, Hazel 11, 49, 51, 91
Scott, Kermit 39
Scott, Raymond 54
Scott, Robert 50, 52–54, 56, 58–62, 64–65, 78
Sent For You Yesterday And Here You Come Today 17–18, 64, 69, 73, 83–84, 100, 107
September In The Rain 13, 14
Serenade In Blue 60
7th Avenue Express 100
Shaw, Artie 11, 78–79
Sherman, James 13
Sherman, Lynn 51, 53–54, 57, 67, 82–83
She's A Wine-O 109
Shine On Harvest Moon 97, 103
Shoe Shine Boy 10, 11
Shoot The Likker 14
Shore, Dinah 54, 62
Shorty George 23, 29
Shout And Feel It 12, 13
Shout And Do It 5
Shout And Scream 10
Shoutin' Blues 109–110
Silent Night 85
Simmons, John 85
Simon, George 100
Sinatra, Frank 81
Sing For Your Supper 25
Singleton, Zutty 84
Six Cats And A Prince 73
Skeleton In The Closet 11
Slack, Freddie 81
Sleigh Ride In July 81
Small Black 5
Smarty 13, 14
Smith, Buster 9, 10
Smith, Carl 'Tatti' 9, 10, 11
Smith, Kate 74, 88
Smith, Tab 38, 41–42, 44–46, 48, 50–56, 59, 67
Smith, Willie 'The Lion' 4
Snoqualmie Jo-Jo 78
Solo Flight 81
Somebody Loves Me 11–12
Somebody Stole My Gal 6, 36, 40
Someday, Sweetheart 33
Someone's Rockin' My Dreamboat 69
Something New 53–55
Sometimes I'm Happy 13
Song Of The Islands 31, 35
Sophisticated Swing 101
Sosnick, Harry 110
South 98
South, Eddie 49

...iskine 6
...atum, Art 8, 49, 84
Taxi War Dance 28, 30
Taylor, Jeanne 101, 104
Taylor, Jimmy 109
Taylor, Louis 65, 73–74, 76–78, 80–81
Tea For Two 10–11, 14
Tea On The Terrace 10
Tell Me More 39
Terry, Clark 102, 105–109
Tess' Torch Song 74, 76
Texas Shuffle 23
Thanksgiving 10, 13–14
Tharpe, Sister Rosetta 24, 35
That Old Feeling 82–83
That's That 106
That Too, Do 6
The Apple Jump 33, 45
The Blue Room 9
The Blues I Like To Hear 23
The Count 6
The Count Steps In 13
The Dirty Dozens 23, 30, 104
The Fives 23, 104
The Glory Of Love 10–12, 14
The Jitters 46
The Jones Law Blues 5
The Jumpin' Jive 75–76
The King 88, 93, 105–107
The Mad Boogie 88, 92
The Man I Love 35
The Moon Fell In The River 44, 46
The Only Girl I Ever Loved 9
The Peacock 106
There'll Be Some Changes Made 46, 53, 75–76
There's A Lull In My Life 14
The Slider 109
The Very Thought Of You 23
The World Is Mad 41, 45
They Can't Take That Away From Me 13–14
The You And Me That Used To Be 13–14
They Say 23
Things Are Looking Up 15
This Heart Of Mine 81–83
This I Love Above All 75
This Is A Lovely Way To Spend An Evening 75
This Time The Dream's On Me 54
This Year's Kisses 11–12
Thompson, Lucky 78, 80–85, 88
Thornhill, Claude 14, 107
Thursday 26, 29
Tickle Toe 36
Tilton, Martha 69
Time Alone Will Tell 75–76
Time On My Hands 39, 58, 67, 75
Time Out 13
Tippin' On The Q.T. 83
Toby 9
Together 81
Tolbert, Skeets 63
Tom Thumb 53–54, 57
Too Bad 11
Too Marvellous For Words 13–14
Too Much In Love 75
Top Man [Man Of The Family] (movie) 69
Topsy 13, 54
Trav'lin' All Alone 14
Troup, Bobby 108

Tuesday At Ten 46, 49, 53–54, 75
Tune Town Shuffle 50, 53
Tush 75, 86
Twelfth Street Rag 28, 31
Two Times 9
Ulanov, Barry 52, 70, 82, 87
Undecided Blues 46, 49
Underneath The Stars 18
Valentine, Billy 109
Vaughan, Sarah 107
Volcano 33
Walder, Woody 5, 6
Walking Slow Behind You 109
Walkin' Through The Park 11
Waller, Fats 4, 11, 31, 74
Warren, Earle 13–17, 21, 23, 25–26, 28–31, 33, 35–36, 38, 41, 44–46, 48, 50–66, 69, 70, 73–78, 80–81, 83–84, 101–103, 105–109
Washington, Booker 5, 6
Washington, Dinah 105
Washington, George 101
...shington, Jack 5, 6, 9, 11–17, 21, 23, 5–26, 28–31, 33, 35–36, 38, 40–41, 44–46, 50, 52–54, 56, 58–62, 64–65, 87–88, 93, 95, 97–98, 100–102, 105–109
...Ethel 60, 65
...Laurel 70
...Blues 60, 76
...Yonder In New Orleans 23
... 6–7, 11, 16, 30, 58
... 8, 9
... 22–23, 25–26, 28–31, 33, 36, ... 44–46, 48, 50, 52–54, 56, 58–62, 64–65, 70, 73–86, 88, 100–102, 105–109
Wettling, George 11, 109
What Can I Say, Dear? 84
Whatcha Gonna Do When There Ain't No Swing? 13–14
What Goes Up Must Come Down 28–29
What's Your Number? 44, 46, 72
When I'm Alone 14
When My Dreamboat Comes Home 13–14
When The Sun Goes Down 25, 30, 104
When They Ask About You 74
Where Are You? 13
White, Dolly 57
White, Gonzelle 5
Whitman, Ernie 'Bubbles' 85
Whitman Sisters 8
Who Am I? 45
Wholly Cats 43–44
Who Wants Love? 14
Why Don't You Do Right? 64
Whyte, Zack 7
Why Was I Born? 11
Wiggle Woogie 46, 54, 73
Wild Bill's Boogie 92, 95, 100
Wild Party 11
Williams, Clarence 76
Williams, Claude 10, 11
Williams, Cootie 44, 46, 56–57, 76, 96, 108
Williams, Elmer 4
Williams, Jack 62
Williams, Skippy 27
Williams, Spencer 76
Wilson, Gerald 101–102, 108–109
Wilson, Shadow 73, 75, 78–80, 83–88, 102, 105–106, 108
Wilson, Teddy 11–12, 15, 23, 38–39, 50, 83
Winslow, Russ 59
Winterhalter, Hugo 54
Wish You Were Waiting For Me 81–82
Without Your Love 13
With Plenty Of Money And You 14
WMGM Jump (Bedlam) 106
Wonderful Thing 109
Won't You Be My Baby? 6
Wrap Your Troubles In Dreams 69
Wright, Eugene 102, 105
Wright, Richard 7
Wright, Steve 4
Wynn, Vivian 7
X-1 105–106
Ya Got Love 6
Yeah Man! 10–14
Yerxa, Ted 84
Yes Indeed! 53–54
You And Your Love 30
You Betcha My Life 109
You Can Count On Me 30–31
You Can Depend On Me 26
You Can't Be Mine 23
You Can't Run Around 38, 42, 53
You Do The Darnedest Things, Baby 11, 13
You Lied To Me 46
You Made Me Happy 6
Young, Lee 51, 60
Young, Lester 9–17, 21, 23, 25–33, 35–36, 38–39, 41, 43–45, 51, 59–60, 71–81, 102
Young, Snooky 59, 67, 79, 84–86, 88, 92–93, 95, 98, 100–101
You're A Lucky Guy 35
You're Just A No-Account 35
You're Precious To Me 14
You're Too Good To Be True 10
Your Red Wagon 101
Yours And Mine 12, 14
Zack, George 29
Zelnick, Mel 106